I'll Do My Own Damn Killin'

Benny Binion, Herbert Noble, and
the Texas Gambling War

GARY W. SLEEPER

BARRICADE
BOOKS

Published by Barricade Books Inc.
185 Bridge Plaza North
Suite 308-A
Fort Lee, NJ 07024

www.barricadebooks.com

Library of Congress Cataloging-in-Publication Data
A copy of this title's Library of Congress Cataloging-in-Publication
Data is available on request from the Library of Congress.

ISBN 1-56980-321-8

First Printing

Designed by India Amos, Neuwirth & Associates, Inc.
Manufactured in the United States of America

CONTENTS

PROLOGUE

IN THE LAST years of his life, old Benny Binion liked to come down to the Sombrero Room and drink coffee, and pass the time with whoever might happen by. Some days he would stay only a few minutes; others he might sit all afternoon. The big leather booth in the back corner was his. Hell, the whole place was his. The sign out front said so. "Binion's Horseshoe Club" flashed in giant gold neon letters on a block-long blue neon background. The hundred dollar chips in the casino had his picture on them. Even the specialty of the house in the Sombrero Room was named after him. "Benny Binion's Jailhouse Chili" they called it. Of course, he didn't own the place officially. After a 1953 felony conviction for income tax evasion, he could never hold a Nevada gambling license.

But that didn't stop him from coming down to the coffee shop whenever he felt up to it, dressed in his big white Stetson hat, his cowboy shirt with the buttons made from three-dollar gold pieces, and his ostrich boots. And it damn sure didn't stop him from talking. He would talk about politics or rodeos or gambling or just about anything a person might care to talk about. He'd tell the story about the time he sashayed out the front door of the Horseshoe Club and into Fremont Street with a million dollars stuffed in his boots and no protection except the .45 automatic tucked under his arm. "Vegas was safe in them days," he would say. "You could stand on a street corner in the middle of the night and holler 'somebody come rob me,' and wouldn't nobody do it." Or he might tell about the fabled poker game between Johnny Moss and Nick the Greek. "Spread the game for 'em right out there in the front of the casino. Damn game went on for almost four months. I think Johnny won about four hundred thousand dollars."

Most of all, he loved to talk about Dallas; about the days when he was "raisin' hell and gamblin' high." He loved the stories about gamblers and bootleggers and rounders and, when he felt good, he would tell stories about Dallas for hours. All you had to do was ask. "Yessir, I can damn sure tell you about Dallas. I'll tell you the truth, too." And then a big grin would flash across his beat-up face, and he would laugh, "I'll tell you the truth, but I ain't gonna tell you everything."

A Killing on Commerce Street

June 14, 1940

Webb's Coffee Shop in the lobby of the Southland Hotel in downtown Dallas was practically deserted. The early morning breakfast crowd had come and gone, and the lunch rush wouldn't begin for almost two hours. The lone waitress on duty busied herself with her morning side work, wiping tables and filling sugar, salt, and pepper shakers. The counterman smoked and stacked coffee cups, and listened to an old yellow Philco near the cash register.

The coffee shop's only two customers sat at the corner table in the back, away from the windows. The younger of the two, Cowboy Benny Binion, wore his silver belly Stetson—the Open Road model—cocked at an angle, gunfighter style. His round, jowly face and mild underbite gave him the look of a slightly perplexed bulldog. Binion's gray suit, expensively tailored at the Model Tailor Shop on Elm Street, struggled against his paunch, and he looked, as he usually did at the end of a long night, as wrinkled and rumpled as an unmade bed. At his right hand, near his coffee cup, a folded copy of the *Dallas Morning News*—which he could not read—concealed a Colt .45 automatic.

The local newspapers referred to Binion as the Dallas gambling "kingpin." The road gamblers, grifters, and hustlers who continually drifted in and out of town, looking for action, knew him as the "boss gambler," a title he had held since 1936. From a simple beginning as a street corner bootlegger in the 1920s,

Binion had charmed, bribed, and shot his way to the top of the Dallas underworld. In a period of not quite twenty years, he had been indicted twice for murder and convicted once. He had been arrested for a litany of other crimes including bootlegging, theft, gambling, assault-to-murder, and vagrancy. Yet, in almost twenty years, he had been sentenced to a grand total of seventy days in jail (not counting suspended sentences) and had actually served only fifty.

More than two dozen illegal casinos operated in Dallas in 1940, and Benny Binion owned, in various partnerships, at least half of them. With his partners, Earl Dalton, Ivy Miller, and Red Scarborough, Benny operated crap games at the Southland Hotel in downtown Dallas, where he held a permanent lease on several second-floor suites and considered his headquarters, and at several other downtown hotels—the Blue Bonnet, the St. George, and the Maurice among them. At least a dozen more downtown Dallas casinos paid a percentage of their profits to Binion in return for his protection and considerable political influence.

Binion maintained a live-and-let-live attitude toward rival casinos. If they chose to run without his protection, they had nothing to fear from him. They would, of course, suffer regular raids by the police or the county sheriff, and their patrons would sometimes be embarrassed by a trip to the lockup. Their confiscated gambling equipment would not be quietly returned to them, as Binion's always was. But these were the costs of doing business without Benny's protection, and most of the downtown casino operators felt that 25 percent of their profit was a small price to pay to avoid such inconveniences.

The numbers racket, which Benny called the "policy business," stood as the cornerstone of the Binion gambling empire. His principal partner in the policy business, Harry Urban Sr., kept the books and distributed the money. Binion's personal income from the policy business exceeded one million dollars a year, and his live-and-let-live attitude toward rival gamblers did not extend to those who sought to muscle in on it. He considered any attempt to run a competing numbers racket as stealing, and when he caught someone stealing from him, his blue eyes went hard and cold as tombstones, his disposition turned ugly, and violence almost surely followed.

Binion's breakfast companion on the morning of June 14 was chunky, forty-seven-year-old Ivy Miller, a ranking associate in the Southland Group, as Binion's gambling syndicate was called. Miller, a gambling operator in Dallas for more than twenty years, was as dapper as Binion was unkempt. In his sharply creased gray flannel trousers and navy blue blazer Miller gave the appearance of a man ready for a light lunch and a round of golf at his country club, although most similarly dressed men did not keep a Colt .38 automatic hidden under a stylish summer straw boater on the edge of the breakfast table.

Just after ten o'clock, the counterman hollered "Benny!" and pointed the telephone receiver at Binion like a pistol. Binion took the phone and listened as the caller, speaking for no more than thirty seconds, reported that Sam Murray was on his way to the Dallas National Bank, just three blocks east of the Southland. Except for his wife, Murray was alone.

Binion handed the receiver back to the counterman and went back to his table, where he spoke quietly to Miller. Binion stowed his .45 in its shoulder holster under his left arm, and Miller slipped his .38 into the pocket of his blazer. The two men left the coffee shop, walking east on Main Street toward the Dallas National Bank, where they intended to kill Sam Murray.

SAM MURRAY HAD come to Dallas from Chicago by way of West Texas in the late 1920s and immediately began making a name for himself as a bootlegger, bookmaker, and gambler. The Dallas underworld circulated the rumor that Murray had been a member of the Capone mob in Chicago, a rumor that was not true, but which Murray did nothing to discourage.* In 1932, Murray made the front pages when he and his brother-in-law, Red Callan, murdered a rival bootlegger named King Watson at a lunch counter and newsstand near Bachman Lake in North Dallas. Callan was convicted and sentenced to twenty-five years in prison, but Murray's indictment was dismissed for insufficient evidence. Although they were not involved in the shooting, Benny Binion and his younger brother, Jack, were present and were held as "material witnesses."

In the mid-1930s, Murray seized control of the Dallas franchise for the horse-racing wire service, which transmitted race results, odds, and other vital information instantly, and was an indispensable tool for any bookie who wanted to stay in business. Murray's wire service franchise afforded him virtual control over Dallas bookmaking.

Bad blood developed between Binion and Murray in 1938 when, through judicious (and generous) campaign contributions, Murray acquired considerable political influence, particularly with Dallas city officials, and began moving in on the downtown gambling territory that Binion considered his own. Ignoring pointed warnings from Binion, Murray not only edged his way into downtown Dallas, he also persisted in moving in on Binion's million-dollar-a-year numbers racket.

Soon, Dallas gamblers began to suspect Murray of using his new-found political influence to harass his rivals. The underworld grapevine whispered that he had furnished information to law enforcement officials that had resulted in a reorganization of the Dallas vice squad, in which, much to Binion's distress, several officers friendly to his interests had been transferred to other assignments. To aggravate matters further, on June 10, 1940, police unexpectedly raided one of Ivy Miller's most profitable crap games, and Binion and Miller pegged Murray as the instigator.

---

* Another Dallas hoodlum, Ted Murray, had actually worked as a Capone bodyguard, and the two men may have been confused.

After the warnings from Binion, the fifty-four-year-old Murray rarely ventured into downtown Dallas—and, in fact, seldom left his ranch—without his bodyguard, a tough gunman from West Dallas named Herbert Noble. But on the morning of June 14, Murray and his young wife, Sue, decided to drive downtown by themselves. Sam had business at the Dallas National Bank, and Sue looked forward to a pleasant hour shopping at the Nieman-Marcus department store, just a few doors east of the bank. Neither of them saw any need for a bodyguard.

At about twenty minutes past ten, Murray left his wife at the Nieman-Marcus entrance, promising to join her for lunch in an hour, and began his walk to the bank, located less than a block west at 1528 Main Street. Outside the department store, Murray met a casual acquaintance, a man named Charles Wilson,* and the two walked together, sharing a joke.

FROM THE SOUTHLAND Hotel at 1200 Main Street, Binion and Miller walked two blocks east to the corner of Main and Browder Streets, where they separated. Binion continued east to the Dallas National Bank's north entrance on Main Street, while Miller walked one block south on Browder and then east to the bank's south entrance on Commerce Street. Each man took up a position commanding a view of anyone going to or from the bank.

Less than five minutes later, Murray approached the bank on the Commerce Street side, still talking with Charles Wilson. With Murray less than fifteen feet from the bank's marble entranceway, Miller, his .38 Colt super-automatic already in his hand, stepped from a doorway and, firing almost point-blank, shot Murray in the stomach. Murray doubled over in pain and slumped to the sidewalk, groping inside his jacket for his own

---

* Some chroniclers of the events of June 14, 1940, have suggested that Charles Wilson served as one of Murray's bodyguards; however, Wilson was not known to be associated with Murray except as a casual acquaintance. He was not armed on the morning of June 14, and all of the evidence suggests he was nothing more than an innocent witness to the events of that morning.

pistol. Miller's next six shots, fired so rapidly that several witnesses later claimed to have heard a machine gun, struck Murray three times in the left leg, twice in the left side, and once in the back. At some point in the fray, Murray fired a single wild shot that slammed into the bank's marble doorway. During the entire gunfight, Miller was silent, and Murray, according to Charles Wilson, said only, "Miller, you dirty bastard."

Two passing policemen, officers D.D. Henderson and J.R. Ragland, abandoned their patrol car on Commerce Street and shouldered through the gathering crowd. Henderson ran to Murray's aid, while Ragland pursued Miller, who had walked into the bank lobby, still carrying his smoking pistol. Recognizing Miller, Ragland shouted, "Put your gun down, Ivy."

"I will," Miller said. "Just don't let them shoot me."

On the sidewalk outside the bank, Murray refused to tell Henderson anything about the shooting. "I'm a dying man," the officer later quoted him as saying, "but just the same, you're not going to find out anything from me."

Murray died before he reached the hospital.

The two officers handcuffed Miller and drove him to the county jail, where he was charged with murder.

Benny Binion walked back to the Southland Hotel.

THE SHOTS THAT killed Sam Murray ignited a war for control of gambling in North Texas that raged until the mid-1950s. For fifteen years, gamblers killed each other with shotguns, pistols, rifles, machine guns, and dynamite. They deposited bodies on country roads and city streets, in back alleys and front yards, and in parking lots and shallow graves. They killed each other for profit, for revenge, and for hire. Theirs was a war of intrigue and double-cross, marked by constantly shifting alliances and shadowy motives. The police knew why the bodies were piling up, and often who the killers were. Yet, not a single gambler was ever tried, much less convicted, for a major crime of violence.

As one former policeman said, "Knowing and proving are two different things."

Before it ended, the Gambler's War would spill out of Dallas and into Fort Worth and even beyond the confines of North Texas. The killings in Dallas were discussed with great concern in the murky backrooms frequented by the Chicago "outfit" and in the plush casinos of Las Vegas. Eventually, the slaughter in North Texas even attracted the unwelcome attention of the United States Senate.

When they talked about the killing in Texas, they talked about Cowboy Benny Binion.

.

The Making of the Cowboy

LESTER BEN BINION, who would come to be known as "Benny," was born on November 20, 1904, near the tiny community of Pilot Grove in Grayson County, Texas, about fifty miles north of Dallas. The Binion clan had settled in Georgia in the late 1700s, after emigrating from Ireland, and began migrating to Texas around the time of the Civil War. Lester Ben's great-grandfather, Thomas Noel Binion, arrived in Texas in 1867 after settling briefly in Iowa. Thomas's son, Zephiner, married Izora Brewer in 1875, and their son, Lonnie Lee, born at the Pilot Grove home place in 1879, was Lester Ben's father.

The Binion men were farmers and carpenters and wagon makers and mill owners. They settled the rich farmland on the northern edge of the Blackland Prairie and produced cash crops of cotton, wheat, and corn. They raised a few cattle and horses and, generally speaking, they were no more and no less prosperous than their neighbors.

As a boy, Lester Ben (he was always called by his full name, in the southern fashion) was what his family called "poorly." Plagued with frequent respiratory illnesses and stricken with pneumonia on at least four occasions, the boy was so fragile that he was not expected to live. He seldom attended school and, in later years, often said that "bad roads and poor health" interrupted his education. Sometimes, when it suited his purposes, he claimed he had no education at all. However, when pressed, he would admit that he could "read readin', but couldn't read writin'." But though his health *was* poor, and the roads *were* bad, it was neither his health nor the roads that ended his formal education. It was his father.

Lonnie Lee Binion was different from the other men of the Binion clan. He had inherited his father's land but not his father's love for the soil. He earned his money from the land by leasing it to his neighbors, leaving the routine of farm life to them. Lonnie's great passions were horses, gambling, and whiskey. Lester Ben, many years later, would describe his father as "kind of a wild man" and "a drunk." Lonnie Lee traveled through North Texas buying and selling horses and mules, gambling and drinking, leaving Lester Ben's mother, Willie, to maintain the household, collect the ground rents on the farmland, grow food in her garden, and otherwise tend to the family's needs.

When Lester Ben was about ten years old, his father decided that an outdoor life might improve the boy's health. "Hell, he's gonna die anyway," Lonnie told Willie. "He might as well come with me." For the next six years, Lester Ben lived the life of a horse trader.

THE TEXAS HORSE trader, according to one old timer, was a man who was apt to "come to town with nothing but a pocket knife and wind up owning everything but the courthouse." The horse trader traveled constantly, dealing in almost anything of value. Although horses and mules were his stock-in-trade, he would often peddle household goods, guns, saddles, and frequently homemade whiskey. Traveling a more or less regular circuit through North Texas, the stockmen would often gather at local events called "trade days." The equivalent of local or county fairs, trade days were (and in some North Texas communities still are) held regularly, affording farmers and ranchers the opportunity to come to town to socialize, shop, and trade. For the horse traders, the trade days offered a chance to trade among themselves, gossip, drink, and gamble on horse races, dogfights, shooting matches, bare knuckle brawls, cards, and dice.

In a 1976 interview with the University of Nevada Oral History

Program, Benny described his days with the horse traders in his own colorful style:

> From a real small kid, I'd go with the horse traders, and became a pretty good horse trader. And then they all gambled when they'd get together. They all traveled in wagons, and they had some of the wagons fixed kinda like trailer houses now, but lived in. So they had known campin' places. And they'd all get together, and sometimes there'd be ten or fifteen there at the time. So they'd gamble and play cards and do this, that and the other, and trade horses . . .
>
> So I kinda got in with more of a gambling type of guy, you know . . . you might say road gamblers. And then I'd go around with them, and I'd do little things for 'em and they'd give me a little money, kinda kept me goin'. Then I'd drift back to the horse traders, maybe stop somewhere and punch cows, or do somethin' a little bit, you know. Always had me a saddle and bed with me.[*]

Young Lester Ben, fascinated with the gambling and the gamblers, especially the dice games, watched carefully and learned. The horse traders and road gamblers played "money craps," which is considerably different from "bank craps," the game played today on complicated layouts in modern casinos. In a money crap game, the "shooter" announces the amount of money he wants to gamble. Any other player may cover (or "fade") all or any part of the shooter's bet. If the other players are unwilling to fade the entire bet, the shooter may roll the dice for the amount the faders are willing to bet or pass the dice to the next shooter. Side bets are permitted, and players are allowed to bet each other either for or against the shooter.

---

[*] University of Nevada Oral History Program, Interview

Observing the crap games, Lester Ben noticed that some players always seemed to win money while others almost always lost. The players who won, he noticed, were the faders, who rarely rolled the dice when it was their turn and always bet against the shooter. Inadvertently, he had discovered a basic mathematical principle of crap games: the fader (called the "wrong bettor," or the "don't bettor" in modern parlance) has a slight advantage over the shooter. Whether this was pointed out to him by the older gamblers, or he discovered it through his own observation, is not known, but the principle of the fader's advantage stayed with him for life.

Lester Ben Binion wandered in and out of the horse trading life until, at the age of sixteen, he decided to strike out on his own. Photos taken on his sixteenth birthday depict a full-grown, robust young man, round-faced and smiling under his newsboy's cap, standing about six feet tall and weighing about 190 pounds.

BY 1922, WHEN he finally made Dallas his home, young Binion had cowboyed and gambled his way across most of Texas. He spent the largest part of the time in El Paso, a wild-and-woolly frontier town tailor-made for his style. With the coming of Prohibition in 1919, the scores of El Paso saloons, brothels, and gambling halls had simply moved across the Rio Grande to Mexico and continued with business as usual. Of course, there were always a few thirsty citizens who, for one reason or another, didn't care to cross the border in search of refreshment, and a large-scale whiskey smuggling trade evolved along the border. In all likelihood, Lester Ben earned a good part of his income bootlegging whiskey from Mexico into the United States. The rest of his living he made at the horse track and gambling dens across the border in Juarez.

The normally talkative Binion was unusually quiet about his El Paso days. A few months before his death, he was asked by a newspaper reporter about the time he spent in El Paso. "I got to be known pretty fast," he said. How? "Well, I wouldn't want to tell it."

Whatever it was that he didn't want to tell, either Lester Ben had enough of El Paso or El Paso had enough of him in short order. He arrived in the Dallas area in 1922 and immediately began bootlegging. As a cover for his activities, he sold newspapers on street corners with two young men who would become his life-long friends: Johnny Moss, later to be recognized as one of the world's greatest poker players; and Chill Wills, the beloved Hollywood character actor. He described those days to Steven R. Reed of the *Houston Chronicle*:

> I bootlegged in and out of town. I'd leave and come back. In and out.
>
> I'd leave town and go out and punch cows, trade horses, do something like that, then come back. Never made no money in nothing. Started making money from about '26.

GAMBLING WAS A fixture of Dallas life in the early 1920s, and the biggest gambler in town was a man named Warren Diamond. Known as a gentleman gambler, Diamond owned real estate and several legitimate Dallas businesses. He lived in Highland Park, a luxurious community on the northern edge of Dallas, where he counted many of the city's wealthiest and most influential citizens as his neighbors.

Diamond operated his game for many years in a wagon yard on Camp Street on the near north side of downtown Dallas. But as his respectability increased and his wealth grew, he moved downtown to the St. George Hotel, where he opened a game in 1914. Eventually, Diamond acquired an ownership interest in the St. George and directed both his real estate business and his gambling operations from an office there. Lester Ben Binion, who by this time had come to be called "Benny" by his Dallas acquaintances, met Diamond in about 1923 and began working for him—parking cars, running errands, and doing odd jobs.* Soon, Benny began "steering" for Diamond's crap games, finding likely players and introducing them to the action at the St. George in return for a commission determined by the amount of the player's losses.

Diamond was known as the highest of the Dallas high-rollers and was famous for never turning down a bet, no matter how large. One incident, in about 1930, cemented Diamond's reputation forever. An East Texas oil operator named Mark Hanna walked into the St. George late one night and tossed a thick envelope on Diamond's crap table. "Diamond," he said, "I'm gonna make you look"—meaning that there was so much money in the envelope, Diamond wouldn't cover the bet. Diamond glanced at the envelope and told the dealer to pass the oil man the dice. Only after Hanna crapped out and fumed out of the hotel did Diamond open the envelope. It contained 171 one-thousand-dollar bills. Legend has it that Benny himself was present at the time, but in fact he was in the hotel lobby. But word reached him almost immediately, and he made up his mind that he, like Diamond, would never refuse a bet.

In 1926, with Diamond's blessing, Benny opened his own crap game in one of the smaller downtown hotels, paying the customary 25 percent for the older gambler's protection. In about 1928, Benny expanded into what he called "the policy business," again with Diamond's blessing. He started his first policy bank with fifty-six dollars in his pocket and made eight hundred dollars on the first day. From that day on, although he continued bootlegging for at least three more years, Benny Binion considered himself a professional gambler.

By 1930, Warren Diamond had completely abandoned any interest he had in the Dallas policy rackets, leaving Binion in

---

* Binion's Dallas police record suggests that some of the jobs he did were odder than others. He was arrested for stealing tires in 1924 and burglary in 1927. Both charges were dismissed.

total control. The policy game had become so popular that Binion had several "policy wheels" operating throughout the city. Each wheel represented a different game, and a drawing for each wheel was conducted at least once, sometimes twice, each day. A player could place a bet on his favorite three digit number on any wheel of his choice, or bet the same number on several wheels. Each wheel paid its own jackpot, usually six hundred times the amount of the winning bet.[*] Numbers runners could be found almost anywhere in the city. Bellhops, taxi drivers, doormen, store clerks, bartenders, and even the occasional policeman took numbers bets for Benny's wheels. Later, during the war years, the numbers game became so popular in factories that a shop foreman or union steward could double or triple his legitimate income by taking numbers bets.

A large portion of Binion's policy business came from an area just east of downtown called Deep Ellum, where black Dallas residents worked and played in a miniature version of Harlem. Deep Ellum extended from Central Avenue, called the Central Track, eastward along Elm Street for a distance of several blocks. Pawn shops, operated by Jewish immigrants who lived above their businesses in the European style, lined the street. Bars, night clubs, music halls, theaters, cafes, and brothels opened their doors around the clock. Except for the pawnshop owners, almost no one actually lived in Deep Ellum, but street musicians, gamblers, hustlers, and streetwalkers crowded the sidewalks and streets at all hours of the day and night.

J. H. Owens, a columnist for the *Dallas Gazette*, a black weekly newspaper, described Deep Ellum:

> Down on "Deep Ellum" in Dallas, where Central Avenue empties into Elm Street is where Ethiopia stretches forth her hands. It is the one spot in the

---

[*] Some numbers, like 777 or 666 or the day's date, paid off at a lower rate, usually 400 to 1, because they were more popular. These were called "cut numbers."

city that needs no daylight saving time because there is no bedtime, and working hours have no limits. The only place recorded on earth where business, religion, hoodooism, gambling and stealing goes on at the same time without friction. . . . Last Saturday a prophet [announced] that Jesus Christ would come to Dallas in person in 1939. At the same time a pickpocket was lifting a week's wages from another guy's pocket, who stood with his mouth open to hear the prophecy.

The police virtually ignored gambling in the black neighborhoods, viewing it as a harmless diversion, an attitude that suited Binion just fine. When the police or the press took notice of black gambling at all, it was with a patronizing sense of superiority, much as a parent would observe the antics of a misbehaving child. This headline, which appeared in the *Dallas Times Herald* in 1936, speaks eloquently of the attitude of the city toward its black citizens:

CULLUD FOLKS JUST GOT TO BET,
EVEN IF THEY CAN'T WIN, SAYS
NEGRO VICTIM OF POLICY RACKET

Although a racist by virtue of his upbringing, Binion located at least two of his policy wheels in the heart of Deep Ellum, one at the Green & White Café and the other above the Tip Top Dance Hall. He considered Deep Ellum and the rest of black Dallas to be his exclusive territory. Once asked why he never joined the Ku Klux Klan, he answered, "because I don't believe in hangin' my customers."

IT HAS BEEN widely reported that "Cowboy" Benny Binion earned his nickname by virtue of his sometime occupation as a horse trader. But the incident that actually gave Binion his nickname occurred during his last days as a bootlegger. He kept a small frame house at 1501 Pocahontas Street in South Dallas for use as a kind of moonshine warehouse, where he sold home brew—which he purchased and hauled in from Freestone County—to local bootleggers. On the evening of October 5, 1931, a black bootlegger named Frank Bolding came to Pocahontas Street to negotiate the purchase of a few cases of liquor. The two men were talking in the back of the house when an argument erupted. Binion described the events of that evening to the *Houston Chronicle*:

> Me and him was sitting down on two boxes. He was a bad bastard. So he done something I didn't like and we was talking about it and he jumped up right quick with a knife in his hand.
>
> Well, the automatic thing would be if I was setting there was that I'd jump up and then he'd cut the shit out of me. But I was a little smarter than that. I just fell backward offa that box and shot the sumbitch right there (pointing to his throat.)
>
> I said "I fooled you, didn't I, you black son of a bitch."

Binion went directly to the telephone to call Bill Decker, the chief criminal deputy constable for Dallas at the time. "Decker," he said, "I just shot a nigger in my back yard. He come at me with a knife."

Decker advised him to stand guard over Bolding's body, making sure that no one removed the knife before the ambulance could be summoned and photos taken of the scene. Both Decker and the ambulance driver later testified that a five-inch switchblade knife was found next to Bolding's outstretched hand. Nevertheless, Binion pleaded guilty to murder and was assessed a two-year suspended sentence.[*]

---

[*] Binion always claimed that he entered his guilty plea as a favor to District Attorney Bill McGraw, who was about to run for Attorney General and did not want to dismiss a high-profile case. The light sentence was purportedly

Word of Binion's acrobatic quick-draw shooting soon spread through both the Dallas underworld and the Dallas law enforcement community. From that day forward, he was known as "Cowboy" Benny Binion.

ON AUGUST 10, 1932, Binion's mentor and friend, Warren Diamond, consumed with cancer and despondent, committed suicide in the bathroom of his Highland Park home.

At about the same time, Diamond's only real competition, old-time Dallas gambler Ben Whittaker, decided to retire completely. He died peacefully several years later. Two of Diamond's partners, Ben Bickers and Earl Dalton, both sportsmen in every sense of the word,* took Benny in as a partner, and soon he was running several downtown games on behalf of the partnership.

In 1933, the Cowboy took a bride. Benny met and courted a tiny, feisty redhead from Oklahoma named Teddy Jane Henderson. "If you marry Benny," Teddy Jane's mother warned her, "you'll spend the rest of your life living in hotels above some kind of gambling game." Teddy Jane's mother, of course, was right. She just didn't know how swanky and how profitable those hotels and gambling games would be.

The Cowboy, now married and, by his definition, "settled down," was well positioned to take control of Dallas gambling. He placed his younger brother, Jack,† who had joined him in Dallas by this time, in charge of Diamond's old game at the St. George and moved his own game to the Southland Hotel at 1200 Main Street. In partnership with Ivy Miller, Earl Dalton, Ben Bickers,

---

justified by the victim's reputation as "a bad nigger, who was known to cut a man." Those less charitable toward Binion suggested that perhaps the photos did not depict the knife as clearly as Binion remembered.

* Ben Bickers was an especially active sportsman. He frequently won skeet shooting competitions and golf tournaments, and was a much sought-after boxing referee. He died in 1967. Dalton died in 1950.

† Jack Binion died in an airplane crash at White Rock Lake, near Dallas, on January 10, 1934. The loss devastated Benny's mother, Willie, who died two years later. Benny said she "grieved herself to death" after Jack died.

Red Scarborough, and several others, he took over Diamond's old games at the Blue Bonnet and the Maurice hotels. By 1934, the gambling syndicate, which by then was known as the Southland Group, had gained total control of big-time gambling in Dallas. Binion himself, with partner Harry Urban, the bookkeeper and financial manager who had filled the same role for Warren Diamond, ruled the Dallas numbers racket unchallenged.

By 1936, Benny Binion was ready for the big time. So was Dallas.

Running Wide Open

IN A MANNER of speaking, Dallas itself was built on a gamble. When John Neely Bryan built his cabin and trading post on a bluff overlooking the Trinity River around 1850, nothing recommended the location except a shallow, hard-rock river ford and a promise from the new state government that a military road from San Antonio to the Red River would cross the Trinity at that spot. Nevertheless, Bryan envisioned a commercial metropolis on the North Texas plains. He soon laid out town lots and began luring settlers with free land and promises of prosperity. Eventually, the young city enticed (bribed may be a better term) two railroads to lay track within a mile or so of the newly established town. Soon, terminus merchants, storekeepers who followed the progress of the tracks and set up makeshift shops at every new railhead, began to make Dallas a permanent location for their businesses.

Located at the convergence of two railroads, Dallas became a natural shipping center for the cotton produced throughout north and central Texas. Dealers and brokers bought and sold cotton in the city streets, and by the turn of the century Dallas had become the world's largest cotton market. Banking, insurance, and finance followed in short order, placing Dallas among the leading commercial and financial centers of the southwest.

By the early 1930s, Dallas vibrated with a sense of its own accomplishment. From no more than a log cabin trading post on the Trinity River, it had grown into a thriving city in less than a century. Its population had swelled to more than a quarter million in 1930, an increase of more than one hundred thousand people in only ten years. The death grip the Ku Klux Klan had held on city politics through most of the 1920s had been broken, returning the city to a measure of political respectability. A mammoth project to redirect the Trinity River channel had been completed, relieving the constant threat of devastating floods. Atop the Magnolia Petroleum Building, Pegasus, the mythological flying horse, outlined in red neon and visible for miles, presided over its downtown maze of steel and concrete. Dallas skyscrapers were the tallest in the South.

While Texas, as well as the rest of the country, foundered under the burden of the Great Depression, Dallas prospered, at least comparatively speaking. In 1930, Columbus Marion "Dad" Joiner, a threadbare seventy-year-old Texas wildcatter, convinced that he could locate oil in East Texas, began drilling in Rusk County, about fifty miles east of Dallas. After two dry holes, Joiner drilled one last well on the spot where his truck had broken down. This third well, the one he called the Daisy Bradford #3, became the first find in the huge East Texas field, the largest in the world at the time. Within a matter of months, a forest of oil derricks covered East Texas. By 1933, the petroleum industry had supplanted the cotton market as the cornerstone of the Dallas economy. The oil fields brought jobs for tool pushers, drillers, roughnecks, roustabouts, and truck drivers, and they all came to Dallas to spend their wages. Almost as soon as the first drop of oil flowed from the East Texas field, new oil-related businesses began to spring up in Dallas. Speculators, drilling contractors, equipment manufacturers, and production companies all found Dallas a convenient base of operations, not only for their East Texas ventures, but also for their continuing activities in the established fields around Beaumont and in West Texas.

IN JUNE 1934, the state legislature appointed a commission to determine how and where to celebrate the upcoming centennial anniversary of Texas independence. The commission decided that the official state celebration should consist of a large exposition to be located at one of Texas's major cities and directed each interested city to submit a plan for the celebration, including a bid representing the city's economic commitment to the project. Three cities—Houston, San Antonio, and Dallas—responded.

Robert L. Thornton, known to everyone in Dallas as "Uncle Bob," took charge of organizing the city's proposal to the centennial commission. Raised on a cotton farm in central Texas, Bob Thornton came to Dallas as a young man with, as he once said, "nothing in my pocket but the holes." Though he had only a few dollars in capital and a minimal formal education, he decided to try the banking business. He noticed that most people had no time to visit a bank during business hours, so he began keeping his new bank open late into the evening. His bank was the first in Texas to make loans on automobiles and among the first to finance oil drilling operations. Given to plain speech—"cotton-pickin' talk"—as he called it, he refused to waste his energy being opposed to anything. If he got an invitation to a civic meeting, Thornton's typical reply was, "If it's a *do* meetin', I'm a comin'. If it's a *don't* meetin', I'm stayin' home." In his business dealings as well as his civic affairs, Thornton believed in doing business with men who could make decisions. He had no patience with a man who needed the approval of a board or committee to make a deal, and he always wanted to talk to the "yes or no men," as he called them.

Thornton attacked the centennial project with typical zeal. Together with two close friends, bankers Nathan Adams and Fred Florence, he lobbied the Dallas City Council tirelessly, until the council passed a $2.5 million bond issue to subsidize the centennial. The three bankers approached their fellow Dallas businessmen, pleading, cajoling, wheedling, and, if necessary, threatening them, until they agreed to provide their financial support. Deals were made, favors brokered, and markers called in. "Partner," Bob Thornton might say to an oil man or an insurance executive, "before long, you're gonna' be askin' me for help on some opera or something your wife wants, and I'm gonna' help you then exactly the same way you help me now."

The tactic was remarkably successful. In a matter of months, Dallas and its business leaders guaranteed funding of more than $7.7 million for the centennial.

When the centennial committee met for the final time to evaluate the three contenders and award the celebration, each city's representatives were asked one question: Should the Texas legislature and the U.S. Congress be unable to appropriate funds for the celebration, would the festivities go on as planned? Houston promptly responded that it would not be interested in the event under those circumstances. San Antonio replied that it would need a guarantee of not less than one million dollars in outside funding, or it would not be able to host the event. Bob Thornton, speaking for Dallas, assured the committee that Dallas would bring off the celebration without a penny in state or federal funds, if necessary. "Dallas will get it done," he said, "because Dallas does not fail."

The committee awarded the Texas Centennial Celebration to Dallas that same afternoon.

THIRTY MILES TO the west, Amon Carter, the patriarchal publisher of the *Fort Worth Star-Telegram*, fumed at the choice of Dallas as host of the Texas Centennial Celebration. Carter was known both for his blind love of Fort Worth and his abiding hatred of Dallas. John Nance Garner, FDR's vice-president, once said of Carter: "Amon thinks the whole government should run for the exclusive benefit of Fort Worth and, if possible, to the detriment of Dallas." Those who were present when he heard the news reported that he unleashed a spectacular torrent of profanity, judged even by his considerable standards.

Dallas, as Carter saw it, was a late-comer, a carpetbagger among Texas cities. San Antonio, in Carter's view, was the sacred ground of Texas, anointed by the blood of Travis, Bowie, and Crockett, and the home of the cradle of Texas independence—the

Alamo. Houston could at least boast proximity to the battlefield at San Jacinto, where General Sam Houston had routed Santa Anna's armies and avenged the Alamo and the Goliad massacre. But Dallas? Dallas didn't even exist during the Great War for Texas Independence.

Carter decreed that if Dallas could have a centennial celebration, then Fort Worth, by God, would have one, too. The Fort Worth version would be called the Frontier Centennial Celebration and it would be an old-fashioned Texas shindig. Carter hired Broadway producer Billy Rose to organize and direct the entertainment. The Paul Whiteman Orchestra would play nightly on the elegant Casa Mañana stage. The leading midway attraction would be Sally Rand's Nude Ranch, a titillating revue featuring a great many beautiful girls wearing a much smaller number of beautiful costumes.

Carter informed Fort Worth officials that, during *his* centennial, if the boys wanted to have a little drink and play a little poker, why that would be fine with him. But this was to be a Fort Worth celebration, and he didn't want any out of town gamblers and bootleggers horning in. Carter even commissioned billboards to be placed along strategic highways around Dallas. They read:

DALLAS FOR CULTURE AND FORT WORTH FOR FUN

THE TEXAS CENTENNIAL Celebration opened in Dallas on June 6, 1936, and the Frontier Centennial Celebration opened its doors in Fort Worth two weeks later. Both events opened to rave reviews and huge crowds. The Dallas celebration was so successful that Bob Thornton told his banking colleagues: "There's money under every bush out there, and we're plantin' more bushes every day." But within a few days, Dallas traffic engineers began to notice an increase in the traffic flow from Dallas to Fort Worth. A quick survey revealed that Carter's billboards were having their desired effect. Fort Worth hotels were full, while their Dallas counterparts reported nightly vacancies. Dallas visitors, and their money, were being siphoned off to Fort Worth.

Alarmed at this development, Dallas civic leaders met with certain Dallas public officials to decide what could be done about the Fort Worth incursion on the Dallas money machine. No agenda for that meeting exists, and no minutes were kept, but it is almost certain that Bob Thornton, Fred Florence, and Nathan Adams were in attendance along with Dallas County Sheriff R.A. Schmid, City Manager Hal Mosely, and Chief of Police R.L. Jones. After careful deliberation, they decided that Dallas would fight fire with fire. Never especially diligent in the enforcement of its laws against gambling, prostitution, and illegal drinking, Dallas would become even more hospitable toward the "friendly vices." Thanks to Amon Carter, Dallas would become a wide-open city.

The decision to let Dallas run wide open was not a particularly radical departure from the norm, especially where gambling was concerned. In 1883, Dallas businessmen had descended on the office of County Attorney Charles Clint, who had announced his intention to run the gamblers out of Dallas for good. Gambling, the civic leaders pointed out, was good for business and a harmless recreation for many of the city's most influential citizens. Besides, they argued, Fort Worth was offering free accommodations and a $3,500 stake to any gambler who might locate there. The county attorney relented.

In the early 1900s, Dallas preachers and businessmen fought a spirited battle over horse racing at Fair Park in Dallas. The Texas legislature had legalized race track gambling in 1905, over the fierce objections of the anti-gambling forces, who immediately began a repeal campaign. They succeeded in 1909, and gambling of all sorts, including race track betting, remained illegal in Dallas and the rest of Texas until 1933, when a law permitting pari-mutuel betting on horse races was surreptitiously passed in the legislature as a part of the state's budget appropriation.

Other forms of gambling, especially slot machines and dice

games, were common in Dallas and in most major Texas cities, although the necessities of politics dictated vigorous anti-gambling campaigns in election years.

Thornton, Schmid, and the others no doubt believed they were acting in the best interests of Dallas. Bob Thornton had told the rest of Texas that "Dallas does not fail," and the city had spent millions of dollars backing his brag. Dallas's reputation was on the line. Surely, with the stakes this high, no harm could come from a little gambling and drinking, and sporting with the ladies.

September 12, 1936

Saturday afternoons were especially active in State Thomas, the predominantly black area northeast of downtown Dallas. Most of the area's residents were paid on Fridays, and they reserved Saturdays for shopping, errands, and socializing. Allen Street, the principal north and south thoroughfare through the district, was lined with grocery markets, cafés, laundries, and dozens of other small businesses, all of them bubbling with activity on this pleasant Saturday afternoon. Quitman McMillan's Pride of Dallas Café, one of the most popular establishments in black Dallas, served the neighborhood as restaurant, beer joint, social center, and hangout for gamblers. The Saturday policy play was by far the largest of the week, and gamblers crowded the café from early afternoon well into the evening, with players consulting dream books[*] and runners writing out betting slips.

On this particular Saturday, Benny Binion cruised through North Dallas in his new Cadillac with one of his chief policy lieutenants, H.E. "Buddy" Malone, at the wheel. Turning north

---

[*] Many superstitious numbers players believed that dreams foretold lucky numbers. For example, dreaming of a dog might signify that the number 6 was about to hit. Dream books were cheap pamphlets sold or sometimes given away by gamblers to assist the numbers players in interpreting their dreams.

on Allen from Ross Street, they drove toward the Pride of Dallas Café, intending to survey the action in their territory. At the curb outside the café, Benny spotted a car belonging to Ben W. Frieden, a forty-six-year-old gambler and bookmaker, who had come to Dallas from California at about the time the oil boom began. With his chauffeur, a black man named George Parker, behind the wheel, Frieden carried on a conversation with Asbury Simmons, another black man, through the open car window. Simmons handed Frieden a large grocery bag bulging with paper and turned to walk away.

Frieden, the proprietor of a successful produce business in the Dallas public market, had recently begun operating a small but growing policy game in North Dallas. His Topnotch policy wheel had not escaped Binion's notice, and the Cowboy had warned Frieden in no uncertain terms to find another city for his policy game, preferably outside of Texas.

Seeing Frieden's car, Binion, whose temper had already become legendary in Dallas,* exploded. Yelling at Malone to stop the car, Benny leapt out of the Cadillac and ran to the passenger side of Frieden's automobile. Reaching through the open window, he slapped Frieden across the face.

"You son of a bitch," Binion screamed, "you're a sucker in the business. You don't know no better and I'm gonna forgive you this time. But don't come around here again or I'll whip your ass."

"You might do it," Frieden replied, "but you won't do it today."

With those words, according to Binion and Malone, Frieden pulled a pistol and fired at Binion, inflicting a flesh wound in the right arm. Binion jerked his .38 revolver and shot Frieden in the heart. Depending on his mood, Benny would say later that he shot Frieden either once or three times.

---

* In 1929, he had been charged with aggravated assault when, after a minor traffic accident, he ripped the bumper from his own car and took a swing at the other driver (a middle-aged woman) that would have made Babe Ruth proud. Fortunately, he missed

Malone, at the sound of the shots, jumped from his boss's car and began firing through the driver's side window of Frieden's automobile. As Binion told a newsman years later, "Old Buddy just shot the piss out of him."

Frieden's chauffeur, George Parker, pressed himself hard into the car seat, trying his best to make himself invisible. He emerged from the gunfight unharmed but nearly deaf, and so severely shaken that he was unable to make a statement to the police.

Binion and Malone calmly climbed back into the Cadillac and drove away. When the police arrived minutes later, they found Frieden dead, shot six times in the chest and back. A .38 revolver, fired once, lay on the seat next to his body. On the floor of Frieden's car, they found a paper grocery bag stuffed with policy slips and cash. Parker, nearly incoherent, still crouched behind the wheel.

THREE HOURS AFTER the shooting, Binion arrived at Deputy Sheriff Bill Decker's office, where he surrendered for killing Frieden. By this time, Decker had learned that two men had been involved in the shooting and he asked Binion to identify the other shooter. "Well," Benny said, "I ain't gonna tell you that, but he'll be in here pretty soon."

True to Binion's word, Malone surrendered on the following Monday morning, telling Decker he hadn't come in earlier because he "had to take care of Mr. Binion's cattle." Malone confirmed Benny's version of the story, swearing that Frieden had fired the first shot and that Binion had fired in self-defense. The police found witnesses, however, who swore they saw Benny throw something into Frieden's car after the shooting, giving rise to the suspicion that the .38 next to Frieden's body had been Binion's. Some even suspected that Binion's flesh wound was self-inflicted and that Frieden had never fired at all. A Dallas County grand jury decided to let a trial jury sort it out and indicted both Binion and Malone for murder.

Unfortunately, the Dallas Police Department's investigation

raised more questions than it answered. Malone's pistol, a .45 caliber automatic, had been fired seven times (or at least was seven shells short of a full clip) when he turned it over to Bill Decker on the Monday following the shooting. Binion's .38 had three expended shells in the cylinder when he surrendered just hours after the shooting. The revolver recovered from the seat of Frieden's car had apparently been fired once, or at least contained one spent cartridge. Thus, taking Binion's story at face value, it appeared that a total of eleven shots had been fired in the melee. However, morticians at the Sparkman funeral home reported that Frieden had suffered six bullet wounds and that all six bullets, four .45s and two .38s, had been recovered from his corpse. This evidence clearly established that Binion had shot Frieden neither once *nor* three times as he claimed, but twice. The discovery of only two of Binion's bullets in Frieden's body raised the very real possibility that Binion had in fact used his third bullet to inflict his own wound.

Eddie Roark, attorney for both Binion and Malone, pointed out, not without a certain logic, that, if Binion had actually wounded himself, it would have required Binion or Malone to have the foresight to bring along an extra pistol, already fired once, for the purpose of tossing it in the car next to Frieden's body. Yet there seemed to be no doubt that Binion and Malone had come upon Frieden quite by accident.*

The disparity surrounding the number and caliber of the shots fired would ordinarily demand an inspection of Frieden's car to determine whether other bullets might be recovered, but apparently this was not done. Finally, as if to put the controversy to rest, the police announced several days later that George Parker, Frieden's driver, had given a statement and he was positive that exactly eleven shots had been fired. Parker's statement, of course, confirmed that the .38 revolver found beside his boss

---

* Roark's argument, though logical, ignores the fact that Binion was often known to carry two pistols and may have provided the "extra" weapon himself.

had been fired exactly once in the battle, accounting for Binion's flesh wound. The revitalization of Parker's memory (it will be remembered he was unable even to talk to police on the day of the shooting) was not explained.

Immediately following her husband's funeral services, Frieden's widow announced that she had no intention of attempting to run his policy wheel. In fact, she planned to leave Dallas as soon as she was able to sell the produce business. When questioned as to possible successors to Frieden's business, George Parker told the police that Frieden had no associates who knew enough about the business to take over. With Frieden's death, the Topnotch policy wheel was gone for good.

Three months later, when District Attorney Robert L. Hurt announced to Judge Noland Williams that the indictments against Binion and Malone were being dismissed for lack of evidence, Benny Binion stood alone at the top of the Dallas gambling world. He would not have another challenger until Sam Murray arrived on the scene in 1938.

4

The Rise of Herbert Noble

June 14, 1940

Commerce Street slowly returned to normal. The ambulance carrying Sam Murray had made its way through the crowds and on to Parkland Hospital, where Murray was pronounced dead. A bystander, fifteen-year-old Jack Kilgore, who had been struck in the leg by a stray bullet, had collapsed between two parked cars and was not discovered until the onlookers began to disperse. He was now on his way to Parkland, where he would recover fully. Ivy Miller had already reached the Dallas County jail. The only indications that a killing had occurred outside the Dallas National Bank were a crimson stain already drying on the sidewalk and the coppery smell of blood lingering in the warm air.

OTHER THAN READILY admitting that he had shot Sam Murray, Ivy Miller had nothing to say to the two detectives who questioned him. When his attorney arrived, Miller said, he would explain everything.

Miller's lawyer, Maury Hughes,* a veteran Dallas criminal defense attorney, arrived less than an hour after the shooting and conferred with his client for more than two hours before making a statement. The shooting, Hughes said, was a clear case

---

* Hughes had replaced Benny Binion's regular lawyer, Eddie Roark, after Roark had been found in a compromising situation with the wife of Guy Nabors, one of his clients. Nabors had killed Roark on the spot.

of self-defense. Miller and Murray had argued some time ago over a livestock deal. The disagreement had become heated, and Murray had threatened to kill Miller on sight. Miller, according to his attorney, so feared for his life that he had begun carrying a pistol. At least a dozen witnesses, the lawyer said, could be produced who would swear they heard Murray threaten Miller on several occasions. Miller's attorney went on to describe a gunfight straight out of the Wild West days of Dodge City, Tombstone, or Deadwood. Miller and Murray had suddenly come face to face on the sidewalk outside the bank; Murray had drawn his pistol and fired one shot, which went wild; Miller then drew his own pistol and fired several shots at Murray in self-defense. With Murray down, Miller, still fearing for his life, had fled the scene toward the bank lobby. In answer to a reporter's question about witnesses who claimed to have seen his client outside the bank several minutes before the shooting, Hughes said any such witness "must be mistaken."

In the course of the attorney's impromptu press conference, not a word was said about the raid on Miller's crap game three days before, or about the telephone call Benny Binion received minutes before the fatal encounter. In fact, Benny Binion's name was not mentioned at all.

FOR MANY YEARS after the shooting of Sam Murray, insiders in both the Dallas Police Department and the Dallas underworld speculated as to who might have made the telephone call that put Murray "on the spot." The only two men who knew the truth, Benny Binion and the caller, had long since taken the secret to their graves. But considerable circumstantial evidence argued that the man who set Murray up was his absent bodyguard, Herbert Noble.

Newspaper and magazine articles frequently refer to Herbert Noble as "a native of West Dallas," but very little is actually known about his birth other than that he was born somewhere in Texas on either April 21 or 22, 1909. The earliest public record of Noble's life, the 1910 United States Census, counted him at the age of eleven months in Palo Pinto County, Texas, about eighty miles west of Fort Worth. His father, Ben Noble, and his uncles, Gus and James, ironworkers by trade, lived an itinerant lifestyle, following the work from town to town, and it is quite possible that Noble himself did not know exactly where he was born. How long the Noble family lived in Palo Pinto County, or where they may have traveled from there, is unknown, but we do know that in 1917 or 1918, when Herbert was about nine years old, they settled in West Dallas.

Officially, West Dallas did not exist. The bastard stepchild of the city of Dallas, it hunkered down on the west bank of the Trinity, almost in the shadow of the downtown skyscrapers. As an unincorporated, unchartered area, it had no government, no police or fire departments, no running water to speak of, and little electricity. Fewer than 10 percent of the structures in West Dallas could boast indoor plumbing. Most of the residents lived in shacks they built from whatever materials they could scavenge from the county dump located at the northwest corner of the community. Some lived in tents or dugouts. The more fortunate owned or rented dilapidated houses that had been carted over the river from Dallas and set down wherever a relatively flat piece of ground could be found.

In rainy weather, the Trinity rushed out of its banks, turning most of West Dallas into a muddy, sticky mess, giving rise to the nickname "the bog." In the heat of summer, the ground hardened and cracked, and dust swirled with the slightest breeze. Smoke and cement dust belched relentlessly from the nearby Trinity Portland Cement Plant and was carried directly over West Dallas on the southwesterly wind. A constant stream of freight trains pounded the community with noise and diesel fumes.

West Dallas streets, unpaved and in most cases unimproved, scarcely deserved the name. Attempts by the county to name the streets and number the structures were entirely unsuccessful; West Dallas residents, having no desire to be easily located, painted over the house numbers and knocked down or stole the street signs.

Most of the small businesses that served West Dallas were scattered among the houses along Eagle Ford Road,* the only paved street in West Dallas. Zoning was non-existent, and in a single block there might be a few houses, a ramshackle apartment building, a café, a trucking company, and a small foundry. Just a mile or so west of the Trinity River, Henry Barrow operated a general store and gas station, selling drinking water (fifty cents a barrel), Nehi soda pop, Bull Durham tobacco, and Star gasoline. His boys—Buck, Clyde, LC, and Jack—ran repeatedly afoul of the law, especially Clyde, who took up with a petite redhead from West Dallas named Bonnie Parker and terrorized the Midwest and Southwest for nearly two years. The Hamiltons—Raymond, who went to the Texas electric chair two weeks before his twenty-second birthday, and Floyd, who earned a measure of fame as one of the few men ever to escape from Alcatraz†—lived not far from Barrow's store.

Noble knew the Barrows and the Hamiltons and dozens of other West Dallas toughs, and shared with them a burning desire to get out of West Dallas. For many of them, the quickest way appeared to be by a gun and a fast car, but Herbert chose to try to bootstrap his way out by staying in school, at least until he was about sixteen. After leaving school, he signed on as a truck driver, first for the Simms Refinery and later for the V.C. Bilbo Trucking Company, both on Eagle Ford Road.

In 1930, Noble married the love of his life, a striking West Dallas brunette named Mildred Bowers. On December 6, 1931, their daughter Freda‡ was born.

---

* Renamed Singleton Boulevard during World War II
† Although he successfully escaped the prison walls, he did not manage to leave "the rock." He was recaptured, near death from exposure, two days after his escape.
‡ Noble's daughter is almost always referred to as "Frieda" in newspapers, books, and magazines, but according to Texas birth records the correct spelling is "Freda."

In March 1932, Noble was arrested and given a two-year suspended sentence for auto theft. After that run-in with the law, his trail goes completely cold. Beyond telling writers and reporters that he had "done some things I'm not proud of," he had nothing to say about his whereabouts or occupation for the next six years. At some point in his travels, he gave up truck driving in favor of gambling, and it is a reasonable assumption that, like most young Texas men in the early 1930s, he spent some time in the oil fields. Noble had a natural talent for things mechanical, and learned to repair and rebuild both automobile and airplane engines. At some time during the period, Noble learned to fly and later acquired a Civil Aeronautics Administration pilot's license. He also met Sam Murray.

By 1938, Noble and his family had returned to Dallas, where they rented a small home at 311 Conrad Street, in a pretty, wooded Dallas suburb called Oak Cliff. He was nominally employed as the manager* of the Santa Paula Hotel at 1710½ Live Oak in downtown Dallas, where Sam Murray operated his gambling casino. Noble served as a pit boss for Murray's games, supervising the dealers, approving credit, and furnishing muscle when needed. In July 1938, Noble was charged with aggravated assault and carrying a pistol in an incident arising from his duties at the Downtown Businessmen's Club, indicating that he managed more than one gambling joint at the time (both charges were dismissed).† He also acted as Murray's personal bodyguard and accompanied Murray everywhere he went, except to the Dallas National Bank on the morning of June 14, 1940.

Those who believed Noble had "dropped the dime" on his boss pointed out that, other than Murray himself, only Noble

---

* The term "employed" is a misnomer. Gamblers were frequently carried on the payrolls of hotels or restaurants where they operated games, in order to avoid vagrancy charges and provide an explanation of their income for tax purposes. Noble almost certainly did not manage the hotel.

† The victim of the alleged assault was one Louis J. Strauss, quite possibly the "Russian Louie" Strauss who later worked as a Binion bodyguard.

could know that Murray would be downtown on Main Street that morning and that he would be unguarded. But it was Noble's meteoric rise in the Dallas underworld after Murray's death that furnished the most damning evidence.

Within days after Murray's death, Noble had taken over the gambling at the Santa Paula. He also operated a game at the Mexico City Café, next door to the Santa Paula on Live Oak, with a partner, Fred Merrill. He later moved this game to the Campbell Hotel, where Merrill and Eddie Wrotan were his partners. By 1943, Noble had expanded his gambling operations to include the Majestic Hotel (with Merrill, Wrotan, Phillip Stein, and Jack Darby) and the Rose and Savoy hotels (with Darby). In the last year of the war, he and Phillip Stein purchased the Santa Paula and opened the Dallas Airmen's Club on the premises. Binion financed all of Noble's operations, and at each location Noble of course paid the usual 25 percent tribute.

Just a year after the Murray shooting, the Nobles purchased eight hundred acres of ranch land in southern Denton County, just a few miles from Binion's own ranch.* Noble's ranch, which he called the Diamond M in honor of his wife, Mildred, boasted a stone ranch house and several matching cabins, where, rumor had it, he operated *very* high stakes crap games. He bulldozed a dirt landing strip on the property and flew gamblers in, using his own fleet of five airplanes. Seeking a measure of respectability, Noble began dealing in used and salvage aircraft equipment and soon had a thriving aircraft maintenance and repair business. Mildred began wearing mink and driving Cadillacs.

Many on the Dallas gambling scene saw Noble's sudden rise in prominence and prosperity as evidence of his reward for putting Sam Murray on the spot. Whether that view is accurate or not, there is no question that Herbert Noble had, by the mid-1940s, become one of Dallas's most powerful and best known gamblers.

---

* They kept the lease on the "town home" in Oak Cliff, as well.

IT WAS ONLY natural that Benny Binion and Herbert Noble should develop a rivalry that would eventually explode into a full-blown feud. The two gamblers were as distinctly opposite as two men can be. Noble was muscular and handsome; Binion was paunchy and plain. Noble was, by the standards of the time, well-educated; Binion was illiterate. Binion was noisy and brash; Noble was quiet and reserved. Most important, Binion had something Noble wanted: power. Binion had the "big fix," the political power to demand tribute from local gamblers and the courthouse clout to get away with murder. In Noble's mind, Binion was an ignorant lout and undeserving of such influence. Binion, on the other hand, saw Noble as ambitious and untrustworthy. If Noble had indeed put Sam Murray on the spot, as the evidence would indicate, Binion might reward him for the service but would forever despise him for the betrayal.

IN THE EARLY 1940s, there was peace in the valley of the Trinity River. Dallas gamblers had forged an accommodation with local officials and, once or twice a week, each protected game would be raided, albeit so quietly that few of those in attendance knew that the raid had taken place. The officers would take a count of the participants and, a day or two later, the gambler or his attorney would show up at the district court to pay a fine of ten dollars for each person present at the game. Benny Binion estimated that, over the years, he paid over $600,000 in such fines. The preachers and reformers "raised holy hell" about this arrangement, according to Binion. But the city needed the money, and gambling remained informally taxed and *de facto* legalized until 1946.

In general, the gamblers repaid the city by behaving themselves. For the most part, the games were honestly run. Occasional skirmishes broke out between gamblers, frequently as a result of personal rather than business disputes. But the Binion-Noble feud had not yet erupted. The gambling war that police had feared following the killing of Sam Murray had not materialized. At least not yet.

The Death of Raymond Laudermilk

NOT LONG AFTER her husband's death, Sue Murray began keeping company with another Dallas gambler, handsome Raymond Laudermilk. Her new suitor had come up from the Dallas streets, beginning his career running errands, parking cars, and steering for crap games. In the late 1920s and early 1930s, he worked for Warren Diamond, guarding games and furnishing muscle when necessary.

When Diamond committed suicide in 1932, Laudermilk signed on with his successor, Benny Binion. Laudermilk worked his way to the top of the Southland Group, eventually becoming the number three man in Binion's policy organization. While Harry Urban looked after the bookkeeping, Laudermilk worked the streets, keeping runners in line, making sure the various wheels were properly guarded, and protecting Binion's money.

Their brief courtship ended in marriage during a trip to California, and Raymond and Sue Laudermilk returned to Dallas with a plan. The scheme, which almost certainly originated with Sue, was simple: they would go into the numbers racket. Sue, who was as intelligent and ambitious as she was attractive, had learned the policy game from her late husband, Sam. She knew how to keep the books and operate the business, and she knew all of Sam's contacts. Raymond knew the streets and how to organize the runners and keep them honest. If needed, Raymond could provide the gun or the brass knuckles to keep things running smoothly. It seemed to Sue that she and Raymond had everything they needed except money, and she had an idea where to get that.

The Laudermilks turned to Sam Murray's old bodyguard, Herbert Noble, for financing. Noble jumped at the idea. With World War II underway, Dallas overflowed with soldiers and sailors and defense workers, and Noble's crap games were making enormous profits. But that was pocket change compared to the money that could be made with a successful policy business. More important, Noble had come to resent the 25 percent that he paid to Binion for the privilege of operating his downtown crap games, and he saw the Laudermilks' proposition as a chance to break free of Binion's organization and establish himself as a big-time independent gambler, perhaps Binion's equal. Maybe even the kingpin.

BENNY BINION LIKED Raymond Laudermilk. The two men were nearly the same age and, in their younger years, had worked together for Warren Diamond. Like Binion, Laudermilk was a street gambler who depended for his livelihood on his wits, his nerve, and his ambition. Binion relied on Laudermilk to keep his policy business running smoothly almost as much as he relied on Harry Urban to keep the books. He had come not only to like but also to respect Raymond when, in 1939, Laudermilk, Urban, and eight of Binion's numbers runners had been arrested and charged with felony gambling.* The district attorney, in an unusual legal move, offered Urban and Laudermilk immunity in return for testimony against the eight runners, who were all black. The two policy bosses accepted the offer, but, with the advice of their attorney, the ever-present Maury Hughes, they soon deciphered the prosecutor's strategy. Under a grant of immunity, Urban and Laudermilk could be compelled to testify not only against the runners but also against Binion himself. When Urban

---

* This was, in Binion's opinion, another attempt at harassment instigated by Sam Murray.

and Laudermilk were called to testify, both men refused. They were each fined five hundred dollars for contempt of court and sent briefly to jail. When they still refused to testify, the felony gambling charges were dismissed, and Binion became almost blindly loyal to Laudermilk.

If another man had attempted to defect as Laudermilk had, Benny would have put a price on his head in an instant. But in Laudermilk's case, Binion kept his famous temper under control. Whenever possible, Benny favored negotiation over violence, although his negotiating tactics were usually of the take-it-or-leave-it variety, spiced with the clear implication of impending murder. But he took a different approach with Laudermilk. He first attempted to persuade Raymond to remain in his employ, offering him a huge increase in pay. Laudermilk refused. Binion then offered the pay increase plus a high-paying job in the Southland Group for Sue. Again, Laudermilk refused. Remarkably, the Cowboy countered by offering Laudermilk the unthinkable: a piece of the action. No one except the indispensable Harry Urban shared Benny's Dallas policy action in those days. Laudermilk turned him down.

There would be no more offers.

RAYMOND LAUDERMILK KNEW he was a marked man, but he had one advantage. He knew all of Binion's guns by sight. He knew their faces, their habits, and their hangouts. If he could stay alive long enough to acquire enough money, power, and influence to insulate him from Benny's revenge, he might survive. Apparently, the thought of leaving Dallas did not occur to him.

BENNY BINION OFTEN bragged that he had never hired anyone to kill a man in his life. "I don't need to hire no goddamn hit man," he liked to say. "I can do my own killin'." Of course, to Benny's way of thinking, putting the word on the street that he would be grateful if a certain person turned up dead—even suggesting, in dollars and cents, how grateful he would be—did not amount to hiring a hit man. After his own gunslingers, particularly Buddy Malone and Cliff Helm, spent nearly a year trying futilely to put Raymond Laudermilk on the spot, Benny put the word out that he wanted Laudermilk looking at the wrong side of a cemetery plot, and he would be indebted to whoever might put him there.

March 19, 1943

In the little room she rented by the week at the Ambassador Hotel, Mrs. M. R. Gelfan prepared for bed. It was nearly nine o'clock, and it was her habit to retire early. The only window in her room faced Ervay Street, overlooking the hotel entrance, and she was accustomed to the noises of the street and seldom noticed them. But on this evening, a series of sharp reports caught her attention. Looking out her window at the street below, she saw a slender man of medium height walking away from a parked car. He climbed into the passenger seat of a second car, which immediately pulled away.

At about the same time, someone called the Dallas Police Department to report a series of loud noises, possibly shots, on Ervay Street near the Ambassador Hotel. Minutes later, the police arrived to find a single car parked at the curb in front of the hotel entrance. In the driver's seat they found Raymond Laudermilk, with six bullet holes in his chest and stomach. They called for an ambulance, but there was no hurry. For the second time in less than three years, Sue Murray Laudermilk was a widow.

Inside Laudermilk's bloody car, on the floorboard of the passenger seat, police found six spent .45 caliber shells. From this evidence, they theorized that whoever shot Laudermilk had been in the car with him when the shots were fired. Later, however, Mrs. Gelfan's story persuaded them that the shooter had leaned into the car, firing the fatal shots through the passenger window.

The presence of a second vehicle, presumably a getaway car, baffled the investigators.

At about nine thirty, twenty-nine-year-old Bob Minyard arrived in a taxi at the Dallas County Sheriff's office and announced that he had just killed Raymond Laudermilk. Minyard told Chief Deputy Bill Decker, who had been called to the office as he always was when a gambling-related killing was suspected, that he and Laudermilk "had some trouble" over money he had borrowed from Laudermilk. He refused to say more until he talked with his lawyer (Maury Hughes, of course).

Hughes arrived at the jail within an hour and, after conferring at length with his new client, gave another of his impromptu press conferences. According to Hughes, Minyard had been leaving the lobby of the Ambassador, where he lived in a furnished room, when Laudermilk parked at the curb and shouted at him. He had gone to the passenger side of Laudermilk's car, and Laudermilk had angrily demanded that Minyard repay some money he had borrowed. When Minyard replied that he was broke, Laudermilk reached inside his jacket for his pistol, and Minyard fired first in a clear case of self-defense. After the shooting, Minyard had flagged down a passing car and hitched a ride to the Baker Hotel, where, anxious to surrender, he had caught a taxi to the sheriff's office.

The whole thing, Hughes said, was the tragic result of an argument over borrowed money.

The next morning, the Dallas County grand jury indicted Minyard for murder but he was never tried.

NEWS TRAVELED FAST in the Dallas underworld in those days, and within hours after Laudermilk's death, Herbert Noble closed his new policy business. Sue Murray Laudermilk, apparently not terribly distraught over Raymond's death—she had filed for divorce only two weeks before he was killed, alleging that he had threatened to kill her—packed her bags and moved on.

JUST AS HERBERT Noble had done after the killing of Sam Murray, Bob Minyard rose rapidly to the top of the Dallas underworld. When he shot Laudermilk, Minyard had been working the South Dallas streets, hustling to scuffle up the money to pay the rent on a furnished room at the Ambassador, once a luxury hotel but in Minyard's day just a step above a flop house.* He guarded crap games for small time gamblers and tried his hand at petty theft. His habit of borrowing money and ducking his creditors whenever possible lends credibility to the story that he owed Laudermilk money.

Shortly after the Laudermilk shooting, Minyard acquired, courtesy of Benny Binion, an interest in a prosperous downtown gambling operation. But this was not just any game. Binion, typical of his style and sense of justice, installed Minyard as Herbert Noble's partner at the Majestic Hotel. Besides the fact that he probably thought it was funny, Binion had good reason for planting Minyard in Noble's back yard. Noble couldn't be killed for backing Laudermilk's policy game—he made Binion too much money—but he could be reminded every day of what happened to those who dared to cross the Cowboy. What better reminder than the man who had killed Laudermilk? Besides, Binion wanted an insider in Noble's game—someone to keep an eye on the ambitious Noble to make sure that Binion got an honest count—and Bob Minyard was just the man. Noble and his pit boss, a lanky gangster named Slim Hays, hated Minyard, but, like it or not, he was their new partner.

Minyard prospered as Noble's partner. In less than two years, he had paid all of his debts and found sufficient extra cash to court and marry a pretty Dallas girl. The newly wed Minyards bought a two-story home near White Rock Lake in the high-

---

* The Ambassador, built in 1905, was considered the finest of Dallas accommodations until the Baker and Adolphus Hotels were built a decade later. The Ambassador deteriorated through time and, by World War II, served as a rooming house. It has since been restored and now houses a girls' boarding school.

toned Lakewood area of East Dallas and filled it with expensive furniture. The Dallas newspapers, which had described him as a "derelict" when he shot Laudermilk, upgraded Minyard to "sportsman," a term reserved for gamblers who had reached a certain level of respectability. He took to buying his suits at the Model Tailor Shop in Deep Ellum, where Binion and Urban bought theirs. In 1945, Minyard listed himself in the Dallas City Directory as a "nightclub operator."

Benny Binion always took care of his friends.

6

The Fort Worth Front Men

Fort Worth, 1942

The beginning of World War II signaled an economic boom unlike any Fort Worth had ever seen. The stockyards teemed with cattle, and the Armour and Swift meat packing plants worked night and day, receiving and processing as many as five million animals a year during peak war years.

Trainloads of soldiers rolled into Camp Bowie on the west side of the city. The Army Air Corps reactivated Hicks Field, which had been decommissioned in 1929, and began training thousands of flyers from the United States and Canada. The Quartermaster Corps established a huge depot in Fort Worth, supplying soldiers in Texas, New Mexico, Oklahoma, Arkansas, and Louisiana with everything from tanks to toilet paper. The Consolidated Vultee Aircraft Corporation built a mile-long manufacturing facility, known to Fort Worth residents as "the bomber plant," and began building B-24 bombers in 1942. On the west side of the bomber factory, the Army Air Force located the Tarrant Field Airdrome, which later became Carswell Air Force Base.

Benny Binion had been fond of Fort Worth since his days as a cowboy and horse trader. With the presence of thousands of soldiers, defense workers, and cowboys, all with fresh paychecks and a natural desire to gamble, his fondness for Cowtown turned to pure love. But he knew his customary style, "raisin' hell and gambling high," would never make him any money in Fort Worth. Not with old Amon Carter in charge.

Amon G. Carter Sr.—oil man, publisher of the *Fort Worth Star Telegram,* and by far the richest and most powerful man in Fort Worth—had nothing against gambling. He played a fair hand of draw poker himself and was known to wager considerable sums on the turn of the cards. In 1936, Carter had insisted that wide-open gambling would be an attraction—unofficial, of course—of the Frontier Centennial Celebration. But he would not abide out-of-town gamblers in Fort Worth, especially Dallas gamblers. Carter hated Dallas and refused even to spend money there. On the rare occasion when he could not avoid Dallas altogether, he carried his lunch in a sack and filled his car with gas before leaving Fort Worth, so that none of his "Fort Worth money" would benefit the Dallas economy. Given the choice, Carter would sooner have Adolph Hitler operating in Fort Worth than Benny Binion.

Benny knew all of this, of course, and simply decided to operate in Fort Worth with a group of local partners and front men, so that he could deny any involvement in gambling on the west side of the Trinity, and Fort Worth could pretend he wasn't there. His three partners were Tiffin Hall, George Wilderspin, and Louis Tindall.

TIFFIN HALL, a native of Missouri, had come to Fort Worth in 1920 and immediately begun his career as a gambler. By the late 1920s, Hall was operating hotel games, including his best known game at the Commercial Hotel in downtown Fort Worth. After opening a restaurant in downtown Fort Worth called the Mexican Inn in 1936, Hall, like two of his Dallas counterparts, Warren Diamond and Ben Whittaker, considered himself more businessman than gambler. Eventually he acquired two more eating establishments and at least one hotel.

Hall never denied his gambling background but never admitted to being a big-time gambling operator. Between 1922 and 1955, he was arrested sixteen times, eight of those for gambling. But it was not until 1951 that Hall was identified as a major Fort Worth gambler—some said the kingpin—and an associate of Benny Binion. Even then, Hall would deny any connection with Binion or other Dallas gamblers.

GEORGE WILDERSPIN WAS a different story entirely. He had known Benny Binion since Benny's days as a horse trader. The two owned cattle together, and Wilderspin frequently visited the 250,000-acre Binion ranch in the "Big Open" country along the Yellowstone River near Jordan, Montana.

A kind of Wild West renaissance man, Wilderspin earned his living over the years as a cattle buyer, horse trader, rancher, restaurateur, nightclub owner, gambler, and rodeo cowboy. He was best known for his accomplishments in the rodeo arena, where he was recognized as a world champion calf roper. With Binion financing, sometime during the war years Wilderspin bought and began operating the East Side Club in Haltom City, an east side suburb of Fort Worth. On the same property, he owned a beauty parlor and barber shop, a service station, a café, a drug store, and a tourist court. Wilderspin readily admitted that he ran a gambling game in the East Side Club, but claimed he only banked the game, telling one news reporter that he didn't know how to shoot dice or play cards. He also claimed he never made any money gambling and often said he regretted that he had ever been involved with it. However he might have felt about his career as a gambler, one thing is certain: George Wilderspin was Benny Binion's closest friend in Fort Worth and he was the man to see if anyone wanted to do business with Benny.

It was in this capacity as Binion's front man in Fort Worth that Wilderspin introduced Benny to his wildest and most troublesome colleague: Louis Tindall.

TINDALL, BORN IN Eastland, Texas, in 1902, became acquainted with Wilderspin on the rodeo circuit. Tindall and his wife, Velma, who made their home in Fort Worth, performed their trick-riding act in rodeos and Wild West shows at arenas in New York, San Francisco, Cheyenne, Calgary, and dozens of lesser known venues. Despite the couple's constant bickering, which at times escalated into physical combat, Louis and Velma kept the act together throughout the 1930s and achieved top billing; however, their rodeo career ended prematurely in 1939 when Louis was diagnosed with severe anemia and hemophilia. Doctors advised Tindall that any injury, no matter how seemingly minor, would be life threatening, if not fatal.

At about the time of Tindall's forced retirement from trick-riding, Benny Binion was on the lookout for someone to run the numbers game in Fort Worth. Wilderspin introduced the two, and soon Tindall had two policy wheels, the Black Cat and Old Glory, up and running from his headquarters behind a barber shop at 907 Jones Street, near downtown Fort Worth. With Binion as a backer, Wilderspin as a fixer, and a Fort Worth Police Department already lax in gambling enforcement, Tindall's position and income should have been assured. Unfortunately, Louis was his own worst enemy. He could not stay out of the courts, largely because of his marital problems, his violent temper, and his inability to keep his mouth shut.

Velma first sued Louis for divorce in 1934, alleging that he had threatened to kill her. In the ensuing legal wrangle, she accused Louis of kidnapping their three-year-old daughter and secreting her in Mexico. Eventually, Louis returned the child to her mother, and the couple reconciled their differences, at least for a time.

Tindall made the papers again when he attacked John B. Davis, the director of Fort Worth's Southwest Exposition and Fat Stock Show and a former Fort Worth city councilman, on Exchange Avenue in the stockyards. Tindall and Davis had been engaged in a running dispute over the Tindalls' contract to appear at the Exposition, and Tindall had promised Davis that he would "whip him the first time I saw him on Exchange Avenue." On January 27, 1936, Tindall did just that. Encountering Davis on the street, Tindall sucker-punched him in the side of the head, knocking him to the sidewalk, then pounded him until he was unconscious and left him with a concussion. Tindall told the police he "was just putting him in line a little."

Velma filed for divorce again in 1941, this time on the grounds that Louis had taken up with a woman named Opal Boyer. Velma dismissed her suit within a few weeks but filed again a few months later. This time the proceedings turned even uglier than usual. Initially, the court ordered Tindall to pay temporary alimony at the rate of $150 per month, but then it scheduled a hearing in November 1942 to set a permanent amount for Velma's support. At that hearing, Velma testified that Louis was the boss numbers man in Fort Worth, employing nearly three hundred runners and earning a personal income of almost four hundred dollars a week. The judge decided that he could not force Tindall to continue an illegal activity and therefore could not fix an alimony payment based on his illegal income; however, he did note that he could make an award to Velma out of whatever money Louis might presently have on hand, and he ordered Tindall not to transfer any assets until another hearing could be held.

Velma took the position that Tindall's assets included any of his property remaining in their home and refused him access to his clothes. Enraged, Tindall charged into the family home and demanded his property at gun point. Velma went for her gun, and shots were fired. No one was injured, but Tindall, now even more furious, destroyed his home, including most of the furniture and at least one wall. He ripped up his ex-wife's wardrobe, leaving, as she later testified, "not enough to make doll clothes out of."

Tindall then locked himself and his former mother-in-law, Anna Callahan, in a bedroom where he pistol-whipped her and beat her with a Bible, breaking her arm. He then called the family doctor and demanded that he "come over here and set this goddamned old woman's arm." Finally, finding nothing left to destroy, he submitted to arrest by two policemen who had arrived on the scene, yelling that his ex-wife and her mother had tried to kill him.

Velma retaliated by accusing her ex-husband of transferring money in violation of the court's order. She told the court that Louis had paid $2,000 by check to T. L. "Curly" Rogers, a Dallas gambler and numbers man. Although she didn't mention him by name in her testimony, everyone in the Dallas–Fort Worth underworld knew that Curly Rogers worked for Benny Binion and that the story of this payment from Tindall to Rogers was a revelation Benny did not appreciate.

Tindall did nothing to help himself when, trying to avoid trial on the charge of assault-to-murder in the beating of Anna Callahan, he checked himself into a Dallas hospital to be treated for anemia and was later asked to leave after he accidentally fired a pistol in his room. It developed that Curly Rogers had smuggled the pistol into the hospital because Louis believed that Velma planned to come and kill him. After this episode, the judge set a new trial date and increased Tindall's bond from $2,000 to $5,000. George Wilderspin posted the new bond.

Benny Binion had had enough. His name had not been mentioned in any of Tindall's escapades, but now, with the involvement of Curly Rogers and George Wilderspin, it was only a matter of time before someone publicly connected Tindall and Binion. Driven by the publicity Tindall's antics generated, the police had begun raiding the policy room at 907 Jones Street every few days, and Tindall had been indicted for gambling. Worse, Tindall had taken to boasting that Velma would never get his money, because she didn't know how much he was taking off the top. Binion expected his front men to steal a little, but bragging about it was another matter. He dispatched a messenger, probably George Wilderspin, to have a talk with Tindall.

Within a few days, the Fort Worth underworld began to

whisper that a "big Dallas gambler" wanted Tindall dead. Tindall apparently took the rumors to heart. He and his new wife, the statuesque former Opal Boyer, went armed at all times, both carrying .44 caliber Colt Peacemakers. Since June 1943, when they had driven two intruders off their property, the Tindalls had developed a routine. If they arrived at home after dark, Opal would leave the car first, her .44 in her hand, and search the house. If all was well, she would turn on the porch light and the numerous outside flood lights, and only then would Louis leave the car and enter the house.

November 12, 1944

Louis and Opal Tindall had enjoyed a quiet dinner and movie in downtown Fort Worth and returned to their home at 5417 Byers Avenue at about 1:00 a.m. on Sunday morning. According to their custom, Opal stepped out of the car to check the house, while Louis, his .44 in his lap, waited for the all-clear signal. Opal had taken no more than two steps toward the house when a shotgun blast shattered the passenger side window of the Tindalls' Cadillac. She turned to her husband and said, "Honey, I didn't shoot at you," but her words were drowned in the noise of three pistol shots. One of the shots missed entirely and embedded itself in the front seat of the car. The second hit Tindall's wallet and lodged in the driver's door. The third struck Tindall in the right side and perforated his lung, just missing his heart as it passed through his body and out his left hip.

Both Tindalls emptied their pistols at two men fleeing under cover of a hedge that separated the Tindalls' property from an adjoining alley, but they did no damage. Opal then drove her husband to the hospital, where doctors pronounced his condition as very grave. His injuries would have been serious for anyone; for a hemophiliac, they were deadly. Yet, after surgery and two days of almost constant transfusions, Tindall was able to talk to the police. He had no idea, he told them, who would want to kill him. He didn't trust banks, he said, and always kept large amounts of money on his person and in his home. He suspected that someone was trying to rob him. He didn't explain the elaborate precautions that he and Opal always took before entering the house, or the rumors that a Dallas gambler wanted him dead.

Tindall's condition continued to improve almost miraculously until the night of November 25, when he was struck by a sudden coughing fit. The coughing spasms broke several stitches and Tindall once again began hemorrhaging. By the afternoon of November 26, 1944, the former trick-riding star was dead.

POLICE HAD NO idea who had ambushed Louis Tindall. They recognized the shooting as the work of two men, one armed with a shotgun and the other with a .45 caliber pistol, and they suspected, but could not prove, the involvement of a third man as a driver. Given Tindall's temper and acidic personality, any number of motives for his killing presented themselves. Robbery might have been the motive, just as Tindall himself insisted, or Velma Tindall and/or her mother, Anna Callahan, might well have hired it for revenge. But speculation centered on the mysterious Dallas gambler who had allegedly offered a reward for Tindall's life. Still, as the police frequently said, knowing and proving are two different things.

The roster of possible gunmen from Dallas or Fort Worth, or even from out of town, was intimidating, and investigators rushed to shorten the list of suspects, quickly checking to see which triggermen were currently in jail or prison and which were at large. Even then, the list remained impossibly long. Bob Minyard was still at liberty, his trial for the murder of Raymond Laudermilk having been continued several times. Cliff Helm, a former rodeo cowboy and close Binion associate, had been no-billed after gunning down his wife's ex-husband in his front yard in October 1941 and was at large. Buddy Malone, after the Frieden murder charges were dismissed, continued in Binion's employ, replacing Laudermilk. Several other Dallas gunmen, not regular Binion employees, were available for odd jobs, as well.

In Fort Worth, the list of possible shooters was even longer. Leroy "Tincy" Eggleston, who always maintained he never killed anyone unless he was paid to do it, was available. So was Jim Clyde Thomas, a well-dressed, soft-spoken bad man who had served time for burglary in both Nebraska and Texas, and was out on bail awaiting trial for the murder of a doctor and his wife in Littlefield, Texas. Frank Cates, an equally violent running mate of Thomas's, was also in the area. Jack Nesbit, an ex-convict known for his skill with shotguns and dynamite, made his headquarters in Fort Worth. The honkytonks and roadhouses out on the Jacksboro Highway teemed with brawlers and street fighters, and any one of them could have been persuaded to kill for money.

The Fort Worth police found the investigation impossible. Tindall had far too many enemies, and Dallas and Fort Worth had far too many killers. The murder of Louis Tindall remains on the books as an unsolved crime.

"I'll Close Down
When Binion Closes Down"

DURING THE WAR years, gambling in Dallas became so flagrant that city officials, determined not to enforce anti-gambling laws, were often hard-pressed to avoid stumbling on it accidentally.

Every downtown hotel, with the possible exception of the Baker and the Adolphus, was home to at least a regular crap game, if not a full-fledged casino. Benny Binion's Southland Group ran the gambling at the Southland, the Blue Bonnet, and the St. George, along with several other lesser operations. Jerry Rosenberg and Johnny Andrews managed the games at the Jefferson. Herbert Noble and his various partners entertained the high rollers at the Majestic, the Savoy, the Rose, the Campbell, and later the Dallas Airmen's Club in the old Santa Paula Hotel. Sherman Little and Bob Fletcher ran a high stakes game at the Maurice.

In his historic interview with the University of Nevada Oral History Program, Binion described the downtown scene this way:

> Well, [the games] were in hotel suites, you know. We'd just have a big suite of rooms have the tables in there, have a bar, and we'd send out to different restaurants and get the food. Everybody knew about it, see them men a-carryin', you know, them things like they carry

hot food in, with a handle on it. They was runnin' up
and down the street with em' all the time.

The main place was the Southland Hotel in Dallas. It's tore down now. That was the famous one.
Then the Blue Bonnet, the Maurice—- that was the
main places. And we all got along good together. . . .
I just run my business to suit me, and I let them do
the same.

Not all of the Dallas gambling, of course, was as sophisticated
as the downtown scene. On the rugged South Dallas streets, a
Friday or Saturday night crap game could be found in almost
every alley, beer joint, pool hall, or walk-up rooming house. If
the winner was lucky enough, and sober enough, he might even
make it home with his winnings. Even in church-mouse-poor
West Dallas, a gambler could find a game at almost any time,
though usually for only nickels and dimes.

On the east side of Dallas, Theatre Row washed Elm Street in
the glow of neon marquees, as the Majestic, the Rialto, the Palace, and a half dozen other theaters announced the latest motion
pictures, variety shows, and road companies of Broadway plays.
Just a mile or so east of Theatre Row, the after-hours clubs and
juke joints of Deep Ellum, scattered among the all-night pawn
shops and cafés, served up food, liquor, gambling, and violence
in more or less equal proportions.

Binion's Policy business thrived during the war years as well.
By 1945, Benny was running twelve policy wheels, each one conducting two drawings a day, seven days a week. Besides the Tip
Top and the White and Green wheels in Deep Ellum, Benny
ran the romantically named High Noon, Silver Dollar, and
Horseshoe wheels, and the more routinely named Hi-Lo, Five
and Ten, Grand Prize, and several others. Each wheel had its
own following and each one could be counted on to generate
one hundred thousand dollars a year in personal income for
the Cowboy.

Hundreds, if not thousands, of slot machines and marble tables, forerunners of today's pinball machines, were scattered through the backrooms of bars, taverns, restaurants, and private clubs from one side of Dallas to the other. Benny Binion had no interest at all in mechanical gambling devices, but their owners, principally Jake Lansky, the brother of the notorious Meyer Lansky, reaped profits in the millions from the machines during the war years.

Horse players could bet legally at the Fair Park race track in Dallas or at Arlington Downs, but bookies all over Dallas prospered, taking bets illegally on races all over the country. Like the slot machines, bookmaking held no interest for Binion, except that the bookies were among his best customers. While bookies seldom play the horses, they are notorious crap shooters and poker players, and a healthy percentage of their profits found a home in Benny's pockets. Binion, however, did not return the favor, following his philosophy of never betting "on anything that eats."

Gambling in all its forms (except at the local race tracks) was, of course, illegal in Dallas, but an accommodation reached with local authorities even before the war insured that the casinos operated with little or no meaningful official interference. The Dallas population had begun to soar with the oil boom of the early 1930s, and the explosion continued through the Depression as farm families abandoned the land and migrated to the cities. With the onset of the war, the migration of rural Texans to the cities increased from a trickle to a flood. Between 1930 and 1950, the population of Dallas increased from 260,475 to 434,462; and the area of the city increased from fewer than forty-two square miles to more than 111. The population expansion, and the accompanying increase in the demand for city and county services, strapped the official coffers. In the hope of averting a potential financial crisis, city and county officials hit upon a scheme to "tax" illegal gambling by conducting periodic raids and levying fines for misdemeanor gambling violations. The resulting gambling tariff generated as much as $200,000 per year in city and county revenues, and Binion estimated that, over the years, he personally paid $600,000 in gambling fines.

Of course, this system of illegally licensed gambling infuriated the segment of the population Benny called "the do-gooders and Bible-thumpers," and occasional sweeping raids were necessary at times to appease the more law-abiding folk. Election years motivated more frequents raids which served a two-fold purpose. The widely publicized raids elevated public confidence in law enforcement officials, making their reelection more likely, and the resulting revenues helped cure any last-minute budget shortfalls, which also helped incumbents' election prospects.

These raids seldom occurred unexpectedly, but some inevitably produced embarrassing results. On the evening of July 31, 1943, the police conducted what they expected would be a routine raid at the Jefferson Hotel. Unfortunately, someone, possibly an overzealous reporter, identified one of the game's patrons as Dallas County Judge Sarah Hughes. The resulting headlines overshadowed the fact that the operators of the game, Jerry Rosenberg and Johnny Anderson, paid the usual fines and were released. Judge Hughes, who achieved immortality twenty years later when she swore in Lyndon Johnson as President of the United States aboard Air Force One on November 22, 1963, was, in fact, not present at the game or even at the hotel. But her efforts to disprove the story occupied the press for several days, and the next few weeks were rockier than usual for the gambling fraternity.

The great danger to the gamblers during the 1940s came not from the police but from hijackers. These desperadoes, invariably either proven killers or murderers-in-waiting, always followed the same modus operandi. Two, sometimes three, masked men armed with sawed-off shotguns would slam through the door of the hotel suite or backroom where a high-stakes game was in progress, and clean out the game and all the players, taking cash, jewelry, and anything else of value. The hijackers would race out of the hotel or restaurant, into a waiting automobile, and disappear. Sometimes, less bold hijackers would wait outside a big game, strong-arm the game's operator as he left the premises, and make off with the night's winnings. A few small-timers would simply find someone associated with the downtown gamblers and, on the assumption that he would be carrying a large amount of cash, rob him at gunpoint in the street. In one such case, Charles Archer, a South Dallas tavern operator and burglar, and a South Dallas police character named Ernest Gamble, set upon a bookie and small-time gambler named Jewel Whitehurst and robbed him at gunpoint at the busy downtown intersection of Commerce and Akard. Not content with robbing Whitehurst, the two then beat him savagely. Whitehurst died several weeks later as a result of the beating.

The most notorious big-time hijacking in Dallas took place in March 1943, when Bob Fletcher and Sherman Little were robbed at the point of shotguns as they left their game at the Maurice Hotel. Fletcher and Little refused to say how much cash they lost in the hijacking and, in keeping with the gambler's code, said that they did not recognize the three men involved. The Dallas underworld grapevine quickly identified the three hijackers as the Norris brothers, Gene and Pete, and one Jack Williams.

The brothers Norris were burglars, bank robbers, murderers, and, in the case of Gene, contract killers. Over the course of his considerable criminal career, Pete Norris accumulated prison sentences totaling more than nine hundred years, and, because of the amount of time he spent behind bars, never truly fulfilled his criminal potential. Brother Gene was another story. Gene was known to have taken revenge on a Houston gambler for testifying against his brother, beating both the gambler and his wife to death in their living room. He also assisted his brother's escape from the Texas prison system (once) and from county jails (twice). After serving six years for aiding his brother's escape, Gene was paroled on the condition that he leave Texas and never return, a condition he ignored entirely. By the time of his death in a rain of gunfire in 1957, Texas Rangers firmly believed that Gene Norris had been responsible for nine murders, and they considered him a prime suspect in nearly thirty more, both in and out of Texas.

Binion solved the problem of hijackings with characteristic Cowboy style. He was most capable of guarding his own games, usually carrying a Colt .45 automatic under each arm and a .38 in his jacket pocket. But for particularly high stakes games, he often hired the worst hijackers he could find to serve as guards, on the theory, as he liked to say, that he "would rather have them on the inside pissin' out than on the outside pissin' in." Following this plan, he frequently hired the likes of Fort Worth gunmen Jim Clyde Thomas, Tincy Eggleston, and Jack Nesbit to stand guard at his casinos. There is no record of one of Binion's games ever being hijacked.*

But hijacking was not the only way to steal from a gambling operation. Skimming went on even before there was a name for it, and dealers and pit bosses have stolen from gambling operators for as long as gambling has existed. Gambling operators expect a certain amount of pilferage from their employees and, although they don't like it, they count it as a cost of doing business. Until it becomes flagrant.

Late in 1945, Benny Binion began to suspect that he was not getting his full 25 percent share of Herbert Noble's gambling profits. By December, he was certain that Noble was skimming the profits at the new Dallas Airmen's Club. Binion waited until New Year's Eve before sending a message to Noble: Beginning with the New Year, Binion would put Noble on a "hard count," meaning one of Binion's men would be in attendance at Noble's club at all times and would supervise the count.

Noble bristled. He was still smarting from the failure of his fledgling policy partnership with the late Raymond Laudermilk.

---

* Binion's partner, Earl Dalton, was approached outside his Highland Park home by a would-be hijacker in March 1946. L.J. McWillie, one of the Southland Group's casino managers, shot the man dead on the spot.

As an added insult, Laudermilk's admitted killer, Bob Minyard, was not only still at large—the district attorney never having found it convenient to try him—but Binion had forced him on Noble as a partner. Just days before, Noble's simmering hatred for Minyard had boiled over. Pioneer Dallas business man Karl Hoblitzelle, whose Interstate Amusement Company owned the Majestic Theatre, complained to the police about the late-night goings-on at the nearby Majestic Hotel, fearing that the public might believe he owned both businesses. At Hoblitzelle's insistence, the police closed down the gambling at the Majestic. Minyard and Eddie Wrotan, at Binion's invitation, moved the operation and its customers to the Blue Bonnet. Noble was not invited to join them. Furious, Noble called Minyard and demanded to know why he wasn't in on the move. "It's none of your damn business why you're out," Minyard told him. The two men exchanged words, including threats to kill each other on sight.

Against this backdrop, Noble's response to Binion's demand for a hard count was as predictable as sunrise. He sent word to Binion that he was able to count his own money and had no need of Binion's help running his business.

In early January 1946, Binion sent word to Noble that his cut of the Airmen's Club business would be 40 percent rather than the usual twenty-five, beginning immediately. Noble replied that Binion could "go straight to Hell."

On January 11, 1946, a Dallas County deputy sheriff paid Noble a visit at the Airmen's Club. After some small talk, the deputy looked carefully around the club and said, "Herbert, you're going to have to close down." Noble wanted to know why. "Gambling's illegal," the deputy told him. "Does Binion have to close down, too?" Noble asked. "Because I'll close down when Binion closes down and not a damned minute before."

The deputy turned and walked out. That night, Noble opened the Dallas Airmen's Club for business as usual.

The Shooting Starts

January 12, 1946

The early morning Dallas skies were clear and cold. Business at the Dallas Airmen's Club had been slower then usual, and by just after two o'clock, the club was deserted, and Herbert Noble was ready to close the doors. Noble, Stetson pulled low and coat collar turned up against the cold, locked the front door and hurried toward his car parked on Live Oak, just a few doors from the club entrance. He had unlocked his car door by the time he noticed a Cadillac sedan parked less than a block away. When Noble wheeled his Mercury coupe away from the curb, the Cadillac followed.

Noble drove two blocks then doubled back, circling back to the front of the Airmen's Club. The Cadillac followed. Noble made several erratic turns through the angled downtown streets. Still the Cadillac followed. By now, Noble had been able to see that two men sat in the front seat of the Cadillac and another sat on the passenger side in the back seat, and he had recognized the car. Noble decided to lead his pursuers toward his ranch in Denton County, away from his wife and daughter at the family home in Oak Cliff.

On the city streets, the Mercury, more nimble than the Cadillac, enjoyed an advantage, and Noble was able to pull away from his pursuers by several blocks. But when the chase reached the open highway, the Cadillac, with its great horsepower advantage, began slowly to gain ground. Noble was within two or three miles of his ranch when the Cadillac pulled up on his rear bumper. The man in the Cadillac's passenger seat wedged himself out the window and fired a sawed-off shotgun at the rear window of Noble's Mercury, showering Noble with shattered glass but doing no real damage. Another shotgun blast riddled the Mercury's trunk lid.

Several shots from a .45 pistol punched holes in Noble's car, and Noble, still uninjured, returned fire, driving with one hand and blasting at his pursuers with the other. About a mile from his ranch, Noble's careening car skated off the road and into a shallow bar ditch, coming to rest on its side. Noble scrambled out of the wreckage and ran toward a farm house, forty yards from the road. With his pistol lost somewhere in the overturned car, Noble was now unarmed. The Cadillac slid to a halt, and two gunmen jumped out and began firing at the retreating Noble. One of the shots found its target, hitting Noble in the back above the left hip just as he reached the farmhouse yard; the gambler went to his knees, crawling under the house.

The shots and barking dogs aroused Noble's neighbor, who stepped onto his front porch, .30-30 rifle in hand, and switched on his floodlights. "Who the hell is making all that racket at this time of night?" he yelled. But by then the two gunmen, not knowing that Noble was unarmed and not being anxious to tangle with the dogs, had climbed back into the Cadillac and were back on the road toward Dallas.

Two days later, from his bed at Methodist Hospital, Noble described the incident to the authorities. He would not, he said, testify against his attackers; however, in a serious violation of the unwritten code among criminals, he did identify the three would-be assassins. Worse yet, Noble talked to the newspapers, and the names of two of the men who had tried to kill him were in the headlines three days after the shooting. For reasons that would become clear, Noble did not identify the third man for the press.

ACCORDING TO NOBLE, the front passenger in the Cadillac, the man who fired the shotgun out the window, had been Johnny Brazil Grisaffi, an employee of Vick's Restaurant, located on Commerce Street about three blocks south of the Airmen's Club. According to police sources, Grisaffi was a triggerman and drug dealer who did frequent work as an enforcer and protector for the Dallas narcotics trade. The presence of several Grisaffi families in Dallas (with numerous spellings that sometimes changed in the city directories from one year to the next) often caused confusion, and the gunman who fired at Noble was usually known simply as "Johnny Brazil" or "Little Johnny."

Johnny Brazil's companion that night, the driver of the Cadillac, was, according to Noble's published statement, Hollis DeLois Green, who preferred to be called "Lois," which was pronounced with the typical Texas twang as "Loyce." Lois Green—already a seasoned career criminal at the age of twenty-seven—and his older brother Cecil had come to Dallas from Oklahoma in the 1920s with their mother, a prostitute named Mary Addie Turner. Cecil and Lois, who had taken the last name of a man named Ollie Green—who may or may not have been married to their mother and who may or may not have been their father—lived in a whorehouse on St. Louis Street in South Dallas. The Green brothers raised themselves on the South Dallas streets, doing odd jobs around the "immoral resorts," as the brothels were politely called in those days, running errands for bootleggers, gamblers, and pimps and, as they got older, stealing bicycles. Neither of them would admit to ever setting foot in school.

By the time he was a teenager, Lois had a long record of run-ins with the law, mostly for shoplifting or petty theft. At fourteen, he was sent to reform school for stealing bicycles; at twenty, he was convicted of auto theft as an adult and made his first visit to the Texas prison system. In early 1942, about a year after his release, he went to New York City and promptly got into trouble again, this time for killing a policeman. There was not enough evidence to convict him, but he spent a term in the

New York jails as a vagrant. Lois Green decided that this term would be his last.

Jail time can be a fine finishing school for a young criminal, and Green took advantage of the opportunity. He listened to the other, more experienced convicts and learned the tricks of the burglary trade. Realizing that the men he listened to were in prison just as he was, Green paid particular attention to the stories about how they had been caught. He soon learned that most of his fellow inmates were behind bars because of the testimony of their accomplices. He also learned that the more powerful the criminal, the more likely the police were to make a deal with a low-level associate to "snitch him off." The key to staying out of prison, as Green saw it, was to leave no witnesses.

Back in Dallas, Green put his lessons to immediate use. He established a hangout in West Dallas that quickly became a clearinghouse for criminal information. Burglaries were planned there, and men were recruited for all manner of criminal enterprises. The police and the newspapers soon came to call the burglars, safe crackers, thieves, tie-up men, pimps, and whores who hung out there "the Green Gang." In truth, the Green Gang never existed, at least not in the sense of the modern gang with its initiation rituals and a formal leadership structure. Green's operation was more like a criminal day-labor pool, where a man so inclined could easily find illegal employment in the Dallas area. Burglars associated with the mythical Green Gang robbed jewelry stores, pawn shops, and payroll safes all over Texas and in at least sixteen other states. They were so proficient that, when Kansas City racketeers found it necessary to break into a vault to steal election returns, Green was called upon to furnish the manpower for the job.

Green personally preferred narcotics robberies, especially of wholesale drug warehouses, where, in addition to cash, he could steal drugs which could be sold on the street or used to entice young women into prostitution. By the end of World War II, Green would become the power behind a prostitution ring that extended into Texas, Louisiana, Oklahoma, and Arkansas. Dallas historian and newspaper man Warren Leslie wrote that, "at one time, there were no prostitutes in Dallas operating independent of Lois Green." This is probably an exaggeration, but Green certainly took his share of the income of almost every pimp and prostitute working in South or West Dallas.

Burglary and prostitution were the mainstays of his livelihood, and the sadistic Green looked at murder as more or less a hobby. He earned his reputation for vicious ruthlessness soon after his last prison sentence. In 1945, an ex-convict and hijacker named Otto Freyer attempted to enhance his bankroll by putting the arm on several of Green's pimps and prostitutes. Green sent two henchmen to dig a grave in the rural country northwest of Dallas and then kidnapped Freyer. At the grave site, Green forced the hijacker to strip naked and shot him in the stomach with a shotgun. Green than kicked Freyer into the fresh grave and covered him, still screaming for mercy, with quicklime before burying him alive. No one ever bothered anyone who worked for Lois Green again.

Green's second companion in the Cadillac, the man Noble identified for the police but not the newspapers, was Bob Minyard.

January 14, 1946

Bob Minyard, who was still awaiting trial for the murder of Raymond Laudermilk, and his young wife, Betty, spent the evening out, perhaps enjoying dinner and drinks at a nightclub. At around ten o'clock, they returned to their new two-story home in Dallas's fashionable Lakewood addition, near White Rock Lake.

The day had been cold and gray, and the mist that settled over Dallas around nightfall had turned to a chilling rain. Minyard first stopped his car in the driveway so that Betty could step into the side door of the house, and then he parked his new Oldsmobile in the detached garage at the end of the drive. Minyard had closed the garage door and turned toward the house when two men, both wearing overcoats and snap-brim fedoras against the chill, stepped from the shadows. One of the two was extremely tall and thin, while the other was of average height and stocky build. The shorter of the two carried a sawed-off shotgun beneath his coat; the other carried a .38 caliber automatic. As Minyard turned, the shorter man leveled the shotgun and fired both barrels nearly point-blank into his chest, lifting him off his feet and slamming him into the garage door. The taller man fired the .38 twice into the gory mess left by the shotgun, as Minyard slumped to the gravel driveway. The gunmen turned and ran to a car parked in a nearby alley while Minyard somehow got off four shots of his own. The *Fort Worth Star-Telegram*, in an uncharacteristic blast of purple prose, reported that Minyard "went down fighting—an automatic belching in his hand."

Betty Minyard, hearing the shots, ran from the house to her husband's side, finding him face-down in the driveway in a widening pool of blood, his smoking pistol in his hand. Her screams for help brought a neighbor who called the police and an ambulance. Less than an hour after reaching Parkland Hospital, the man who had been called a derelict and a vagrant when he shot Raymond Laudermilk died with $2,400 in cash in his pocket.

WORD OF MINYARD'S shooting buzzed on the underworld grapevine, probably even before he reached Parkland.

With his connections in the sheriff's office and the police department, Benny Binion knew that Bob Minyard had been shot within minutes after the shooting occurred. In fact, Chief Deputy Sheriff Bill Decker had made a quick stop at the side entrance of the Southland Hotel, where he collected Binion on the way to the scene of the shooting. Binion, of course, did not know who had fired the fatal shots, but he didn't need to. The

Cowboy may have been illiterate, but he could add two and two and he knew that no one but Herbert Noble would have a reason, or the nerve, to kill Bob Minyard.

THE POLICE NEVER made an arrest in the Minyard killing, although they knew the killers' identities within a few days. As the police said more than once in those days, "knowing and proving are two different things."

According to statements made years later by a Dallas police detective, the tall, thin killer was Owen Nelson Hays, who, at 6 feet 3 inches and 143 pounds, was naturally called "Slim." Hays had been employed for years by Herbert Noble as a dice-dealer, pit boss, and bodyguard, most recently at the Dallas Airmen's Club. Both local and federal authorities believed that Hays, in addition to his gambling activities, was a major figure in Dallas marijuana distribution.

The same detective identified the shotgun-wielding second gunman as a West Dallas police character named Charles M. Lefors Jr., known as "Sonny."

Sonny Lefors owned Sonny's Food Store on Singleton Boulevard in West Dallas, a well-known hangout for burglars and safecrackers; Lefors himself was known not only as a burglar but also as a major fence. Lefors had grown up in West Dallas and had known Herbert Noble for many years. Although it was not common knowledge at the time of the Minyard killing, later developments established that Lefors engaged in several criminal enterprises with Noble, including concealing large amounts of stolen property.

The driver of the getaway car, police would learn much later, was the red-headed girlfriend of Slim Hays. She burned up the motor in Hays's Cadillac in her haste to leave the scene and, years later, produced the receipt for repairs in support of her statement to the police about the Minyard killing.

With the involvement of Slim Hays and Sonny Lefors, and the timing of the shooting, which occurred only two days after the attempt on Noble's life, the meaning of Bob Minyard's murder was clear. From his hospital bed, Herbert Noble had avenged Raymond Laudermilk and sent a declaration of war to Benny Binion, all in one murderous stroke.

IN THE AFTERMATH of the killing of Bob Minyard and the attempted murder of Herbert Noble, Binion's Southland Group quickly came to resemble an armed camp. When he learned that Minyard had been killed, Binion quickly called Johnny Grisaffi. "Johnny," he said, "you're carrying a lot of heat on this deal. You'd better come to the hotel and stay awhile." Binion made similar calls to Lois Green and George "Junior" Thomas, whose car had been used in the attempt on Noble. In short order, the Southland was full of the toughest thugs in Dallas.

All over Dallas, underworld characters searched their memories for any real or imagined wrong they might have done to Noble, fearing they might be next on his list. Eddie Wrotan, who had joined Minyard in defecting from Noble's operation only a few weeks earlier, was so terrified that he left Dallas without even stopping to pack his clothes.

A LITTLE MORE than three months after the attempt on Noble's life and the murder of Bob Minyard, one of the most puzzling of the long list of unsolved Dallas and Fort Worth gambling murders occurred.

In the late evening of April 30, 1946, a resident of a small community located just west of Arlington was disturbed by the sound of something scratching at his front screen door. He opened the door to find forty-six-year-old ex-convict Ivan Poole dying on his front porch. Judging from appearances, Poole had been in a horrible fight. Several of his teeth were broken or missing, and his nose was broken. His knuckles were bruised and bleeding, and in one hand he clutched a bloody switchblade knife. He had been shot once in the right leg and once under the chin. The bullet that would prove fatal had entered under his left arm and lodged in his heart. Poole survived long enough to reach the hospital, but he never regained consciousness and died a few hours later.

Among Poole's personal effects, police found a key to a room at a tourist court on the east side of Fort Worth. There they found that Poole, who had a wife and a home in Dallas, was sharing the room with a "friend," a prostitute named Louisa Johnson. According to Johnson, Poole claimed that he made his living as a gambler. Only three days before, she said, Poole had engaged in a violent argument with a "big Dallas gambler." None of this surprised the police. Poole had a long history of involvement with gambling, prostitution, and violence. In 1933, he had been the leading suspect in the murder of a Dallas gambler named Nick Rapasky. He also had a total of six convictions for violation of various white slavery laws. In other words, he was a small-time thug and pimp and, as far as the police could see, the world was a better place without him.

The police *were* surprised, though, when Poole's car turned up a few days later in a Dallas parking lot. They were even more surprised when they found clothes in the back seat belonging to Dave Jarvis, a twenty-five-year-old cattle thief. Jarvis explained that he had borrowed Poole's car and was taking a few clothes to the laundry. He was sorry, he said, to hear that Poole was dead, but he didn't know anything about it. The police didn't believe him, but they let him go. Police never made an arrest in the Poole murder, but they did, eventually, come to know what had happened. Poole had gotten into an argument on an East Fort Worth street with Jarvis and Slim Hays. The argument became a fist fight, and Poole pulled his switchblade. In the struggle for the knife, Jarvis or Hays—or both—started shooting.

The probable participation of Slim Hays led investigators to strongly suspect that they knew the identity of the "big Dallas gambler" Poole had argued with three days before his death: Herbert Noble.

THE KILLING OF Ivan Poole was of little significance in the war for control of gambling territory in Dallas and Fort Worth. As Deputy Sheriff Bill Decker commented, "Poole was not known to be connected to any large gambling operation in Dallas or Fort Worth." But in terms of timing, it was a major event. Nineteen forty-six was an election year in Dallas, and law and order forces were waging a vigorous campaign against gambling and prostitution. For the reformers, the killing of Ivan Poole couldn't have come at a more opportune time.

"My Sheriff Got Beat"

BENEATH ITS HIGH-POWERED economy and fussy manners, Dallas at the end of World War II had become as dark and dangerous as any city in the United States. The friendly vices that the city fathers had tolerated, even encouraged, since the 1936 Centennial had turned ugly. Big-time gamblers like Ben Frieden, Sam Murray, and Raymond Laudermilk were gunned down on the city streets every few months. Lesser gamblers, pimps, and police characters shot, stabbed, and beat each other almost weekly. Safecrackers, burglars, and armed robbers—"yeggs" the newspapers called them—terrorized the city.

By 1944, the Dallas crime wave had become such an embarrassment that Texas Governor Coke Stevenson, responding to the demands of church and civic groups, called on the Texas Rangers to shut down the gambling in both Dallas and Fort Worth. Stevenson chose Ranger Captain M.T. "Lone Wolf" Gonzaullas to lead the clean-up. The flamboyant Gonzaullas, his Ranger uniform heavily starched and sharply creased, belonged to the old time one-riot-one-Ranger school of law enforcement. He carried a matched pair of nickel-plated, ivory-handled Colt .45s in quick-draw holsters slung from a hand-tooled gun belt, and he made no secret of the fact that he had used them before and wouldn't mind using them again, should the need arise. Fresh from quelling an oil field riot near Beaumont in 1943, Gonzaullas announced that the gambling and whoring in Dallas were going to stop or he would know the reason why.

The Rangers, led by Gonzaullas, began conducting raids at

known gambling spots all over North Texas, all to no avail. Each time the Rangers struck, they found empty hotel rooms, abandoned warehouses, and back rooms used for nothing more sinister than an occasional gin rummy game. Gonzaullas concluded that the gamblers were being tipped off in advance of the Rangers' raids. His suspicions were confirmed when he and his men arrived at the site of a well-known Dallas crap game to find the hotel suite completely stripped of gambling equipment of any kind. The telephone began to ring just as the Rangers rushed in the door, and Gonzaullas picked up the receiver. The voice on the line said, "They're on the way right now." "We're already here," Gonzaullas replied. The caller said, "Oh, damn," and hung up.

The raids ended in early 1946 when Gonzaullas was called away from Dallas to investigate a gruesome series of late-night murders near the northeast Texas town of Texarkana. Before leaving Dallas, "Lone Wolf" put the best possible spin on the Rangers' abortive anti-gambling campaign. The Rangers, he said, hadn't found any gambling going on and, if the gamblers weren't out of business, they were certainly slowed down. This, of course, was not true. The Rangers' activities in North Texas had been almost entirely unsuccessful; nevertheless, the end of wide-open Dallas gambling was in sight. Dallas voters were about to do what the Texas Rangers could not.

AT THE END of World War II, thousands of returning veterans swarmed into Dallas in search of the American Dream. Anxious to forget the war years and put down roots in a thriving, forward-looking community, they wanted houses with picket fences and parks where children could play. A wide-open town might be fine for a soldier on a weekend pass, but it wouldn't do for a family man. The politicians and civic leaders who had supported a wide-open Dallas understood that the city's future lay in banking, insurance, and commerce, and there was no place in their vision of the modern Dallas for gamblers, bookmakers, prostitutes, and pimps. The soldiers who had fought for democracy now wanted to participate in it, and the watchword in the 1946 Dallas County elections was "reform," with a new emphasis on law and order.

Benny Binion's long-time friend, Dallas District Attorney Dean Gauldin, announced that he intended to retire to private practice and would not stand for reelection in 1946. With no incumbent on the scene, six candidates announced for the vacancy. By the time the Democratic primary election approached (Dallas had no truly viable Republican Party at the time, and victory in the Democratic primary was tantamount to election to office), the field had narrowed to three serious contenders.

Former U.S. Army Major Will Wilson, a thirty-three-year-old Southern Methodist University graduate, was generally considered the front-runner. Wilson, who was on leave of absence from the Texas Attorney General's staff, had law enforcement experience, a war record and the support of his influential Highland Park[*] neighbors. His platform consisted essentially of promises to bring law and order to Dallas County and he pronounced himself a staunch foe of "organized crime" (meaning, of course, Benny Binion).

Henry Wade boasted an even more elaborate law enforcement background, as a former FBI agent and district attorney of nearby Rockwall County. A veteran of the Navy, Wade, like Wilson, promised to run "organized crime" (meaning Benny Binion) out of Dallas; however, Henry Wade was not a true resident of Dallas County, as ordinarily required by law. He had established his eligibility for election by taking advantage of an obscure statute permitting returning veterans to declare residency wherever they might choose, and many Dallas County voters saw him as an outsider. His reputation as something of a carpetbagger dimmed his election prospects.

---

[*] Highland Park was and is an exclusively residential, incorporated city located entirely inside the city limits of Dallas. Citizens of Highland Park have for years been among the wealthiest and most influential in North Texas.

Local attorney Andrew Pierce, a part-time preacher and full-time bigot, based his constituency on the remnants of Dallas's once powerful Ku Klux Klan. Pierce, like Wilson and Wade, jumped on the reform bandwagon, but he seemed far more concerned with Wilson's support among black voters. "Will Wilson is roundin' up them Negroes," Pierce ranted, "and votin' 'em like he was dippin' sheep."

BENNY BINION REMAINED unconcerned with all the talk of reform and law and order. For most of his life, prosperity had depended on the outcome of local elections, and he knew that, in an election year, law and order talk was as common among Texas courthouse politicians as cheap suits. But he *was* a bit concerned that none of the leading candidates for district attorney would take his money.

WILSON WON THE Democratic primary, but he failed to secure a majority and was forced into a run-off with Andy Pierce. Wade finished a close third.

During the run-off campaign, Wilson and Wade struck a deal. Wilson's ambitions lay in state politics, and he intended to occupy the Dallas District Attorney's office for no more than a single term. He offered Henry Wade a position in his office as chief prosecutor and promised to support Wade as his successor in four years. Wade accepted and quickly announced his endorsement of Wilson's candidacy. Wade's support assured the election, and Wilson defeated Pierce easily in the run-off. One of the men who had refused Binion's campaign contributions was now the district attorney-elect, and another would be his chief prosecutor. The Cowboy had lost a little of his grip on Dallas, but, always the careful gambler, he still had an ace in the hole.

RICHARD ALLEN "SMOOT" Schmid had served as Dallas County Sheriff since 1933. Before his election as sheriff, Smoot (he had legally changed his name so that voters would not be confused at the polls) had operated Smoot's Guaranty Cycle Company on Commerce Street in Dallas, where he sometimes bought and sold used bicycles. Apparently, the soon-to-be lawman wasn't particular about the origins of his merchandise. One of his steadiest suppliers had been a young West Dallas thief named Raymond Hamilton, who ran for a year or so with Bonnie and Clyde and met his end in the Texas electric chair at the age of twenty-one. Hamilton and his friends stole bicycles and sold them to Smoot, who cleaned them up and resold them in his shop, sometimes buying and selling the same machine several times.

The sheriff's live-and-let-live attitude made him an extremely popular law enforcement officer with some elements of Dallas society, and with Benny Binion in particular. Benny had known Smoot since his bootlegging days and frequently dropped by the sheriff's office to visit and drink coffee even when he hadn't been arrested. When election time rolled around, Smoot could always count on Benny for a generous campaign contribution. In return, the sheriff was always happy to help Benny's rivals see the error of their ways and, if necessary, escort them out of his county.

Smoot's chief claim to fame was that two of his deputies, Bob Alcorn and Ted Hinton, had joined the legendary former Texas Ranger Frank Hamer in the posse that eventually tracked down and killed Bonnie and Clyde. Smoot was not a member of the posse and was not present at the ambush, but ever the politician, he arrived in Louisiana only hours after the shooting and appeared in many of the hundreds of photos taken that day. A good many Dallas voters were under the impression that their sheriff had led the posse in the hunt for the outlaw pair, and Smoot did little to correct the misconception.

Smoot's chief deputy, Bill Decker (who did lead the group of lawmen that captured Raymond Hamilton), may have been the only lawman in Dallas who was more popular than Smoot himself. As a lawman, Decker was so effective that he frequently needed only to put the word on the street that he wanted someone and his man would appear at his office in a day or two ready to be questioned. Decker had known Binion since the young boot-legger's earliest days in Dallas and probably first introduced him to Smoot. As was the case with many policemen and criminals of the time, Binion and Decker had developed, over the years, a friendship based upon mutual respect. If Decker wanted Benny or one of his men, all he had to do was call. By the same token, Benny and his men knew that they would get a fair shake from Decker if he arrested them. Decker knew almost everyone in Dallas and was generally regarded as honest and fair. With his support, Smoot's reelection seemed virtually certain.

The sheriff's principal opponent was a young former policeman and Army Air Corps veteran named Steve Guthrie. Like Will Wilson and Henry Wade, Guthrie campaigned on the "reform" platform. He cast the incumbents as villains, characterizing Smoot Schmid as part of "the biggest political machine ever known in Dallas County." Guthrie, too, promised to rid the county of "organized crime" (meaning, as usual, Benny Binion).

As expected, the incumbent Smoot won the Democratic pri-mary by a margin of more than eleven thousand votes over his young challenger. Still, with four other candidates in the race, Smoot's total fell short of a majority. He would face Guthrie in a run-off. ·

During the run-off campaign, Guthrie campaigned relent-lessly, speaking anywhere he could gather a crowd. He appeared often on radio broadcasts, appealing for help in his crusade against the Dallas County "political machine." In an exhaustive door-to-door campaign, Guthrie attempted to visit every Dallas household and very nearly succeeded.

Smoot Schmid, on the other hand, was so confident of reelec-tion that he conducted the bulk of his run-off campaign with his size fourteen boots (he was sometimes known behind his back as "Bigfoot") propped on his desk in the sheriff's office.

GUTHRIE, THE HEAVY underdog in the run-off election, received an unexpected windfall when Herbert Noble, always in pursuit of the "big fix," offered the young dark-horse candidate a campaign contribution of $15,000. In those pre-television days, when local political campaigns largely consisted of speeches at public events and a few newspaper ads, $15,000 was a huge contribution— nearly sufficient to finance an entire campaign—and Guthrie accepted Noble's offer. Noble's generosity clearly implied that, should Guthrie win, he expected to enjoy a relationship with the sheriff's office similar to the one Binion had shared with Smoot and Decker.

When word of Noble's enormous contribution to the Guthrie campaign reached him at his ranch near Jordan, Montana, Binion's notoriously volcanic temper erupted. Benny believed that Noble had been shorting his count from their various gambling ventures, stealing from him on a daily basis, for several months. Now, adding insult to injury, Noble was giving his stolen money to a candidate sworn to clean up Dallas gambling and to jail Binion in the process. Binion dispatched Buddy Malone, who had been in Montana helping with Binion's horses and cattle, to Dallas, with instructions to get rid of Herbert Noble immediately.

Malone, although he had proved himself willing to use his gun in the Ben Frieden killing, was not an assassin. He was a good man with horses and cattle and a competent street man for Binion's policy racket, but it was not in his character to lie in wait for a victim and kill him in cold blood. Even if Malone had been willing, Noble, of course, knew him on sight and, after the attempt on his life in January, was not about to let any of Binion's regulars get within killing distance. Malone needed someone close enough to Noble to kill him—and greedy enough to do it. The man he picked was Jack Darby, a Dallas gambler and a part-time associate of Noble in several hotel crap games. Malone offered Darby $15,000 and a Dallas crap game to kill Noble, and Darby accepted the proposition.*

---

* Malone always denied attempting to arrange Noble's murder by Darby or anyone else, but whether it was arranged by Malone or someone else, the attempt on Noble described here was confirmed by both Noble and Darby.

On the evening of August 19, 1946, at about five o'clock, Darby called Noble from the Biltmore Recreation Room near the corner of Knox and Travis in downtown Dallas. A few days earlier, Noble and Darby had won $12,000 in a crap game from Eddie Gilliland, a gambler who ran a game in the back room at the Biltmore. Darby called Noble to tell him that Gilliland had paid off. Darby said that he had been drinking and was afraid to take that much cash out on the street; he suggested that Noble come to the Biltmore and get the money.

As Noble entered the door, Darby stuck a .38 snub-nosed pistol under his chin and began cursing him, ordering him to an upstairs office. On the way upstairs, Darby fired twice into the stairs at Noble's feet, apparently trying to force Noble to draw his pistol. Upstairs, Gilliland and a man named Bill Holcomb waited at a small table. For the next half hour, Darby kept the gun cocked and pointed at Noble, calling him "everything but a white man," trying to get Noble to draw the pistol tucked in his belt. Apparently, Gilliland and Holcomb were present so that they could later testify that Darby had killed Noble in self-defense. After a tense half hour, Noble finally talked Darby out of killing him, and Holcomb took Darby's gun away from him. Noble took the $12,000 and left. For the second time in less than a year, he had survived an attempt on his life.

Eddie Gilliland was not so lucky. His body, severely beaten and shot twice in the head, was dumped on a dirt road in eastern Tarrant County just two months later. The murder was never solved.[*]

UNBELIEVABLY, GUTHRIE BEAT the heavily favored Smoot in the run-off election by just over eight hundred votes. "My damn

---

[*] Gilliland's murder, though never officially solved, bore all the earmarks of a Lois Green execution. Gilliland had been taken to a rural location, where he was relieved of a wad of cash and then beaten nearly to death with a piece of lumber. Two shots to the head finished the job.

sheriff just sat on his ass and pissed away the election," was the way Benny Binion put it.

At one minute after midnight on January 1, 1947, the district attorney's office would be swarming with reformers publicly sworn to put Benny in jail. His strongest ally, Smoot Schmid, would be replaced by yet another reformer. In the interest of harmony in the sheriff's office, Bill Decker, Benny's last hope, tendered his resignation as chief deputy effective at midnight on December 31, 1946.

To make matters worse, if possible, the city council had appointed a new city manager, V. R. Smitham, who, in turn, had appointed a new police chief, Carl Hansson. Several years earlier, Hansson, then a Dallas detective, had incurred Binion's wrath, and Benny had pulled enough stings to have Hansson transferred to the graveyard shift at the city zoo. Benny had taken great delight in calling Hansson at home in the early morning hours to ask if the monkeys were in bed yet. "When I saw Hansson was the new police chief," Benny said years later, "I just went to hollerin' and lit out a-runnin'."

10

The Syndicate Makes Its Move

EVEN BEFORE THE new sheriff and district attorney took office, the 1946 reform movement faced its first serious challenge. Surprisingly, the challenge came not from local gamblers but from outsiders with greedy eyes for Dallas gambling profits.

IN SPITE OF its booming economy and phenomenal growth, Dallas had never been considered a major center for organized crime. Being landlocked, it had no shipping and no dockworkers, a traditional focal point for organized criminal activity. Its labor unions, another traditional breeding ground for criminal enterprise, were small and relatively weak. This is not to say, however, that organized crime had no interest in Dallas.

In the national structure of organized crime—variously called "the Syndicate," "the Mob," "the Outfit," "the Mafia," or "la Cosa Nostra"—Dallas served during the 1930s and 1940s as a distribution point for narcotics smuggled into the United States from Mexico or through the Galveston seaport. Usually considered a satellite of the New Orleans mob, the Dallas "family" was founded in 1921 by Carlo Piranio, a Sicilian Mafioso who had originally settled in New Orleans before establishing the rackets in Dallas. He remained in power until February 1930, when he died of natural causes. His underboss and younger brother, Joseph Piranio, took over the Family and served as New Orleans's man in Dallas for twenty-five years.

In Galveston, the Maceo brothers, Sam and Rosario, controlled the drug traffic, gambling, and prostitution and reported, at least nominally, to the New Orleans crime boss Sylvestro "Silver Dollar Sam" Carolla.* The Maceos also controlled the corporation that owned the Southland Hotel in Dallas and thus were Benny Binion's landlords.

During the late 1930s, the coming world war imperiled the mob's established sources of narcotics. With Benito Mussolini in power, the Sicilian Mafia was driven into hiding, and the flow of drugs from Italy into the United States, once a torrent, slowed to a trickle. The Japanese invasion of China ended the availability of narcotics from the Far East almost overnight. To satisfy the demand for drugs in New York, Chicago, Detroit, and other major markets, the mob turned to South America and Mexico. The natural point of entry for contraband of any kind from Mexico or South America would be the bustling seaports at New Orleans and Galveston, and the hundreds of miles of Texas's virtually unguarded Mexican border.

But the New Orleans mobsters and their Galveston allies, still steeped in the clannish traditions of the Sicilian Mafia, distrusted even non-Sicilian Italians—Sam Carolla once refused to do business with Al Capone—and could hardly be expected to participate in a national smuggling operation with Jews and Irishmen. Thus, Dallas became a kind of middle ground, where the New Orleans smugglers sold their goods to the Chicago mob for distribution in Denver, Kansas City, St. Louis, Hot Springs, and, of course, Chicago. The scope of this arrangement became apparent as early as 1937, when Joe Civello, who would later become the Dallas mob boss, and his brothers Sam and Leon were convicted of possessing heroin with a wholesale value of more than three hundred thousand dollars.

Given this connection between New Orleans and Chicago, it was not surprising that a similar gambling arrangement would also exist.

---

* During the 1920s and 1930s, Galveston was so lawless that it was known to law enforcement as "the Free State of Galveston." In those days, absolutely nothing illegal transpired in Galveston without the blessing of the Maceos.

In 1934, New York Mayor Fiorello LaGuardia began a campaign to rid his city of slot machines, forcing New York mobster Frank Costello, who owned almost all of the city's slots, either to move the machines out of New York or see them destroyed. Costello struck a deal with Louisiana Senator Huey Long to move the slots to New Orleans. Costello nominated "Dandy" Phil Kastel, a New York gambler and con, as his man on the scene in Louisiana. As his local lieutenant, Kastel recruited a young gangster named Carlos Marcello, who would ten years later become the absolute ruler of the New Orleans mob. Soon New Orleans and the surrounding territory were saturated with slot machines. With still more machines warehoused in New Orleans, Kastel and Marcello began shipping the machines to Texas. The Maceos in Galveston owned their own machines and the New York slots were not welcome there. But it was 1936, and Dallas was a wide-open market for gambling action of any kind.

Jake Lansky, the brother of the mob's financial wizard, Meyer Lansky, opened a Dallas amusement company and began distributing slot machines, pinball machines (called marble tables), and jukeboxes to bars, restaurants, and clubs all over Dallas. Lansky was joined in this enterprise by Dave Yaras, a well-known Chicago hoodlum and contract killer. It was on a visit to Dallas to see his brother Jake that Meyer Lansky first met Benny Binion, a connection that would be important to Benny in years to come.

The bagman and fixer for Chicago's Dallas operations during the war years was a veteran hoodlum named Paul Roland Jones. A native of Pittsburg, Kansas, Jones came to Dallas in late 1940, after receiving first a parole and then a pardon following a 1931 Kansas murder conviction. Beginning in 1942, and continuing through the war, Jones worked with ranking Chicago hoodlum Nick de John and his Chicago bosses in the black market, selling gasoline and sugar rationing coupons. During the same period, Jones's duties also included overseeing the distribution of drugs smuggled from Mexico and destined for St. Louis, Denver,

Kansas City, and Chicago. On de John's instructions, Jones also began looking into the possibility of colonizing Dallas gambling, including craps, bookmaking, and numbers.

After surveying the local situation for several months, Jones advised de John against any attempt to take over Dallas gambling, telling him that the syndicate composed of Benny Binion, Earl Dalton, and Ivy Miller was too strong and too closely connected with law enforcement to be overthrown; however, Jones, did recommend expanding the slot machines and related activities. Soon after, de John financed Jones's interest in the Southwest Amusement Company, a distributor of jukeboxes (which were perfectly legal), pinball machines (which were marginally legal), and slot machines (which were completely illegal).

Around 1945, another Chicago gangster, Marcus Lipsky, whose career dated back to the days of Al Capone, arrived in Dallas. Lipsky contacted Jones, telling him that he had "the OK from the Chicago boys" to take over Dallas gambling, and he described a plan to kidnap and murder Benny Binion, Ivy Miller, Earl Dalton, and Buddy Malone. Determined to show the Dallas rubes how the boys in Chicago did business, Lipsky intended to leave the four bodies in a stolen car outside the sheriff's office. Jones wisely persuaded Lipsky to abandon the plan, but the two did purchase interests in several more amusement businesses, extending Chicago's control over North Texas slot machines even further.

In the summer of 1946, James Weinberg, Paul Labriola, Martin Ochs, James Barcells, and Danny Lardino, all Chicago hoodlums, arrived to assist Jones in whatever criminal activities he could arrange. The Dallas police quickly spotted and arrested this crew, and Deputy Sheriff Bill Decker and Dallas police officer Will Fritz, together with several very large deputies, took the five men to the Dallas county line, pointed out the general direction of Chicago, and told them never to come back. Undoubtedly, it was incidents like this one that Binion referred to in a revealing exchange during his interview with the University of Nevada Oral History Program:

Q: Well, wasn't there some kind of competition there [in Dallas]?

A: No, we had it all. We didn't have no competition.

Q: How did you keep your competition out?

A: Well, they just didn't come there.

Q: Why not?

A: Well, I don't know.

Q: The Mafia was into every other place, trying to be.

A: Well, to tell you the honest truth about the Mafia, I think it's a overestimated thing. I actually never knew anything about the Mafia. I've knew some people that [the newspapers] said was in it, knew 'em personally, but they never did tell me they's in it, so I just don't know.

Q: There were some rumors that they were trying to move into Dallas, and your organization was too strong for them, that they couldn't move in there. I just wondered how you managed that.

A: Well, I wouldn't want to go into *that*.

In late October 1946, Paul Roland Jones asked Lieutenant George Butler of the Dallas Police Department to arrange a meeting with Sheriff-Elect Steve Guthrie. At first glance, such a request would seem ludicrous, but it makes much more sense in light of Herbert Noble's contribution to Guthrie's campaign and his relationship with George Butler. Noble enjoyed a relationship with Butler very similar to Benny Binion's friendship with Bill Decker. While on opposite sides of the law, Noble and Butler trusted and respected each other and must be considered to have been friends.[*]

---

[*] Relationships of this nature were the rule rather than the exception. In the 1930s, 1940s and 1950s, lawmen and criminals frequently came from the same neighborhoods and shared the same cultural background. As in the Old West, some of the worst outlaws of the era began their careers as lawmen. In Dallas,

For at least two years, Chicago's organized crime interests had greedily eyed Dallas gambling, but had been warded off by Binion's informal alliance with local law enforcement officials, principally Smoot Schmid and Bill Decker. After Guthrie's election, Noble believed he had the "big fix" he'd wanted for years, and he believed he had the political muscle to deliver Dallas to the Chicago interests. Noble almost certainly instigated the meeting between Jones and Guthrie, and it is only natural that he would suggest his friend George Butler as a go-between.

Shocked to hear that the notorious Jones wanted a meeting, Butler told Jones that Guthrie would agree to such a meeting only if he, Butler, was present. Demonstrating why he had not risen higher in the ranks of organized crime, Jones not only agreed to a meeting with both Guthrie and Butler, he also agreed that the meeting could be held in Guthrie's home. Butler contacted the Texas Rangers, and in no time Guthrie's living room was wired for sound.

The meeting between Jones, Guthrie, and Butler took place at Guthrie's modest home on the east side of Dallas on November 1, 1946. Jones laid out his plan:

> Here is my proposition to you. You pick a man, a local man, we will put him in business. We will rent him a building but we will finance it. We will put in some juke boxes, some marble tables, some sort of slot machines. We will get him a mechanic and a pickup truck. We will start hustling, getting him some locations, legitimately, no muscles attached. Somebody that you trust. If you trust him, I trust him. We will furnish him all the slot machines, marble tables, punchboards, etcetera. We will operate and there will be only one gambling house in the county.

most of the police and the sheriff's deputies were on a first-name basis with the city's most notorious criminals.

Jones went on to explain that the new exclusive gambling operation would be run by only one man from Chicago, a man who "looked like a preacher" and was neither a "Dago" nor a "Jew." Local gamblers like Bob Fletcher and Sherman Little would be involved as the actual operators and would front the operation. Sheriff Guthrie, who would be paid forty thousand dollars a week to take care of all the necessary payoffs, would serve as "the money man" for the entire operation. Since this was to be a long-term arrangement, Guthrie would enjoy the benefit of having his total campaign expenses covered by the Outfit every election year. Any significant opposition would be discouraged and, in most years, Guthrie could expect to run unopposed.

Guthrie expressed interest in the proposal, but told Jones he wanted to meet some of the "higher-ups" from Chicago. Jones called from Chicago on November third to arrange another meeting, this time with two of the "head men" from Chicago in attendance. These two turned out to be Jack Knapp (true name: Romeo Jack Nappi) and Patrick Manning (true name: Pat Manno). Both Nappi and Manno were ranking Chicago mobsters, particularly Manno, who was close to Chicago boss Joe "Joe Batters" Accardo. The second meeting, on November 7, also took place in Guthrie's home.

At this meeting, Guthrie told Jones and the others that four men would have to be run out of town because they could jeopardize the take-over. He named Lois Green, Johnny Grisaffi, Junior Thomas, and Mack Barnes. To this list, Butler added Monk Wright, another of Green's lieutenants. Jones identified Grisaffi as "a local boy who handles dope." Butler added that Grisaffi was a trigger man. Not surprisingly, all of these men (except Barnes) had been implicated in attempts on Herbert Noble's life.

Guthrie wanted to know how the current gambling bosses would be handled. "We all know Bill Decker is a pay-off man with Benny Binion," he said, and Butler agreed. Jones replied that there was nothing to worry about with Decker, that he was "an old bootlegger around here and a bagman" and he would be taken care of. Binion, he said, was already "under control." Again, not surprisingly, Herbert Noble's name was not mentioned, even though he was clearly one of the Dallas gambling bosses, probably second only to Binion himself. On the tape of that meeting, Paul Jones is heard to say:

> We control Binion. We won't shoot nobody; we won't have to shoot nobody. They [the local gamblers] are not as tough as they think.
> I'm not going to put the heat on you like they put on Gauldin to drop murder charges.

Later in the conversation, Guthrie asked Jones why the local gamblers were closing.

Jones answered: "It is over. The fix goes off. . . . They ain't got the district attorney, and the city is scared to death unless they figure they got the county cooperating."

ONCE AGAIN, GUTHRIE pressed for another meeting, asking to meet more "higher-ups." A few days later, Jones produced two men he claimed to be top-ranking Chicago mobsters: Jake "Greasy Thumb" Guzik and Murray "the Camel" Humphries. When these two proved to be imposters, Guthrie decided he had caught the biggest fish he was likely to catch and sprung the trap. The incriminating tapes were turned over to the Texas Rangers, and Jones, along with several others, was arrested and indicted for bribery.

In one of Will Wilson's first major prosecutions, Jones was convicted and sentenced to eight years in prison. But the State of Texas had to wait for Jones. Before he could be tried in Dallas, Jones was arrested, convicted, and sentenced for smuggling narcotics from Mexico. In short order, the Chicago mob sent another representative to Dallas. The new man had been a strikebreaker, collector, and all-around Chicago hoodlum since the Capone days. His name was Jacob Rubenstein. Shortly after his move to Dallas, he changed it to Jack Ruby.

WITH THE ARREST of Paul Roland Jones, not only had Herbert Noble's quest for the big fix failed once again, but also the reform movement had passed the test. It was now clear that the reform talk had been much more than the usual campaign rhetoric. On December 19, 1946, Dallas civic leaders Bob Thornton, Nate Adams, and others met with Dallas city and county officials Smitham, Hansson, Wilson, and Guthrie. They decided that the 1946 elections had truly mandated a new law-and-order stance for the city of Dallas. The wide-open gambling and prostitution of the previous ten years had served a purpose, but beginning on January 1, 1947, the wild and woolly days were over. Dallas was closed.

GAMBLERS LEFT DALLAS like the town was on fire. Herbert Noble closed down the open gambling at the Airmen's Club . (although the club remained open as a private club with a good bit of "sneak gambling" in the back room) and announced his intention to spend most of his time at his Denton County ranch, raising turkeys and peacocks and tending to his aircraft salvage business.* He was, he said, a "retired gambler."

Benny Binion decided that he would leave Texas entirely. "There wasn't no other way to go," he told an interviewer more than thirty years later. "My sheriff got beat."

AND SO IT was that on a crisp morning in the first days of 1947 Benny Binion's chauffeur, an enormous black man called "Gold Dollar," guided Benny's Cadillac limousine westward out of Dallas. His cargo, in addition to Benny, included Cliff Helm

---

* Noble also owned a joint called the New Orleans Club on West Davis in Oak Cliff, where sneak gambling went on frequently.

and Johnny Beasley—both very heavily armed—two steamer trunks filled with Benny's clothes, and several suitcases stuffed with more than three million dollars in cash.

Cowboy Benny Binion was on his way to Las Vegas.

Raisin' Hell and Gamblin' High— Las Vegas Style

IN 1946, LAS Vegas was little more than a wide place in the nar-row stretch of highway snaking its way from Los Angeles to Salt Lake City. A few visitors, mostly from California, came for the high-speed divorces that the Nevada legislature had autho-rized in 1931, and they fled the desert as soon as their unwanted spouses had been legally and properly discarded. Those who could afford it whiled away the brief waiting period at the Last Frontier and El Rancho Vegas, two dude ranches located south of the township on U.S. 91. Those who couldn't afford the luxury resorts on the highway stayed downtown on Fremont Street and passed the time at sawdust-floored saloons. Most came and went by railroad; what automobile traffic there was shared the roadways with the sand and tumbleweeds driven by the incessant wind. Its sixteen thousand permanent residents sweltered in the dusty, smothering heat that radiated from nearby Death Valley and tried to scratch a living out of one of the most Godforsaken places on earth. As one old-timer put it, the place was "hotter than Hell and a little drier."

By the end of World War II, the little town's brief flirtation with prosperity was over, or so it seemed. The men who had constructed the magnificent Hoover Dam forty miles to the south had spent their paychecks in Las Vegas's clubs, saloons, and bawdy houses during the Depression, saving the town from complete disaster. But by 1941 their work was finished, and they were gone.

During the war, the U.S. Army established a gunnery school north of the city, and four thousand trainees swarmed into town every six weeks. Like the construction workers before them, the soldiers found that Las Vegas offered ample entertainment for young men with money to spend. But as soon as the war ended, the soldiers, too, went home.

Benny Binion arrived just in time for the grand opening of Ben Siegel's glitzy Flamingo Hotel, five miles south of Las Vegas on U.S. 91. Siegel, who was known (but never to his face) as "Bugsy," had spent more than five million dollars building a great resort of imported marble and mahogany in the middle of nowhere, envisioning a European-style palace where entertainment, food, glamour, and divorces would be secondary to the main attraction: gambling. Binion called the grand opening "the biggest whoop-de-do you ever saw." But Siegel's partners, Frank Costello, Charley Luciano, and Meyer Lansky—all top-ranking East Coast mobsters—were not as impressed. Bugsy's joint, as they called it, actually lost huge amounts of money during its first days. The Flamingo's hotel accommodations had not been finished in time for the opening, and all of Bugsy's invited high rollers, who had booked rooms a few miles north at the Last Frontier and El Rancho Vegas, gambled away much of their bankrolls (and a good deal of the Flamingo's) with Siegel's competition.

Aside from the spectacle of the grand opening, Benny Binion wasn't particularly impressed, either. He was much more at home with the cowboys, miners, prospectors, and desert rats on Fremont Street in downtown Las Vegas, the area we now know as "Glitter Gulch." Benny's first venture in Las Vegas was a storefront saloon and gambling hall called the Las Vegas Club, which he operated with a partner, J.K. Houssels, a pioneering Nevada gambler. Benny got along well with Houssels, and the two remained friends for many years, although differences in gambling philosophies eventually led to the dissolution of their partnership. Houssels believed in grinding out the profits, strictly enforcing table limits, and catering to high rollers; Binion, as always, believed in "raisin' hell and gamblin' high" and favored taking any bet any player was willing to put down. If a high roller wanted to bet a million, Benny, like his Dallas mentor Warren Diamond, would take the action. But he also believed in accommodating the low-end player. "You never know," he would say, "somebody might die and leave that fifty-cent player some money. I want him to spend it here." Benny also pioneered the idea of "comps," free food and drinks for the players, a notion that irritated his never-give-away-anything-you-can-sell partner. When the time came to dissolve the partnership, neither Binion nor Houssels was heartbroken.

In truth, Binion never saw his move to Las Vegas as perma-nent. One of his last stops before leaving Dallas had been in the sheriff's office, where he had a long talk with his old friend Bill Decker. In the course of their conversation, Benny urged Decker to run for sheriff in the 1948 elections. Benny knew that Decker, still extremely popular throughout the county, could win easily, even against an incumbent Steve Guthrie. Decker's old boss, Smoot Schmid, would not be a factor in the 1948 race. Smoot was already angling for a position on the Texas Pardon and Parole Board and would not run again for sheriff under any circumstances. "Decker," Benny promised, "if you decide you want to do it, just raise whatever [money] you can, and I'll damn sure make up the rest." Binion knew that no district attorney, no matter how dedicated, could prosecute a man who hadn't been arrested, and Decker's election as sheriff, he believed, would once again hand Benny the keys to Dallas.

Not long after his arrival in Las Vegas, another episode took place that underscored Binion's dissatisfaction with his new home. Two bodyguards had accompanied Benny and his suitcases full of cash from Dallas. One, Cliff Helm, had been a long-time friend of Binion and his family. The other, Johnny Beasley, had been released from prison a few weeks before Benny decided to leave Dallas. Beasley, a drug addict who swore he had reformed, pestered Benny for handouts and eventually for a job. Benny was concerned about leaving Beasley behind when he left Dallas, because he feared Beasley would bother Teddy Jane and his children, who were staying behind until Benny could find a suitable home in Las Vegas. Rather than leave Beasley in Dallas, Binion decided to take him along.

Binion, Helm, and Beasley had been in Las Vegas only a matter of weeks when Beasley began using drugs and generally causing trouble. Finally, Benny, at home with the flu, called Beasley at the Las Vegas Club. "I told him he had to leave town," Benny said later. "I said I'd buy him a ticket wherever he wanted to go. He said he thought he could get a job at some Wild West show in New Jersey, so I told Cliff [Helm] to buy him a ticket and put him on the train."

On the way to the train depot, Beasley changed his mind, telling Helm that he would take a bus to Kingman, Arizona (about a hundred miles south of Las Vegas), and hitchhike East from there. He demanded that Helm give him the rest of the ticket money, which Helm refused to do without talking to Binion. The two went back into the Las Vegas Club and headed to a back office so that Helm could call Binion at home. On the way, Helm stopped at a boiler room to reset a thermostat. Benny explained what happened next to the University of Nevada Oral History Program:

> So Cliff walked back there and did this [reset the thermostat] and when he turned around, Beasley was standin' in the door with a knife. And I guess he was full of that dope, and he went to cussin' Cliff about this thing. And he cut at him with a knife, and Cliff was a security guard, and he had the pistol. So Cliff shot him. And I know two guys that seen it, absolutely, but they were "hot." You know, they couldn't be seen because they was wanted somewhere. But I knew 'em

good. So they told me Cliff was absolutely in self-defense. But when Cliff shot him and knocked him down, well, he just hauled off and shot him right in his head, and him layin' down there. Well, he knows, in his own mind, and this frame of mind Cliff's in, if you don't kill him, you've got to kill him sometime, 'cause this is the most dangerous son of a gun in the world. So he just went ahead and done a good job of it.

Cliff was as honorable and as honest as any man I ever had anything to do with, Cliff Helm. And I did everything I could for him, but the thing was stacked agin' him in them days there. They was wantin' to get rid of me, too, really. They didn't want me around here. I was a little too strong in competition right then.

Even Benny's best efforts were not enough to keep Cliff Helm out of the Nevada State Penitentiary, a fact Binion always regretted. In the old days in Dallas, Helm would have been indicted and a few months later, when things cooled off, the charges would have been dismissed for lack of evidence. But Binion did not have that kind of "juice" in Las Vegas, and it made him homesick for Dallas, where he had always been able to help his friends.

The other casino owners wanted Binion out of town as well. He was paying dealers a good bit more than the going rate (although he didn't know it), and his flamboyant, high-rolling, no-limit style grated on his more conservative competitors. And so, when Bill Decker called in early 1948 with the news that he had decided to run for sheriff of Dallas County and had raised about half of the campaign funds he would need, Benny did not hesitate to let out a trademark whoop and tell Decker, "You just tell me what you need, and I'll damn sure give it to you."

BENNY'S INTENTION OF returning soon to Dallas, to reclaim his position as the "Boss Gambler" in North Texas, becomes even clearer if we take an inventory of what he left behind.

The notorious downtown Dallas casinos at the Southland, the Blue Bonnet, and the St. George may have closed their doors forever on December 31, 1946, but Benny's beloved policy business went on without a hitch. Largely because the numbers gamblers were blacks and poor whites, rather than the high rollers who patronized the casinos, the authorities had never been particularly interested in pursuing this aspect of Binion's empire, and Harry Urban Sr., who had been left in charge of the operation, continued sending enormous amounts of money to Benny every week, long after Benny had relocated to Las Vegas. With twelve policy wheels running seven days a week, Binion would not lack for income on his return to Dallas.

In Fort Worth, with his connections to Tiffin Hall's numbers game and George Wilderspin's gambling operation in east Tarrant County, the Cowboy remained a power, although a less visible one than he had been in Dallas.

In addition to his other interests, he had for several years been quietly acquiring a substantial interest in a gambling house (and alleged brothel) called the Top O' the Hill. Located in Arlington, Texas, about midway between Dallas and Fort Worth, the Top O' the Hill was a forerunner of the modern Las Vegas casino. Its patrons, once they had made their way through a maze of complex electronic security devices, entered an elegant bar and dining room, where the best steaks money could buy were served on fine china, and bonded Bourbon whiskey was poured in crystal glasses—all at no charge. After dinner, the invited guests—and there were no uninvited guests—were shown to the basement, where another bar, complete with white-jacketed bartender, awaited. Adjacent to the bar, a fully carpeted casino, lit by crystal chandeliers and staffed by as many as twenty tuxedoed dealers and pit bosses, offered three pool tables, several slot machines, three blackjack tables, two roulette wheels, and two crap tables. On weeknights, the gambling stopped at 2:00 a.m. On weekends the action went on until dawn or after.

Unknown to the gamblers at the Top O' the Hill, a third

floor was sandwiched between the dining room and the casino. Virtually soundproof and accessible only by a carpeted ladder, this floor was equipped with several wide-scale viewing devices, permitting casino security men to view the action at any of the tables on the floor below. This early version of the famous Las Vegas "eye-in-the-sky" kept both the players and the dealers honest. At one end of the hall above the casino, a large closet hid an elaborate arrangement of switches and levers, which, in a matter of seconds, could move the casino walls in such a way that all of the gambling devices were completely hidden, and only the bar and pool tables remained in sight. In the unlikely event that a police raiding party should penetrate the club's extensive outside security and gain access to the basement, they would find only a few well-dressed and very wealthy friends enjoying a cocktail and a quiet game of pool.

At the back of the casino, hidden behind a key-operated moving wall, a tunnel led some fifty yards out into the Texas brush. In an emergency, all of the gamblers could be evacuated in a matter of seconds and the wall closed behind them, leaving no trace of the evening's action. On the hillside above the club, a mounted guard armed with a .30-30 rifle patrolled the only outside entrance to the tunnel.

Nominally, Fred Browning, a former plumber, owned the Top O' the Hill, but after World War II the club was often referred to as belonging to Benny Binion. There are also references to be found indicating that Binion and Browning were partners (which is the more likely scenario). Browning, unfortunately, was a gambler with a taste for buying, and betting on, racehorses. Worse, his wife shared his passion. Even though the Top O' the Hill regularly entertained movie stars like Don Ameche and Gene Autry, and high-rolling oil men like H.L. Hunt, Billy Byars, and Howard Hughes, much of the club's profits went to the nearby Arlington Downs race track, and the Brownings were constantly in debt. For several years, Binion had been buying Browning's markers. Whether this was a favor to Browning, a business arrangement, or a hostile takeover is unknown, but by 1946, Benny had become the power behind the Top O' the Hill.

Of course, Binion couldn't openly operate in Tarrant County without risking a head-on collision with Amon Carter, which Benny knew he could not win. But he did see to it that many of the veterans from his Dallas operations found employment at the swanky Arlington club. Ivy Miller, who had gunned down Sam Murray, ran dice games at the Top O' the Hill. So did Earl Dalton, an original member of the Southland Group whose gambling associations went back to Warren Diamond. L.J. McWillie, a true gambling professional who had learned his trade in illegal games in Tennessee and Mississippi before coming to the Blue Bonnet Hotel in Dallas, worked as the casino manager at the Top O' the Hill for more than six years. At one time or another, former Dallas dealers, floor men, and pit bosses Bob Floyd, Jerry Rosenberg, Meyer Panitz, and Johnny Anderson all worked the Top O' the Hill.

Out on Fort Worth's infamous Jacksboro Highway, where several miles of roadhouses, honkytonks, after-hours clubs, and cut-and-shoot joints offered every sort of legal or (more often) illegal diversion, Binion was reported to have an ownership interest in Bert Wakefield's 3939 Club and, later, in the Four Deuces Club at 2222 Jacksboro Highway. Both of these operations stood a cut above most of the joints along the highway, but were nowhere near the splendor of the Top O' the Hill.

Outside Dallas and Fort Worth, Binion had staked gambling operations in Midland, Odessa, Lubbock, and Sherman. If and when the Cowboy should decide to return to Texas, his empire was waiting.

Dallas Closes Down, and Fort Worth Runs Wild

May 21, 1948

The emergency room at the Dallas Methodist Hospital was quiet in the early hours of Thursday morning, when a husky, silver-haired man walked in with a bloody towel wrapped around his right arm. He politely gave his name—Herbert Noble—and asked to see a doctor. In the examining room, Noble told the doctor that he had been handling a pistol, a .38 automatic, at his Denton County ranch and had dropped it. The pistol went off accidentally, wounding his arm. On closer examination, the doctor found much greater damage than he expected, given Noble's description of the accident. Noble's arm was, in fact, mangled. Noble explained by saying that the pistol had accidentally fired *five times.*

Since the "accident" had occurred in Denton County, the hospital called the Denton County Sheriff and reported the incident. Noble repeated his story about dropping the pistol to Deputy L. A. Brackenridge. County Sheriff Roy Moore, far from convinced, decided that a late-night visit to Noble's ranch was in order, and it was there that he learned the truth from Mildred Noble.

At about 10:30 p.m., Noble had made the sharp turn onto his ranch road from the county line road several hundred yards from his house. At the corner, as Noble slowed for a cattle guard, someone rose up from a clump of bushes and fired at Noble's Mercury. A load of double-aught buckshot struck Noble in the right arm, wrist, and hand. The wounded gambler drove on to his ranch house, where he told his wife what had happened, and then drove to a neighbor's home and was taken from there to the hospital.

The sheriff found three buckshot pellets inside Noble's car and found the front passenger seat soaked with blood. A deputy investigating the bushes near the cattle guard found shotgun wadding and footprints. A short distance away, he found fresh tire tracks.

The police were not especially surprised to discover that someone had tried to kill Noble. It was, after all, the third time. But they didn't understand why Noble, usually forthcoming about the attempts on his life, had tried to conceal this incident behind the flimsy story of an accidental shooting. Noble's high stakes crap games had been going on for several years at his ranch cabins, and there had been no hint of trouble. He had been operating sneak games at the Airmen's Club since the 1947 shutdown in Dallas, and again there had been no sign of trouble. There were, however, rumors that Noble was involved in other activities that he didn't care to discuss. Indeed, Noble himself had told close friends that he was involved in "some things he didn't want his family to find out about."

What those things were, he would not say, but the police suspected Noble of using his ranch to help his long-time friend Sonny Lefors store stolen property, especially items too large to be sold out of the back door of Sonny's Food Store. It would take several years, but this theory would eventually prove to be absolutely correct. Noble's many private airplane trips to Mexico and South America had led the police to speculate that he might be flying in large quantities of drugs—marijuana in particular—to the makeshift landing field at his ranch. The fact that Noble's pit boss and bodyguard, Slim Hays, was suspected of being a major marijuana dealer added to the speculation.

Either fencing stolen property or dealing in drugs could well explain the attempt on Noble's life on May 20, 1948, and would also explain his reluctance even to admit that someone had tried to kill him. Investigators did not know, and would not find out until many months later, that, a few nights before a shotgun blast shattered Noble's right arm, someone had emptied a pistol into Johnny Brazil Grisaffi. The shots had wounded Grisaffi, but not seriously enough to require a hospital visit. Instead, a cooperative doctor visited the Grisaffi residence for emergency repairs. The police would never have learned of the incident had the doctor not first gone to the wrong house. Months later, a neighbor told police about a doctor knocking on the door late one night saying he had been called because Grisaffi had been shot.

After speculating and chasing rumors for months, the authorities, when they finally learned of the Grisaffi shooting, unofficially laid this most recent attempt on Noble's life at the feet of Lois Green, reasoning that Green and Grisaffi were still trying to fill the contract on Noble after their failed attempt in January 1946.

IN MID-1948, DISTRICT Attorney Will Wilson and his chief prosecutor, Henry Wade, began making good on their election promise to prosecute Dallas gamblers. On May 27, 1948, as a result of his work as a pit boss for Bob Fletcher at the Maurice Hotel, James Worsham became the first Dallas gambler in more than twenty years to be convicted of felony gambling. The same series of arrests resulted in the prosecution of Maurice Hyams, the owner of the Maurice Hotel, for allowing gambling on public premises—also a felony. After numerous legal delays, Hyams was finally convicted on November 1, 1948.

The Hyams conviction drove a stake through the heart of professional gambling in Dallas forever. For the first time, owners of hotels, night clubs, recreation halls, and bars, realizing that allowing an open game on the premises would result in a prison sentence rather than the customary one-hundred-dollar fine, had a real interest in preventing gambling in their places of business. Private clubs like the Cipango and the Dallas Airmen's Club continued to run occasional "stag nights" on the sneak, but only rarely and with very little profit. Dallas had announced on January 1, 1947, that its doors were closed to gamblers; on November 1, 1948, it announced that the doors would never reopen.

IN THE EARLY fall of 1948, while Will Wilson and his staff were delivering the death blow to Dallas gambling operators, Herbert Noble plotted revenge. Of the three men who had tried to kill him on that cold night in February 1946, only Lois Green remained unharmed. Bob Minyard was dead, presumably on Noble's instructions. Johnny Grisaffi had been wounded, but not as seriously as Noble would have liked.

Believing that the attack at the ranch on May 20 had been accomplished on Green's orders, if not by Green himself, Noble concluded that he could never live peacefully in Dallas so long as Green was alive. Since he had no intention of leaving Dallas, Noble could see but one solution: he would have Lois Green killed.

Through Sonny Lefors, one of the gunmen who, according to police, had murdered Bob Minyard, Noble propositioned a small-time West Dallas operator named S.J. "Baldy" Whatley* to kill Green. Noble offered $5,000, and Whatley, a burglar, armed robber, and one-time escaped convict, eagerly accepted. Whatley devised a simple plan. He would find someone who knew Green and have Green "put on the spot." For the setup, Whatley approached a Dallas hoodlum named Foy Crowell.

---

* Surely one of the most inept criminals in Texas history, Whatley had been jailed at various times for shoplifting and stealing chickens. He became briefly well known in 1934 when he was one of twenty-two persons convicted of harboring Bonnie and Clyde. In 1938, Baldy tried to kill West Dallas hoodlum Joe Francis, but mistook Clyde Barrow's brother LC for Francis. Whatley fired a shotgun at Barrow but missed and hit Cumie Barrow, LC's mother, instead. The enraged Barrow went for his gun and shot Whatley in the back. Everyone survived the fracas.

Whatley couldn't have made a worse mistake; Crowell was one of the few Dallas gangsters who actually liked Lois Green and he immediately informed Green of the plot.

Crowell reported to Whatley that he had arranged a meeting with Green on the pretense of buying a quantity of drugs. Instead, Whatley was to lie in wait and shoot Green from ambush. At the appointed time on October 4, 1948, Whatley found, not the unsuspecting Green as promised, but Green and Johnny Grisaffi, both armed with shotguns. Late that night, Whatley was found beside a road near Irving, Texas. He had been shotgunned in one leg, beaten, and stomped. Somehow, Whatley escaped the trap alive and was placed under police guard at Parkland Hospital. The hapless thug told the police he knew the men who had tried to kill him, but refused to identify them. Whatley had the good fortune, soon after his release from the hospital, to be arrested on a narcotics charge. He pleaded guilty and was sent to prison, prolonging his life for at least a few years, although Green and Grisaffi were expected to kill him at the first opportunity.

EVEN THOUGH BILL Decker had been elected Dallas County Sheriff by a landslide in the 1948 elections, Benny Binion began having second thoughts about returning to Dallas.

The successful prosecutions of Worsham and Hyams had proven that a dedicated district attorney, using investigators assigned to his office and bypassing the sheriff and even the police, could almost single handedly send gamblers to prison. Decker would have been a friendly face in the sheriff's office, but the power of the sheriff had been greatly diminished in the years since the end of the war, and even Decker's friendship would not be enough to protect Benny's operations in this new, reformed Dallas.

By early 1949, Binion was negotiating the sale of his interest in the Las Vegas Club and planning the purchase of a downtown gambling joint that would become, after extensive remodeling, the Westerner. He had taken to spending summers at his

Montana ranch, away from the oppressive Nevada heat. He had invested in oil leases in Montana, Wyoming, and the Dakotas and for a time he operated the gambling at the notorious Log Cabin Club in Jackson Hole, Wyoming. All of this, in addition to his Dallas policy business, his Fort Worth policy and gambling interests, and his West Texas operations, made Benny Binion an enormously wealthy man.

With all of the money he was ever likely to need, Benny might well have forgotten Texas entirely. But he was homesick. He and Teddy Jane both missed Dallas terribly, and Benny often told friends how much they wanted to raise their children back home in Texas. He, however, was plagued by the specter of the only man who had ever defied him and lived: Herbert Noble. Noble had made it clear that he did not intend to leave Dallas and he often said that, when Dallas opened up again, he intended to be as big as Binion ever was. Maybe even bigger. More quietly, Noble also told his friends that he intended to kill Benny Binion.

February 14, 1949

The downtown Dallas streets were practically deserted as Sunday night became Monday morning. Outside the Dallas Airmen's Club, Jimmy Jordan, a customer leaving the club, noticed someone moving around under Herbert Noble's black 1949 Mercury. The man raced back into the club and upstairs to Noble's office. Breathlessly, he told Noble what he had seen. Noble first called the police and then grabbed his pistol. By the time Noble and Slim Hays reached the car, there was no one to be found.

The police arrived minutes later and began a search of the area. Under the Mercury they found two blasting caps and several sticks of dynamite partially attached to the ignition wires. Clearly, someone had been disturbed in the process of attaching a bomb to Noble's automobile and, with the help of an observant customer, the silver haired gambler had survived a fourth attempt on his life. When the story hit the newspapers, reporters began calling Noble "the Cat" and wondering in print how many lives he actually had.

The two witnesses (police located another passerby who had seen someone under the car) had managed only a brief glimpse of the man tampering with Noble's car and were able to give police only a general description; nevertheless, they looked at photographs of dozens of Dallas police characters, thugs, and hoodlums. They picked out several that "might" have been the man they saw, and the police dutifully checked out each suspect, only to find that each of them had a solid alibi.

The underworld grapevine whispered that there was an open contract on Noble, and that his life was worth fifteen thousand dollars. The man to see about the money was, according to the rumors, Harry Urban Sr., Benny Binion's long-time partner. When questioned by the police, Urban denied any knowledge of any bounty on Noble's head, saying he had "nothing against" Noble.

More than two years later, Lieutenant George Butler had a long talk with a Dallas hoodlum named Foy Crowell, the same police character who had put Baldy Whatley on the spot. Known as a drug dealer, pimp, and small-time thief, Crowell was at the time on his way to the penitentiary following a conviction for narcotics violations. Crowell, a close friend of both Lois Green and Johnny Grisaffi, told Butler that, about two years before, he had been offered fifteen thousand dollars to kill Herbert Noble, and that Harry Urban had been holding the money. Crowell refused to identify the man who delivered the proposition, but hinted that it had been Lois Green. Although Crowell insisted that he "wouldn't touch the proposition," Butler's notes describe him as "an exact match" for the description of the man who attempted to dynamite Noble's car.

AFTER FOUR ATTEMPTS on his life, another man might have given up and left North Texas, or at least quit gambling. But not

Herbert Noble. Texas was his home, and he insisted he would not be driven away by Benny Binion or anyone else. On at least one occasion, he even called Binion in Las Vegas to tell him so.

Although he described himself as a "retired gambler," Noble continued to run the sneak games at the Airmen's Club and New Orleans Club, as well as the more open and profitable games at his Denton County ranch. In 1949, he expanded his operation to include a crap game in a secluded barn owned by Buddy Crawford on Dallas's Northwest Highway, near the Tarrant County line.

By 1949, gambling in Fort Worth had become as widespread and open as it had been in Dallas during the war years. Crap games ran with virtually no interference from the police at the Blackstone, Seibold, Madoc, Westbrook, and Commercial hotels. George Wilderspin, Fred Merrill, and Chick Fluornoy ran the East Side Club in Haltom City for Benny Binion. Almost every Jacksboro Highway joint offered gambling of some type, and Tarrant County could boast more than fifteen hundred registered (as amusement devices) slot machines and countless unregistered one-armed bandits. In nearly every pool hall, newsstand, lunch counter, or drug store, a sportsman could make a bet on a horse race anywhere in the country or place a few coins on the day's lucky number.

The kingpin in all this was Tiffin Hall, the restaurant and hotel owner who fronted Binion's numbers racket, and the members of his syndicate, including, among others, Wilderspin, Merrill, Fluornoy, Bob Floyd, and Red Oden. Hall's status, and particularly his relationship with Benny Binion, were closely guarded secrets.

A separate syndicate, run by Tincy Eggleston and Nelson Harris, operated just as openly as the Hall syndicate. A petty criminal since his teens, Harris had been a delivery boy for the Green Dragon narcotics syndicate and was sentenced—coincidentally on the same day Ivy Miller was indicted for killing Sam Murray—to two years at Leavenworth Federal Penitentiary for narcotics violations. After his release, Harris returned to Fort Worth, where he worked as a bouncer at various downtown and Jacksboro Highway joints. His brief employment as a "yard-man"—an outside security guard—at the Four Deuces Club ended when club owner W.C. "Pappy" Kirkwood caught him running a prostitution racket out of the club's parking lot. For a time, Harris operated an after-hours club called Nelson's Place out of his own home.

After joining forces with Eggleston, Harris began running crap games at the Town House Hotel near downtown Fort Worth and at the Skyliner Annex (sometimes called the Annex Club) on the Jacksboro Highway. The Skyliner had once been a supper club featuring big bands, dancing, and floorshows, but in later years, after it was purchased by W. D. Satterwhite, it had degenerated into a hard-drinking, anything goes kind of joint featuring a floorshow made up entirely of female impersonators—a genuine scandal in Fort Worth in the late 1940s. Satterwhite built the Annex behind the Skyliner as an after-hours and gambling club, for patrons in search of more action after attending the Skyliner's unique floorshow.

Jack Blackman, a veteran Texas gambler who had spent a few years in Nevada, returned to Fort Worth in mid-1948 and began operating a crap game at the Town House Hotel. Blackman, never a friend of Benny Binion, had left Nevada shortly after being acquitted on a charge of murdering one of Binion's associates. His association with Harris and Eggleston remained largely unknown to the public, but well-known in Fort Worth gambling circles.

Any muscle that Harris and Blackman may have needed was provided by their partner Tincy Eggleston. One of Fort Worth's toughest and most versatile street criminals, Leroy "Tincy" Eggleston, had been variously convicted, indicted, charged, jailed, or suspected for burglary, hijacking, armed robbery, assault, gambling, and murder. Tincy's Fort Worth police file began in 1926 with a robbery conviction and, by the time he joined up with the Harris gambling faction, was as thick as a telephone book for a good-size city. Tincy, who was known as extremely polite, once robbed a man at gunpoint, telling his victim, "You ought to be damn glad it's me robbing you. I ain't gonna kill you. I don't kill nobody unless I get paid to do it."

The source of financial backing for the Harris-Blackman-Eggleston operation remains a matter of some dispute. Fort Worth newspapers reported several years later that Harris had been "an associate" of Herbert Noble. In his reports, Lieutenant George Butler stated unequivocally that the man named Noble who backed Nelson Harris was, in fact, Lewis Noble, a Dallas and Fort Worth fence who was not related to Herbert. Benny Binion, Tiffin Hall, and their associates didn't especially care who was backing Harris—although the mere possibility that it was Herbert Noble would have enraged Binion—they didn't like the competition. In mid-1949, Binion's Fort Worth associates sent an emissary to call on Nelson Harris. Jim Clyde Thomas, a well-dressed, soft-spoken, hired killer, visited Harris with a suggestion. In a nutshell, Thomas told Harris to wise up and throw in with Hall and Wilderspin. Thomas didn't make any threats, but in those days it was not considered healthy to ignore a friendly suggestion from Jim Clyde.

Thomas's criminal career had begun in earnest with a conviction for bank robbery in Nebraska in 1931. Released from the Nebraska Penitentiary after serving his time, Jim Clyde then walked straight into the waiting arms of Texas authorities brandishing an indictment for a Texas holdup committed before the Nebraska robbery. After a brief trial, Thomas went to the Texas State Penitentiary, where he was locked up until early 1942. He remained at large only a few months before attempting to kill Maitland Jones, a Lubbock businessman, only to run afoul of Jones's bodyguard, a former deputy sheriff named Baxter Honey. Thomas and Honey engaged in an all-night running gun battle through the streets of Lubbock until, their ammunition completely shot up, they stood toe-to-toe and tried to pistol-whip each other to death. Apparently Jim Clyde got the worst of it. Not only did he return to prison for assault-to-murder, he also suffered life-threatening wounds.

In 1943, prison doctors decided that Thomas would die in prison if not properly treated and ordered him released from custody so that he could obtain medical care. Shortly after his release, Thomas was hired to kill Dr. Roy Hunt and his wife in Littlefield, Texas. The doctor and his wife were found bound and gagged in their home: the doctor had been shot in both eyes; a blow to the skull had killed his wife. Thomas was arrested, tried, and convicted of the murders, but his conviction was overturned on appeal. Eventually, he would be tried and convicted twice more, and twice more his convictions would be reversed on appeal.

Between trials and appeals, Jim Clyde worked on occasion as a guard for Benny Binion's crap games in Dallas, although he was such a notorious character that the Dallas police soon asked Benny to discontinue his services. In Fort Worth, Thomas guarded games for his close friend, Frank Cates, and engaged in an amazing variety of other illegal activities. In Odessa, Texas, he owned an interest in a tourist court and a nightspot called the Rambling Rose, generally believed to be a front for both gambling and prostitution. With a partner in crime named Hubert Deere, Thomas ran con games and scams in Oklahoma, Texas, and Louisiana. In his spare time, he bought and sold counterfeit money and stolen cattle.

When a man like Jim Clyde Thomas made a suggestion, smart men listened. But Nelson Harris was known more for his mouth than his mind. He told Thomas that he had no use for Tiffin Hall, George Wilderspin, or any other friend of Benny Binion. He intended, he said, to take over Fort Worth gambling and he had the money to do it.

13

A Gunfight in Grapevine

DURING THE SUMMER of 1949, Herbert Noble stayed close to his ranch, feeding his peacocks and turkeys and taking care of his cattle. He made occasional trips to Mexico and South America, supposedly in connection with his airplane parts business and—having heard of Nelson Harris's reply to Jim Clyde Thomas—avoided both Dallas and Fort Worth as much as possible. In keeping with his image as a self-proclaimed retired gambler, Noble began negotiating for the purchase of the Hicks Airfield near Fort Worth. With a group of partners from New York, he planned to convert the old military training field, which had been decommissioned after the war, into a private airport and small-aircraft maintenance facility.

In early September, Noble's neighbors began to report seeing a strange automobile near his ranch. About three hundred yards south of the main ranch house, a section line road ran east and west through the Diamond M. This road, which connected with the southbound county road leading to the town of Grapevine, provided the only access to the narrow, graveled lane that led to Noble's driveway. Since it was used almost exclusively by Noble and the other ranchers in the area, any strange automobile on this road was likely to be noticed, especially if it returned more than once. On September 6, a black Ford was seen several times driving slowly along the section line. Two days later, the same car was back again.

September 8, 1949

Sometime after dark, one of Noble's neighbors arrived at his front door to report that the black Ford was again in the area, driving slowly back and forth along the section line. Noble stuck his pistol in the waistband of his pants and grabbed the .30 caliber carbine he kept behind his front door. With one of his ranch hands, reportedly a man named Tom Ellis, Noble drove down the lane and parked, lights out, near the intersection of his ranch road and the section line. Minutes later, the black Ford cruised by again. Noble flashed on his lights and pulled out behind the Ford, which immediately raced off toward Grapevine. Noble chased the Ford for almost six miles, at times reaching eighty miles an hour until, just north of Grapevine, the Ford skidded off the road, coming to rest in a ditch.

Rifle in hand, Noble jumped out of his car and yelled at the occupants of the Ford to get out of their car. Three men jumped from the Ford, two of them firing pistols at Noble. The third, the driver, aimed a shotgun and fired twice, hitting Noble in the right leg just above the ankle. With blood filling his shoe, Noble stood his ground, returning fire until he had emptied his carbine and then drawing his pistol. While Noble was changing weapons, the three men abandoned their car and ran into a stand of trees a few yards from the highway, while Noble blasted away at their backs.

When the Grapevine police and a Tarrant County sheriff's deputy arrived to investigate the ruckus, Noble, ignoring his wounded leg, insisted on riding with the deputy while he searched the area, hoping to find some trace of the three shooters. Finding nothing, the deputy finally persuaded Noble to go to Methodist Hospital, where he was rapidly becoming a familiar face, for repairs to his leg wound. His injury, although not serious, would leave him limping for almost a month.

The next day's investigation of the shooting proved more productive than usual. The police traced the black Ford, which had been abandoned at the scene, to a veteran Fort Worth hoodlum named George R. "Jack" Nesbit. Sporting a police record that dated back to the 1920s and included a Kansas forgery conviction and a grand larceny conviction in Oklahoma, Nesbit had spent the 1940s working as a bouncer in various Jacksboro Highway joints, and as a bodyguard and hired gun for Fort Worth gambler Frank Cates. Nesbit, who was also known by the police to be an expert with dynamite and nitroglycerine, was promptly arrested.

Nesbit generally denied any knowledge of any attempt to kill Noble at any time and specifically denied any intent to kill him on the evening of September 8. He reminded the police that he had been driving alone on a public road, where he had every right to be, when Noble began chasing him. When his car skidded off the road near Grapevine, Noble had approached him with a rifle. He had simply fired his gun at Noble to protect himself, he said. If anyone should be charged in the incident, according to Nesbit, it should be Noble. In response to Noble's assertions that three men had been in the black Ford, Nesbit again claimed that he was alone.

When the police searched Nesbit's car, they found a box of 12-gauge shotgun shells, a box of .30 caliber rifle ammunition and a .30 caliber military carbine. Most damning, they found a piece of heavy cardboard, cut in the exact shape of the Ford's passenger side window with a three-inch rectangular hole cut in the center. When placed over the car window, this device would make it possible to see out of the car, but impossible to see in. Unable to envision any legitimate use for this piece of equipment, police charged Nesbit with assault-to-murder.

Three days later, Noble was called to testify before a Tarrant County grand jury. He told the story of the high-speed chase and the shooting that followed just as he had told it to the police, but he refused to name names, saying he did not recognize the two men in the car with Nesbit. After his grand jury testimony, he told the local press that he would testify against Nesbit, if the DA could make a case against him. Although the police were relatively certain that the two men with Nesbit were Jim Clyde Thomas and his friend Frank Cates, no other charges were filed.

EVEN THOUGH JACK Nesbit had no known connection to Lois Green, Noble persisted in his belief that Green was trying to fill the contract that Benny Binion had given him in 1946.

Noble was aware of the price on his head, reputed by this time to be twenty-five thousand dollars, and was certain that every thug in Dallas or Fort Worth would eventually try to kill him. Noble desperately wanted to retaliate, but he had no way to strike directly at Binion, who was in Las Vegas and heavily protected. Neither could he get to Jack Nesbit, who was hiding out near Snyder, Texas, at a tourist court owned by Jim Clyde Thomas. But Lois Green was handy in West Dallas, and Noble decided to try again to have him killed.

In late October or early November 1949, Noble approached his friend Sonny Lefors with a proposition: as he had a year earlier, he wanted Sonny to find someone who would kill Lois Green. Green disliked Lefors and would have nothing to do with him, and of course Noble himself couldn't get anywhere near the West Dallas gangster. They needed someone who could get within killing range of Green without arousing suspicion, and Lefors decided that J.R. Gilreath* would be the perfect man. Noble provided a .30 caliber carbine, a .38 caliber Colt automatic pistol, and a five-hundred-dollar down payment on the job, all of which Lefors passed on to Gilreath with instructions to put Green on the spot and "blow his goddamn head off."

The heavyset (5 foot 7 inch, 203-pound) Gilreath owned a record of arrests for burglary, auto theft, arson, and carrying a concealed weapon. He had learned to work with explosives in

---

* Gilreath is usually referred to in police reports as "J.R. Gilreath," but his true name was James Nathan Gilreath.

the military and specialized in blowing safes with nitroglycerin. He was also known as an excellent mechanic and, caught up in the post-war auto-racing boom, he drove race cars in Dallas, San Antonio, and Houston.

Gilreath never got around to killing Green and, months later, told police that he had never intended to. "One time we were at a nightclub in West Dallas, and I was close enough to reach out and touch him," Gilreath said. "Another time he was at a café on Singleton Road, and I was outside in a car. I could have shot him easy." But Gilreath told the police he only wanted Noble's money and had never given any serious thought to killing Green.*

BY LATE 1949, Benny Binion was as frustrated as Noble, although for very different reasons. Even though he was making huge amounts of money, he still had not found his niche in the Nevada desert. After winding up his Las Vegas Club partnership with Kell Housells, Binion leased a building from the widow of an old-time Las Vegas gambler and began remodeling it as the Westerner Club. It was the first time that Benny had the opportunity to design a gambling house from scratch, using his own ideas about the look and atmosphere of the place. He enjoyed the role and would undoubtedly have been happy there had he been able to be entirely his own boss. But Benny had taken in a partner.

Emilio "Gambo" Georgetti came from a background distinctly different from Binion's but in many ways remarkably similar. Georgetti was an old-time Sicilian Mafioso, a "Mustache Pete," from San Mateo, California. Like Binion, Georgetti was rough-talking, blunt and functionally illiterate. Also like Binion, Georgetti had been forced out of his position as the boss gambler in his hometown by a change in the occupancy of the sheriff's

---

* Actually, this plot on Lois Green's life was much more advanced than Gilreath admitted. Lefors hired Bob Braggins, another West Dallas hoodlum, to break into an elementary school across the street from Green's home. After Braggins located a key to one of the school's doors, Lefors gave the key to Gilreath, who planned to use the school to ambush Green.

office, and had relocated to Nevada, where he could practice his trade legally. But there the similarity ended. Georgetti was a clannish, suspicious member of the Sicilian Mafia, and unlike Binion, a figure in national organized crime. Where Binion liked the company of old-time gamblers like Johnny Moss and Nick the Greek, and eccentric desert rats like "Doby Doc" Caudill, Georgetti insisted on surrounding himself with "made men." Binion favored using his old Texas gambling cronies as pit bosses and dealers; Georgetti wanted to employ veterans of his San Mateo operation and their friends.

Since 1946, the West Coast faction of organized crime had coveted a place in the Las Vegas sun and a share of the enormous wealth the city had already begun to produce for their East Coast counterparts. True, Bugsy Siegel, the patriarch of the Las Vegas strip, had lived in Hollywood and had hobnobbed with movie stars, but his allegiance was to his Eastern partners, Luciano, Costello, and Lansky. The West Coast mob, in the constant throes of a battle for leadership between Jack Dragna ("the Capone of Los Angeles") and Mickey Cohen, an abrasive ex-prizefighter, found itself frozen out of the goldmine in its own backyard. Emilio Georgetti was to be the West Coast point man in Las Vegas and he intended to use the Westerner to establish his beachhead.

After a little more than a year, Binion sold out to Georgetti entirely and began pondering his next move. He seriously considered retiring to his ranch in Montana. Instead, he began work on a new venture that would become the legendary Horseshoe Club. He told the *Houston Chronicle*:

> Me and my son (Jack) went out to the Desert Inn. They hustled me out there to sell me the Horseshoe. It was called the El Dorado. It was closed. They'd fooled around there and they'd had an $870,000 tax loss. So I bought it for $160,000.

Finally, Benny had exactly what he wanted, a gambling house of his own, entirely family-owned (except for tiny percentages he gave friends like Doby Doc). He could run the place his own way and do anything he pleased. Anything except go home to Dallas.

14

"At Least She Won't Have to Worry About Herbert Anymore"

November 29, 1949

Herbert Noble dressed in his finest suit and most conservative tie for his trip to downtown Fort Worth. Negotiations for the purchase of Hicks Air Field by Noble and a group of partners from New York had been successfully completed, and he was about to leave for the United States Attorney's office in Fort Worth, where he would meet his bankers and sign the papers that would truly make him a retired gambler. Noble's group intended to use the old Army training field as a private airport, and as a facility for the sale, maintenance, repair, and storage of private aircraft. Eventually, his partners intended to establish an airplane parts manufacturing facility in Fort Worth, using Hicks Field as their local headquarters.

Noble planned to take the bankers to lunch to celebrate the deal after all the paperwork was completed, and he decided to travel in style. In honor of the occasion, he drove Mildred's dark green 1948 Cadillac.

Mildred Noble could not have been more pleased. For years, she had prayed that Herbert would give up the life that had nearly gotten him killed a half dozen times. Tired of waiting for the phone call that would tell her that Herbert had finally been murdered, Mildred had begged him to go ahead with the Hicks

Airfield deal and quit the gambling life entirely. To celebrate, she planned a special dinner, all romance and candlelight, for that evening. While Herbert signed the papers, Mildred intended to drive to the ranch to pick up their maid, so that she could help with the evening's arrangements. Since Herbert had taken her Cadillac, she would drive his Mercury.

THE EXPLOSION WAS heard eight miles away. Windows shattered for blocks in all directions. One of the Mercury's fenders flew over the roof of the Nobles' home and into a neighboring yard in the next block. Both of the car's seats were blasted into the middle of the street. The engine was reduced to a gnarled mass of metal. Pieces of glass and steel shrapnel were imbedded in houses, fences, and trees as much as two hundred feet away. The black 1949 Mercury sedan, now nothing more than a twisted chassis and four mangled wheels, sat smoldering at the curb.

Mildred Noble's body, scorched and crushed by the blast, lay on the sidewalk ten feet from the car. Her right leg had been blown off below the knee. Blood from the wounds inflicted by hundreds of shards of glass and steel covered her body. Her face, once beautiful, was unrecognizable. She had been thirty-six years old.

A neighbor, Mrs. G.E. Thompson, rushed to help. She later told the police that she could tell the body was that of a woman, but could not recognize her friend. She returned to her home to call the police and then walked back to cover Mildred's body with a sheet.

THE TELEPHONE CALL reached Herbert Noble in the United States Attorney's office just as he finished signing the last of the papers that made him the co-owner of Hicks Airfield. He listened for a minute in silence and then said only, "Dead?" The retired gambler put down the phone and turned to face the room, his face looking as if his features had been etched on a tombstone. "The bastard killed my wife," he said.

IN A COLD fury, Noble drove his wife's Cadillac at breakneck speed to the Lamar & Smith Funeral Home where Mildred's body had been taken. Over the protests of the undertakers, he demanded to see his wife's body. In the back of the funeral home, he cradled Mildred's body in his arms, moaning and crying in an unearthly wail. At that moment, some said, Herbert Noble lost his mind.

Noble left the funeral home and rushed to the Dallas Police Department where, disheveled, wild-eyed, and covered with his dead wife's blood, he was mistaken at the front desk for an assault victim trying to report a crime. While Noble stood at the desk trying to explain who he was and what he wanted, Captain Will Fritz, who was heading the investigation, frantically searched West Dallas and Oak Cliff, fearing that Noble might be on a killing rampage. Rumors that Noble had appeared and created a disturbance at the Methodist Hospital emergency room (later proved false) fueled Fritz's desire to find the grief-stricken gambler before more trouble broke out.

Eventually, officers at police headquarters reached Fritz and told him that Noble was at the station waiting to talk to him. By the time Fritz arrived, newspaper reporters had cornered Noble, and he had blurted out his story. "The man who did this to my wife," he ranted, "is a kill-crazy man who lives 1,500 miles from here. He's killed a lot of people and he wants to kill me." Reporters pressed for more information, and Noble further identified the man he blamed as "a gambler who has run a big policy racket here for years." He didn't mention names, but he didn't need to: everyone knew he was talking about Benny Binion.

George Carter, a reporter Noble trusted, came to the house on Conrad Street later that day and found Noble, stunned and enraged at his wife's death, sitting alone in the darkened living room. The silver-haired gambler held out his hands, still bloody, to the reporter. "See that," he said, "that's my wife's blood."

Three days later, seven hundred mourners crowded the Lamar & Smith chapel for Mildred Noble's funeral, and four hundred more stood outside in a chilly mist. The funeral procession extended for two miles through the streets of Dallas to the Sparkman Hillcrest cemetery where Mildred, in a solid-bronze casket, reportedly the most expensive ever purchased in Dallas, was laid to rest. As they left the graveside, one mourner, a woman who had been a friend of Mildred's, said to another, "At least she won't have to worry about Herbert any more."

THE POLICE INVESTIGATION of Mildred Noble's murder proceeded with uncommon intensity. The Dallas police didn't particularly care if the gamblers killed each other, as long as they disposed of the bodies discreetly and innocent citizens didn't get hurt. But an explosion in Oak Cliff, a quiet residential section, and the killing of an innocent woman was another story entirely. Many Dallas policemen knew Mildred personally. They liked her and they knew that she had nothing to do with Herbert's business. Unlike the fictionalized gun molls portrayed in the pulp detective magazines, she had been a devout, churchgoing housewife who worried about her husband and accepted with dignity the fact that she loved him but could not change him.

A good many of the West Dallas police characters knew and liked Mildred Noble as well. She had grown up in West Dallas, and her brother, Delbert Bowers, was himself a three-time convicted felon. She had little or no contact with Delbert, but she never "got above her raisings," as the West Dallas saying went, and she was always kind and polite to anyone she met, rich or poor. West Dallasites who ordinarily wouldn't give a starving policeman directions to a free lunch were willing, even eager, to talk to the police about Mildred Noble's death.

At the scene of the blast, investigators confirmed the obvious. A homemade bomb wired to the automobile's generator and placed directly behind the dashboard had caused the explosion. The most likely explosive, they concluded, was nitroglycerin gel, a substance made by combining liquid nitroglycerin with cotton. The gel, which had been used for years in the oil fields, had been appropriated for use by safe crackers because it was more powerful and easier to conceal than dynamite, and much more stable than liquid nitro, which was prone to explode when even slightly jostled. Safe crackers called the gel "grease" or "soup."

Police quickly learned that two explosives experts from Kansas City, Bob Pinkerman and Henry Ramsey, had been in Dallas about two weeks before Mildred Noble's death, apparently attracted by the large price on Herbert's head. But both had left town before the fatal explosion. A local safe blower, a burly member of the Lois Green gang named Roy Sistrunk, who happened to live less than three blocks from the Noble house, was questioned and released when his alibi proved solid. Just three days before the blast, Clarence Bourg and John Forrest Lowe, both from Houston and both considered explosives experts, had been arrested at a West Dallas motor court for vagrancy—or, as they said in West Dallas, "charges of unemployment." They had been released and sent on their way back to Houston, but police found it interesting that their companion when they were arrested had been Lois Green.

Always high on the list of suspects when a major crime was committed in Dallas, and at the very top of the list when the crime involved an attempt to kill Herbert Noble, Lois Green immediately became the leading suspect in Mildred's death. The police theorized that Green had met with the two Houston safe blowers for the purpose of purchasing the nitro gel that had killed her. They had no useable proof, but the information they were wringing from the underworld grapevine indicated they were on the right track.

The police also believed that the murder had been a three-man job, with one man planting the explosives, one keeping a lookout, and a third manning the getaway car. They soon arrested twenty-nine-year-old R.D. Matthews, another Green gang member. Matthews had served in the Marine Corps during the war and had missed the wide-open years in Dallas, but upon his discharge in late 1945, he had returned to Dallas and immediately began compiling an extensive record on the local crime scene as a bookmaker, drug dealer, and burglar.*

On November 21, just eight days before Mildred's murder, Matthews made several attempts to contact L.J. McWillie, Benny Binion's man at the Top O' the Hill in Arlington and, reportedly, one of the men to see about a payoff for killing Herbert Noble. On November 25, four days before the blast, Matthews called a man named Hugh Street in connection with an Arkansas burglary in which Matthews had been charged. According to police reports, Matthews told Street he had to stay out of jail because there was "$10,000 on Noble."

On the day of Mildred Noble's funeral, an informant told police that Matthews and Junior Thomas, another Green gangster, had been furious at Green because Green talked in front of a prostitute about "blowing up that woman."

Relatively sure that Green had planted the bomb, possibly with Matthews acting as lookout, the police had two strong suspects for the driver. One, Junior Thomas, a burglar and drug dealer, was a long-time friend of Lois Green and was considered one of Green's most trusted lieutenants. Thomas had provided the car that Green, Johnny Grisaffi, and Bob Minyard had used on the night of the wild car chase from downtown Dallas to the Noble ranch in 1946. Ten days before Mildred's murder, Thomas was reported to have had some trouble with Ray Woods, a mechanic, over a car repair bill. He was overheard to tell Woods, "take a mortgage on my life if you want to, I can pay it off in two weeks."

Obviously, Thomas, like Matthews, expected to come into money at about the time Mildred Noble was killed. But the grapevine reported that the driver had been George Washington "Jettie" Bass, another of Green's lieutenants and one of the best and most active safe burglars in the country. Handsome, well-

---

* FBI reports refer to Matthews as a "hired killer" but there is no record that Matthews was ever arrested for, or charged with, murder.

dressed, and an expert golfer, Bass hardly fit the mold of the Dallas hoodlum. Up to this time, he had limited his criminal activities to robbing safes and jewelry stores, always at night, and was never known as a hijacker or gunman. But Bass had several charges pending in Georgia and Alabama and, according to the word on the street, desperately needed money for lawyers and, presumably, bribes. When Green, again according to underworld rumor, asked Bass if he wanted to make some money, Jettie agreed to drive the car but said he "didn't want anything to do with killing anyone." A fine distinction, but apparently one that soothed Bass's conscience.

ALTHOUGH MILDRED NOBLE'S murder had occurred in Dallas County, a Tarrant County grand jury invited Herbert to testify at a hearing on December 12, 1949. His grand jury testimony is, of course, secret, but he repeated most of it in statements to reporters. The gist of Herbert's testimony was that an unnamed "kill-crazy man" who lived fifteen hundred miles west of Dallas was behind Mildred's murder as well as several attempts on Herbert's own life. He repeated his assertions that this man owned and continued to operate a large numbers racket in Dallas. Noble went on to tell reporters that the man who wanted to kill him hated him because he wouldn't "bow down to him."

Once again, Noble refused to speak the name, but he left little doubt in the minds of either the reporters or grand jurors that he referred to Benny Binion. When Dallas and Fort Worth reporters called Binion for his reaction to Noble's charges, the Las Vegas gambler said he had never met Mildred Noble, but he had heard that she was a fine woman. He was, he said, "sorry as hell to see her killed like that . . . terrible thing." Binion said that he knew Herbert Noble well and had done business with him in Dallas during the war, but he wasn't trying to have him killed and didn't have any idea who was. Binion admitted that he was acquainted with Lois Green, but said he'd never hired Green to kill Noble or anyone else.

With Noble's charges and Binion's denials, the murder of Mildred Noble faded quietly out of the headlines. The two Dallas police officers in charge of the investigation, Will Fritz of the homicide squad and George Butler of the vice squad, continued to pound the pavement, squeezing informants for information and hoping to find evidence that would support prosecution. Butler eventually summarized the investigation by saying that "information was received to the effect that Lois Green, R.D. Matthews and Jettie Bass had planted the bomb. One arrest was made, but there was insufficient evidence, and no charges were filed." Once again, the old police axiom held true: knowing something and proving it are two different things.

Officially, the murder of Mildred Noble remains unsolved.

Lois Green's Last Party

December 23, 1949

The party started just after ten o'clock. Lois Green and several members of his gang, together with their girlfriends—wives were not welcome—gathered at the Sky Vu* nightclub to have a few drinks and enjoy the pre-Christmas floor show. The Sky Vu, located at 542 West Commerce in a wedge of land created by the fork of Commerce Street and the Fort Worth Pike, was owned by Joe Bonds (true name: Joseph Loturo), a newcomer to Dallas with a New York background. The Sky Vu had become a popular hangout for Green and his associates and served as an informal headquarters for the gang that the newspapers had begun to call "the Forty Thieves."

No one kept a list of those who were on the premises on that particular evening, but most of the burglars, dope dealers, pimps, thugs, and police characters who associated with Green were present at one time or another. Jettie Bass was on hand with his girlfriend, Gladys Harvey, who, besides being Jettie's girlfriend, served the important function of helping Green and Bass keep track of Herbert Noble's whereabouts through her husband, Red, who worked as a dealer for Noble at the Airmen's Club. James R. "Jack" Todd, a safe burglar who was rumored to be Green's top lieutenant, was there for most of the evening. So was Junior

---

* Sometimes referred to as the "Sky-View," the club closed after a 1950 fire and reopened as the Sky Club.

Thomas. Others drifted in and out during the evening, staying to drink and talk for an hour or two before leaving to go about other business.

Duane Smith, a car thief, safe cracker, and burglar, left the party around midnight. Stopped at a traffic light less than a mile from the Sky Vu, Smith glanced at a black Ford rolling to a stop next to him and found himself looking down the barrel of Herbert Noble's shotgun. Noble smiled at Smith but did not fire. Smith ignored the red light and raced away.

Less than an hour after Smith's encounter with Noble, at about one o'clock on Christmas Eve morning, Green himself left the club. Nattily dressed in a dark gray topcoat with a snap-brim fedora, Green walked to his new Oldsmobile parked in an alleyway separating the Sky Vu from its neighbor, the Semos Drive-In Restaurant. As he unlocked his car door, a sound of some sort attracted Green's attention to the shadows between the buildings. Perhaps someone called his name, or possibly he heard the unmistakable sound of a pump action shotgun racking a shell into place. For whatever reason, he turned toward the shadows just as the first blast of 12-gauge buckshot struck him in the left side, a few pellets lodging in the inside of the Oldsmobile's door. A second shot ripped into the left side of Green's neck and throat. Still on his feet, Green staggered away from the gunman and around the front of his Oldsmobile, where he slumped near the right front wheel. The gunman fired at least once more, blowing away the top half of the side door of the drive-in, before escaping into the darkness.

Jack Todd and Junior Thomas heard the shotgun and rushed into the alley, where they found Green mortally wounded but still conscious. Todd ran back into the Sky Vu, shouting for someone to call an ambulance. Thomas took care to remove Green's pistol from his pocket so that he would appear to have been unarmed.

The sheriff's deputies arrived first, followed seconds later by Sheriff Decker himself. Decker knelt to question Green, but the buckshot-riddled hoodlum had already lost consciousness.

An hour later, doctors at Parkland Hospital pronounced Green dead on arrival.

Decker's investigators found one witness to the shooting, a bus boy from the Semos Drive-In who had stepped outside for a smoke. The young man described the shooter as medium height and stocky, a description that effectively eliminated Slim Hays but scarcely anyone else. According to the witness, the gunman had walked back into the shadows after the shooting and may have left the scene on foot, although the witness heard several cars leaving the area soon after the shooting and thought the killer might just as easily have driven away. Other than this vague information, the only eyewitness to Green's murder had nothing to offer.

Searching the scene, deputies found five shotgun shells in the alley, marking the spot where the gunman had stood. Strike marks on the shells indicated that they had all been fired from the same gun, leading to the conclusion that only one shooter had been involved. Party-goers still inside the Sky Vu told Decker that Green had left the club alone just before one o'clock. Seconds after he walked out the door, shots were heard from the direction of the parking lot. The number of shots was in dispute, with witnesses claiming to have heard from as few as three to as many as eight.

In a parking lot across Commerce Street from the Sky Vu, Sonny Lefors parked next to a taxi and asked the driver what all the commotion was about. The driver told him that Lois Green had been shot, and Lefors drove away.

BILL DECKER ORDERED his deputies to bring in anyone they could think of who may have been involved with Green, either friend or foe. Any shotguns found in the sweep were to be confiscated and brought in as well.

By the next afternoon, Decker had questioned more than twenty Dallas hard cases, among them Herbert Noble, Sonny Lefors, Jack Todd, and Junior Thomas. No one, of course, offered any helpful information. Duane Smith, keeping to the under-world code, did not mention that he had encountered Noble, who was armed with a shotgun, near the Sky Vu shortly before the shooting, a fact that would certainly have interested Decker and his investigators. No one could locate the cab driver who had spoken to Lefors minutes after the shooting. By the time of Green's funeral, nearly every police character in Dallas had been questioned, and the sheriff's office was knee-deep in shotguns. Still, the police had no decent leads.

Green's funeral service may well have been the largest legal gathering of criminals ever to take place in Dallas. At the time of his death, Green himself had been under indictment for burglary in Idaho and the subject of a fugitive warrant in that state for failure to appear at trial. He was also under indictment in Dallas County for the robbery of a Highland Park oil man, and his trial for the tie-up robbery of Grover Furr, a McKinney automobile dealer, was scheduled to begin just weeks after Green was killed. The Reverend Alfred Palmer, who officiated at the service, had been released just a few weeks earlier on parole from the federal correctional facility at Seagoville, Texas, where he had been serving a two-year sentence for mail fraud.

The pallbearers boasted equally colorful histories. Olen Tyler, a drug dealer from Irving, Texas, had been convicted of murder in 1935. Jettie Bass had been convicted for burglary in 1933 and violating federal rationing laws in 1943. He was, at the time of the funeral, under indictment for burglary in Hillsboro, Texas. R.D. Matthews had been indicted for burglary in Hot Springs, Arkansas, just weeks before Green's death. Jack Todd had received a five-year suspended sentence for burglary in 1943. Duane Smith's record included convictions for a 1942 Texas burglary and a 1944 federal narcotics violation. Junior Thomas was the only pallbearer without a record at the time of the funeral and he would find himself in prison less than a year later.

Cecil Green did not attend his younger brother's funeral.

He had been unable to arrange a furlough from the state penitentiary in North Carolina, where he was serving ten years for burglary.

The day after Green's funeral, Dallas Police Chief Carl Hansson held a press conference. While there were no solid leads, he said, the police had developed several theories as to why Green had been killed. One possibility, according to Hansson, was that members of Green's own gang had killed him. Green was well known for disposing of accomplices who might testify against him, and some investigators thought that his murder grew out of his pending trial in McKinney. Another theory held that Green had been hired to kill Herbert Noble by someone—meaning Benny Binion—and had been killed because he botched the job. The third, and most credible, theory was that Green had been murdered in retaliation for the attempts on Noble's life, especially the bombing that killed Mildred Noble. Hansson, who didn't want to admit that Dallas might be on the verge of a full-scale gang war, did his best to downplay the idea that Green had been killed by Noble (or someone hired by Noble), even though this was by far the most logical supposition.

The deluge of grief at the passing of Lois Green was short-lived. On January 5, 1950, Green's widow, Betty, a prostitute named Phyllis Hudson (usually known as "Dixie Ewert"), Angelo Casten, and R.D Matthews were arrested at Matthews's home with twenty vials of cocaine.

ON THE DAY of Lois Green's funeral, Herbert Noble walked into Sonny's Food Store and laid on the counter an eight-by-ten glossy photograph of Green on a morgue slab. "There he is," he said to Sonny Lefors. "There's the dirty son of a bitch." He refused to say how he had obtained the photo, taken minutes after Green's death, before the gore had been cleaned up. Perhaps Noble, an avid amateur photographer, had somehow managed to slip into the morgue and take it himself.

SHORTLY AFTER GREEN'S murder, Noble sent Sonny Lefors to Las Vegas, to "look over Binion's security." In case an opportunity to kill Binion might present itself, Noble supplied Lefors with a .38 Colt super-automatic. Lefors wouldn't promise to try to kill Binion, but he did agree to make the trip. This may well have been the most serious error in judgment Herbert Noble ever made.

Noble could not have known it at the time, but Sonny Lefors had for some time been keeping Bill Decker informed of the criminal activities in West Dallas in return for relative immunity for his own burglary and fencing operation. Years later, a Dallas police officer called Lefors a "fink" and a "double-crosser." The same officer referred to Lefors as "the sorriest punk we had around here." Considering his close relationship with Decker, Benny Binion no doubt knew that Lefors was on his way to Las Vegas as soon as he left Dallas.

Only hours after Lefors arrived in Las Vegas, a black Cadillac sedan pulled up to the curb as he walked along Fremont Street. One of the three men in the car, Cliff Helm, stepped out of the car and herded him into the back seat. Sonny didn't recognize the driver, but he knew the man he was sitting next to: Benny Binion.

As the four men drove west out of Las Vegas toward Death Valley, Lefors was convinced that he would never see Dallas again. But before they reached the desert, the driver turned in to a sprawling area of ranch-style houses and then into a long driveway leading to a small building behind Binion's home. Inside, the driver, who has never been identified, stood silently by the door while Cliff Helm begged Binion to let him kill Lefors. Helm, who was waiting until his appeals were exhausted before beginning a life sentence for the murder of Johnny Beasley, told Binion he had nothing to lose. He could just take Lefors out into the desert, he said, and blow his head off. Chances are, he argued, no one would ever even find the body. Binion finally turned on Helm. "Shut up," he said. "I don't want no unnecessary killing."

Jetty Bass

Baldy Whatley

Foy Crowell

Sonny Lefors

Lt. George Butler (l) with Senator Estes Kefauver

Dallas District Attorney Henry Wade (r) with captain Will Fritz.

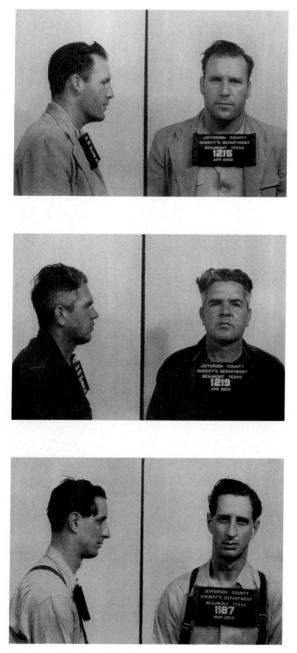

Top: J.R. Gilreath; middle: Finley Donica; bottom: Bob Braggins

West Dallas slums like this one spawned criminals like Bonnie & Clyde and Herbert Noble. The Dallas skyline is visible in the background.

Dallas and Fort Worth gambler Bob Floyd.

Noble points out the holes in his "bullet proof" Ford the day after the ambush by Franklin Strong and Leroy Goss.

Noble examines a piece of shrapnel from the exploded engine of one of his airplanes. At forty years old he could easily have passed for sixty.

Mildred Noble's sheet-covered body lies near the wreckage of her husband's car. Their home at 311 Conrad St. is in the background.

Herbert and Freda Noble at Mildred Noble's funeral.

Mildred Noble's casket was, at the time, reported to be the most expensive ever sold in Dallas.

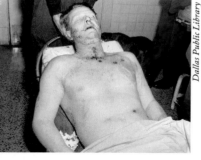

Lois Green in the morgue.

Lois Green swaggers out of jail after one of his many arrests.

Herbert Noble after his fight with Jack Todd. Fifty-six stitches were needed to repair his ear.

Jack Todd

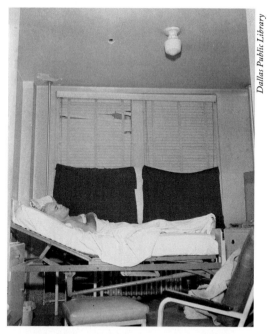

Herbert Noble in his hospital bed after he was wounded on New Year's Eve 1949. The bullet hole in the blinds above the bed and the hole in the ceiling are the result of the attempt to kill him in the hospital.

The shots at Noble's hospital room were fired from this spot.

*Cowboy Benny Binion at the height of
his career as Dallas's "boss gambler"*

*This stable in northwest Dallas County served as headquarters for Binion's multi-
million dollar policy racket.*

Benny Binion (r) with his friend Sheriff Bill Decker.

George Wilderspin, Benny Binion's man in Fort Worth.

The Southland Hotel in downtown Dallas served as headquarters for Binion's gambling operations.

District Attorney investigators examine evidence at Binion's policy headquarters. The documents gathered in this raid sent Binion to prison.

Benny Binion at his sentencing for income tax evasion.

The scene of the Louis Tindall ambush. The fatal shots were fired from behind the hedge on the right.

Jim Clyde Thomas

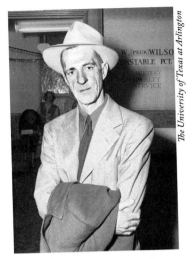

Jack Nesbit, the only man ever charged with attempting to kill Herbert Noble. He was never tried.

Tincy Eggleston

Tincy Eggleston's car was found dripping blood in a supermarket parking lot. His body was found several days later at the bottom of an abandoned well.

Map showing the location of the Noble murder.

MAIL BOX

300 yds.
TO NOBLE'S
HOUSE
ROAD

CAR WITH
NOBLE, BLOWN
TO BITS HERE

60 yds.

KILLER'S
TRUCK

ROAD

150 yds.

KILLER HID
HERE

Texas Ranger Lewis Rigler demonstrates how the ground wire was touched to the barbed-wire fence, setting off the blast. In the background, a group of men surround the demolished car.

An unidentified man gathers cash scattered in the Noble explosion. The battery used to trigger the bomb is in the foreground at lower left.

Noble's Ford after the fatal explosion. Note the ace of diamonds in the foreground.

As Lefors later described it, he and Binion had a pleasant conversation. "Benny was very nice and polite," Sonny said. "He just asked me a lot of questions." Binion told Lefors that he was sorry that Mildred Noble had died the way she did and swore that he had nothing to do with it. He also denied any knowledge of anyone trying to kill Herbert and told Lefors that he "damn sure wasn't behind any of it."

Finally, Binion allowed the relieved Lefors to go. Before he left, Lefors told Binion to call on him if he ever needed anything. From that point forward, the Cowboy had a spy inside the Noble camp. Binion laughed and said he didn't think he'd need to do that. Less than two years later, he may have changed his mind.

THE LOCATION OF Benny Binion's Dallas policy wheels had never been much of a mystery. Some, like the Tip Top at the Deep Ellum Dance Hall, were actually named for their locations. Others, though less helpfully named, were equally easy to find. On the other hand, the location of his headquarters, where each day's take was divided and records were kept, was a carefully guarded secret. Or it was until the early morning of December 28, 1949.

At eight thirty that morning, a hand-picked team of lawmen chosen from the ranks of the Dallas Police Department, the Dallas County sheriff's office, and the district attorney's investigative squad kicked through the front door of a riding stable located a few miles west of the Dallas city limits on Highway 183. In the tack room, a small storage room in the back of the stable, they found six men with bundles of cash, policy slips, adding machines, and other paraphernalia of the numbers business. Harry Urban Sr., who owned the riding stable, had been associated since the 1930s with Binion in the Dallas policy racket. Buddy Malone had been at Binion's side in 1936 when the two of them pumped a barrage of fatal shots into policy rival Ben Frieden. Curly Rogers had acted as the go-between for Binion and Louis Tindall in the early 1940s, when Tindall ran Binion's

Fort Worth numbers operation. The other three, Ernest Fivecoat, H.T. "Jelly" Jordan, and J.W. Smith, were all known gambling associates of Binion and Urban.

Besides an impressive haul of evidence and highly placed gamblers, the raiders found an open safe containing rudimentary financial records of the operation. Among these were copies of Benny Binion's income tax returns for the last three years and a few cancelled checks and bank deposit records.

On that morning, four other groups of officers raided a total of fourteen other locations, including all twelve of the Binion-Urban policy wheels, Harry Urban's Urban Distributing Company (a vending machine distributorship at 2823 Main Street in Dallas), and Urban's residence on Preston Road, north of the Dallas city limits. The twelve policy wheels were locked up, nearly thirty policy runners and counters were arrested, and more business records were seized.

By Friday, December 30, warrants had been obtained for bank records, cancelled checks, and safe deposit boxes from two Dallas banks. The records, taken as a whole, revealed every detail of the complex financial structure of Benny Binion's policy business. With the damning evidence in hand, District Attorney Will Wilson quickly secured the (reluctant) cooperation of Urban's accountant, A.A. Eads, and his bookkeeper, Jesse Palmer. An internal police department memo described the policy organization:

> [Binion] and Urban organized the policy operation into a business like enterprise, they retained an accountant and a legal staff, divided the town up into territories and put salesmen into each territory and protected them by keeping out all other competition and fixing their fines at the city hall. It is stated that at one time he [Binion] had a representative on the city commission, it was well known that various enforcement officials were greatly influenced by him.

Through the years he has had various partners, but at all times he kept the larger percentage of the take from these operations; one partner, Harry Urban, has been constant since the beginning. In 1945 he organized the policy set-up into its approximate present form, it consists of two partnerships, but both operate together using the same facilities, offices, and salaried personnel. Binion has retained from 51% to 66⅔% of the net take from these operations since that time. The present organization is as follows:

Binion owns 66⅔% of a partnership composed of himself, Harry Urban, T. L. Rogers, and Ernest Fivecoat operating 8 wheels known as Horse Shoe, Tip-Top, East & West, North & South, Hi-Lo, Red & Green, Five & Ten, and Silver Dollar. Although this partnership operates 8 of the 12 wheels owned by Binion, its income is smaller than the 4 wheel partnership which is as follows:

He owns 66⅔%* of the partnership composed of himself, Harry Urban, James W. Smith, H. E. Malone, and H. T. Jordan, Jr. which operate the White & Green, High-Noon, Grand Prize, and the Gold Mine policy Wheels.

Urban's records established the method of distribution of the profits as well. Urban maintained a bank account at a local bank, which was used exclusively for the deposit of profits from the policy wheels. Urban transferred his personal income to another account at the same bank. Binion's share was transferred to his personal account at another Dallas bank. With these records in hand, the district attorney was able to determine the exact income from the policy racket for both Binion and Urban, over

---

* This percentage was later determined to be incorrect. Binion's interest in these four wheels was actually 51 percent.

a period of several years. District Attorney Wilson couldn't call the IRS fast enough.

Within a few days after the policy raids, Binion, Urban and their five partners had been indicted for felony gambling in Dallas and, within a few more days, for federal income tax evasion.

When the news of the raids reached Binion in Las Vegas, he immediately concluded that someone had tipped off the police to the location of Urban's riding stable. He decided the culprit could be only one man: Herbert Noble.

16

"I Suppose They'll Get Me Someday"

December 31, 1949

In Oak Cliff, New Year's Eve passed quietly. The tree-lined streets of this peaceful neighborhood were undisturbed except for the occasional sound of fireworks in the distance as Dallas geared up for the final celebration of a turbulent decade. Like most of his neighbors, Herbert Noble intended to greet the New Year at home. His daughter, Freda Lou, would be returning to her boarding school in Virginia in only two days, and when she announced that she intended to spend the evening with a friend, Herbert urged her to invite the young man to the house at 311 Conrad. Just after eight o'clock, a friend of Herbert's called and invited himself over for a New Year's drink. Noble wanted to make a quick trip to the drug store and he decided to run the errand before his friend arrived.

As he stepped out of his front door, a spotlight flashed on, lighting Noble like an actor on a stage. An instant later, a high-powered rifle bullet shattered his left arm below the elbow, ripped away a piece of his hip, and lodged against his spine. Noble staggered back to the house, banging on the door as a second shot ricocheted off the brick front of the house. Freda opened the door, and Noble collapsed into the living room, alive but seriously wounded.

Ambulance attendants responding to Freda's call arrived in minutes, but Noble, suspecting a trick, held them at gunpoint, refusing to allow them in the house until a policeman he recognized arrived and took charge of the situation.

Noble was able to tell the police that the shots had been fired from a new Hudson, equipped with a spotlight and parked at the curb almost exactly where the explosion had killed Mildred just five weeks before. There had been two men in the car, Noble said, but he could not identify them.

At the hospital, Noble's doctors pronounced the wounds serious but not life threatening. Five hours of surgery were required to rebuild his arm and probe for the bullet near his spine, which, ultimately, the surgeons were unable to remove. During the surgery, police went through Noble's effects and found in his pocket a carefully drawn map to Benny Binion's Las Vegas home, including a snapshot of the property.

In a fitting conclusion to the bloodiest decade in Dallas history, Herbert Noble welcomed the New Year and the new decade from a bed at Methodist Hospital.

SEVERAL DAYS AFTER his surgery, Noble called his brother Robert, who was called "Runt," to his bedside. He told Runt that he had become acquainted with an Italian who was identified in police reports only as "Mike." According to Noble, Mike was closely connected to the Chicago mob through his father, an undertaker who presided at mob funerals. Mike's brother was, in turn, acquainted with Ralph Capone, the brother of the notorious Al Capone. Ralph Capone had, in fact, stopped in Dallas to visit Mike while on his way to Arizona only a few months before. Herbert had directed Runt to take a sum of cash to Mike as a down payment on a hit on Benny Binion. Mike was to forward the money to Ralph Capone, who was to arrange the killing.

Runt did as he was told, but whether the money reached Capone, or whether any attempt was ever made to hire someone to kill Binion, remains unknown. Noble, however, was sufficiently optimistic that he bragged about the plan to George Butler some time later. Butler recalled the incident in a departmental memo written months after the fact:

> Noble told this investigator about 18 months ago that he had tried to make some contacts in an effort to get someone to kill Binion. That he had put up a lot of money and might bring the deal to a close sooner than anyone expected. Apparently the contact was made through an Italian in Grapevine who lived in Webb City. The man's name was Mike. Mike was supposed to have been associated with the Capone family directly. His father was a funeral home director in Chicago and handled funerals for the Mob there. While Noble was in the Methodist Hospital during the time a sniper took a shot at him, he, Noble, was supposed to have given Mike $400.00. Mike then went to Grand Prairie and telegraphed the money up the country. This was reported to the Chief but no further investigation was made at that time to find out who the money was sent to. Mike was reported as entertaining Ralph Capone when he was on his way from Wisconsin to check on some of his investments in Arizona. . . . Apparently the information previously received to the effect that Noble had used connections of the Grapevine Dago to get himself a man to kill Binion was not a well kept secret.

February 7, 1950

Late in the evening, a man dressed in a dark overcoat and hat took a position in a small courtyard situated between two of the wings of Methodist Hospital. He may have been alone, or another man may have waited in a car parked nearby. Practically invisible in the shadows of a large oak, the man commanded a clear view of the window of Herbert Noble's fourth floor hospital room.

Around eleven, Noble switched on a small bedside lamp and got out of bed, bound for the bathroom. In the courtyard below, the man in the overcoat swung a .30 caliber military carbine into position and took careful aim at Noble's silhouette. He squeezed the trigger gently until the weapon fired.

The bullet crashed through the window of Noble's room, ripped a huge hole in the Venetian blinds, deflected off the ceiling, gouged a chunk of wood out of the doorframe and, finally spent, fell to the floor. At the sound of the shot, which he said "sounded like a canon," Noble dropped to the floor and crawled to the nightstand, where he unplugged the table lamp. In the process, he re-injured his mangled left arm, still in a cast after the New Year's Eve shooting. Otherwise, Noble was badly shaken but unhurt.

A contingent of police officers, led by Sheriff Bill Decker and Captian Will Fritz of the Dallas homicide squad, searched the courtyard below Noble's window for several hours, but found no trace of the shooter.

"God took care of me," Noble told his friend George Carter of the *Dallas Times Herald* the next morning. "They'll never give up," he said. "They could have their guns trained on me at any time." Noble repeated his assertion that the men who tried to kill him were paid by "a gambler 1,500 miles from here," but, as always, he did not name Benny Binion. He told Carter again that he would not leave Dallas. "I suppose they'll get me someday, but they won't run me out of town."

The failed attempts on Noble's life on New Year's Eve and later at Methodist Hospital served to underline the reason that the killers had not been able to get the silver-haired gambler. They couldn't shoot.

The roster of gangsters who had tried to kill Noble was made up exclusively of city men. Green, Grisaffi, Minyard, Nesbitt, and all of the others had been born and raised in the city, most of them in the streets of Dallas or in the hardscrabble slums of West Dallas. They were accustomed to killing at close range with a pistol, a knife, or a shotgun, and their targets were usually seated in a car, tied up, or otherwise obligingly immobile. The task of shooting a man—a moving target—with a rifle at a distance was foreign to them, and they proved time and again that they weren't up to the chore. None of them, except the ex-Marine R.D. Matthews, had any military training. They might have gotten the job done with heavier firepower, but they lacked the machine guns and automatic rifles that had made the bank robbers of the 1930s so deadly.

Apparently, they understood their shortcomings. In the future, they would resort to more effective methods.

ON THE DAY after the shooting at Methodist Hospital, Dallas newspapers reported that a porter at a local hotel had been arrested for selling policy slips for the Green and White wheel. Despite the arrests and indictments for felony gambling and income tax evasion barely a month before, Benny Binion's policy business was back in full swing. No one seemed particularly surprised.

AFTER HIS DISCHARGE from Methodist Hospital, Noble seldom returned to the house on Conrad Street. Instead, he spent most of his time living as a near-recluse at the Diamond M Ranch. Unable to sleep during the night, he would prowl the house from sundown until dawn, his .30 caliber rifle always at hand. He kept pistols in every room and stationed shotguns at strategic points near the doors.

In the bedroom he had shared with Mildred, he kept a large color photo of her flower-covered casket. In the tradition of the time, Mildred's portrait had been placed atop her closed casket, and Noble sat for hours staring at the picture of the coffin, Mildred's portrait smiling back at him. Her clothes remained in the closet, exactly as she had left them on her last night at the ranch. Her green silk nightgown still hung on a hook inside the closet door.

At first light, he would take a sleeping pill and fall exhausted into bed, where he would sleep a few hours, usually rising before noon. Never before a heavy drinker, he took to pouring back at least a case of beer on most days and was frequently drunk by dark. On those nights, he would drive to Dallas, where he would roam the streets aimlessly, sometimes for hours, running into parked cars, telephone poles, and the occasional bar ditch. Many of those late-night trips ended in West Dallas, where he would cruise the streets looking for anyone he thought might have had a hand in Mildred's murder. His Dallas excursions almost always ended at Sonny's Food Store, where he would find Sonny Lefors, and Lefors would follow him to make sure he made it safely back to the ranch.

Noble stopped using his Jeep to travel around his ranch, fearing that he would present an inviting target in the open vehicle in broad daylight. Instead, when he needed to check on his cattle, he flew one of his small planes. When he did use his car, even if it had been left unattended for only a few minutes, he would check carefully all around and beneath the Ford sedan, looking for any sign of tampering. Any time his business required him to leave his car parked on a public street, he would pay someone to watch it.

On one day each month he ventured a trip to Dallas in the daylight. Afraid of possible delays in the mails, he went personally to pay the premium on his life insurance.

17

Kefauver Scares the Boys,
and Shimley Comes to Dallas

WHILE HERBERT NOBLE recuperated from his New Year's Eve
wounds, a lanky, hard-drinking young United States Senator named Estes Kefauver prepared to launch an investigation
that would threaten the underpinnings of gambling, both legal
and illegal, throughout America. Elected to the Senate in 1949
after two terms as a United States Representative from Tennessee, Kefauver, whose ambitions extended to the White House,
immediately began searching for a cause that would propel him
into the national spotlight. Organized crime, he decided, would
do nicely.

During his service in Congress, Kefauver had paid particular
attention to the sensational news coverage of two events: the
murder of Bugsy Siegel in Los Angeles and the killing in Chicago of James Ragen, the head of the Continental Press racing
wire service. Both had received detailed coverage in newspapers
throughout the country and both were connected, as Kefauver
saw it, with gambling at a national level. Kefauver postulated
the existence of a national crime cartel, connected by the racing
wire service that allowed bookmakers from coast to coast to
operate with instantaneous race results. In the case of the Ragen
murder, he was absolutely correct. Ragen had been killed because
he refused to sell the Continental Press to the old Capone syndicate in Chicago. Siegel had been sent to the West Coast by
his East Coast mob associates to develop a wire service, called

Trans-American Press, as a rival to Ragen's operation. After Ragen's death, when the mob had gained control of Continental and no longer needed Trans-American, Bugsy refused to close Trans-American unless his partners paid him for his lost profit, a demand that nettled the East Coast mob. But Siegel's death was primarily motivated by the fact that he and his girlfriend, Virginia Hill, were stealing from his partners in the new Flamingo Hotel in Las Vegas.

Other killings across the country, although not related to bookmaking or the wire service rivalry, received extensive and sometimes graphic news coverage, and even the most tenuous connection to gambling brought these murders within Kefauver's view of organized crime. The spectacular murders of Mildred Noble and Lois Green, and the ambush of Herbert Noble, all occurring during the last five weeks of 1949, were among the instances of "wanton slaughter" that Kefauver cited to his Senate colleagues as he drummed up support for his national investigation.

In the spring of 1950, the Senate authorized and funded the United States Senate Subcommittee on Organized Crime, which was to become popularly known as the Kefauver Committee. Beginning on May 10, 1950, and continuing for almost exactly one year, Kefauver's traveling investigation would set up shop in fourteen cities, question more than six hundred witnesses, and produce more that eleven thousand pages of testimony.

All of this concerned the boys in Las Vegas greatly. In those formative years of the desert gambling mecca, almost every casino of any size was connected to some degree with gambling and organized crime outside Las Vegas. Bugsy Siegel's legacy, the Flamingo, had finally achieved success under the direction of Gus Greenbaum and his right-hand man, former Minneapolis gambler Dave Berman. The sprawling Thunderbird opened in 1948 under the complete control of Meyer and Jake Lansky, well-known for their involvement in racketeering in New York, Miami, and Havana. The Desert Inn, nearly completed by this time, would be operated by Moe Dalitz, a Prohibition-era bootlegger in Detroit and a prime mover in Cleveland's notorious Mayfield Road Gang. Downtown in Glitter Gulch, former bootleggers and outlaw gamblers from Ohio, Tennessee, Kentucky, California, and Texas owned or managed nearly every gambling joint on Fremont Street.

But it was not exposure of their former criminal activities that worried these men. With the exception of the Lanskys, who preferred to remain out of the limelight, all of the casino owners and operators conducted business openly, and some, like Benny Binion, even capitalized on their notorious pasts. The boys in Las Vegas were worried that Kefauver might uncover "the skim."

The racketeers, and the hotel and casino owners-in-name-only who fronted for them had invented in Las Vegas a money machine—a seemingly endless flow of untraceable, tax-free cash. Every week—and sometimes more often—couriers carrying suitcases stuffed with cash departed Vegas for Chicago, New York, or Miami. This untaxed cash would make its way to secret bank accounts in Switzerland or one of the emerging off-shore banks, or would be used to purchase narcotics or other contraband, or would finance mob investments in legitimate businesses.

Concealing money from taxing authorities (or business partners) was hardly the invention of Las Vegas. In the plush illegal gambling joints of Miami, New Orleans, and along the Ohio-Kentucky border, gamblers had skimmed for years to avoid taxes. But in Las Vegas, for the first time, the money could flow in both directions. Enormous amounts of cash could be skimmed from the casino counting rooms, funneled through legitimate business investments, and then returned to Vegas as "show money"* to finance new casino construction or for expansion of existing

---

* The term "show money" refers to capital that can be accounted for as legitimate income. The IRS carefully monitors major criminals in the hope that they can be caught spending money which they can not account for on tax returns. In order to finance a multimillion-dollar hotel casino, an investor either had to be able to show enough income to make the investment appear legitimate or borrow the "show money" from a disclosed source.

casinos. Hotel gift shops, coffee shops, and retail stores, as well as the casinos themselves, were used as handy fronts for laundering money or in many cases providing "legitimate" income to racketeers who seldom, if ever, set foot on the premises.

The boys in Vegas were very worried that Kefauver and his little committee might reveal the existence, scope, and economic impact of their money machine.

Any notoriety which might serve to connect Las Vegas with illegal activities outside Nevada terrified the newly respectable Vegas mobsters. And so it was that Dave Berman of the Flamingo, once called "the toughest Jew in Vegas," invited Benny Binion to the strip for a visit. Berman explained that the boys were concerned about all the publicity surrounding Binion's feud with Herbert Noble, especially Noble's insistent references to his would-be assassin as "a big gambler out West." With Kefauver's investigation just around the corner, Berman said, the attempts on Noble's life had to stop. Legend has it that Berman told Binion to leave Noble alone or he, Berman, would have Benny killed. In truth, it is far more likely that Berman's threats would have been more implied than spoken. Berman knew Benny Binion better than to threaten him openly, but Berman undoubtedly conveyed the idea clearly that the Noble situation in Dallas could no longer be tolerated.

Enter Harold Shimley.

A MOON-FACED CON man with a traveling-salesman smile, Harold Shimley claimed to be a big-time gambler and a protégé of the legendary Titanic Thompson. In truth, he was neither. Shimley traveled the country under at lease five aliases, running con games, forging checks, and making book. He first arrived in Texas in 1938 and was promptly arrested in Houston for buying clothes on credit at a store where he had neglected to open a charge account. The Houston police escorted him out of town, and he headed for Dallas, where he was soon arrested for gambling and vagrancy. It was during this, his first time in Dallas, that Shimley probably became acquainted with both Benny Binion and Herbert Noble.

From Dallas, Shimley went on to compile a gaudy arrest record for petty crimes in Indiana, Missouri, Illinois, and Ohio. He settled in Oklahoma City in 1946 and began running a marginally successful crap game and bookmaking operation at the Farmers' Market, near the stockyards. His limited success in Oklahoma City having apparently gone to his head, he attempted to expand into Tulsa, where he had been in business only a few weeks when local gamblers pistol-whipped him, smashed his equipment with axes, and ran him out of town at gunpoint. Back in Oklahoma City, Shimley hit the criminal big-time when he became involved, along with two thugs from Chicago, in the kidnapping of a local bootlegger and his "telephone girl."*

Shimley played a relatively minor role in the kidnapping, acting as a local guide for the Chicago kidnappers. But his participation earned him a two-year sentence in the Oklahoma Penitentiary.

After his release from prison in 1949, Shimley appears to have drifted between Dallas and Las Vegas. He is known at one point following his release to have received money from Benny Binion and possibly to have stayed briefly in Binion's home. Shimley was definitely in Dallas and in contact with Herbert Noble in late 1949. There is persuasive evidence that he was with Noble at some time on New Year's Eve not long before Noble was shot on his front porch, and that he drew the map to Binion's home found in Noble's pocket that night.

---

* In this bizarre incident, two Chicago thugs came to Oklahoma City with the intention of collecting a debt of $5,000 arising out of the sale of bootleg whiskey. They decided to kidnap the local bootlegger, one Willie Joe Kelly, and his telephone girl, Claudie Sams, and hold them for ransom. The Chicago men hired Shimley and a local bootlegger, Harold Byford, as local guides. Kelly was held for eleven hours, during which time he was pistol-whipped and threatened, before he was released. All four kidnappers went to prison.

WHEREVER HE TRAVELED, Shimley kept himself finely attuned to the local underworld grapevine. In Las Vegas, he heard the whispers about Dave Berman's thinly veiled threat to Benny Binion and, being a con man by nature, quickly devised a scheme to profit from the situation.

In early March 1950, Shimley called Herbert Noble to arrange a meeting. Noble agreed to meet with Shimley but, wary of Shimley's intentions, he insisted on meeting somewhere away from his ranch. He also insisted that Phillip Stein, his partner in the Airmen's Club, join the meeting. They agreed to meet on March 10 at a tourist court near Love Field. Noble took the additional precaution of notifying Lieutenant George Butler of the meeting, and Butler arranged to have the entire conversation recorded.*

Shimley began by telling Noble, "Your name and his name [Binion's] is the talk of the goddamn country," and he had been approached by Dave Berman to "straighten this thing up." Shimley recounted a conversation—probably fictitious—between himself, Berman, and Binion, in which Binion, tears running down his cheeks, spoke of the attempts on Noble's life. "I hope my five children will die this minute if I know one thing about it," Binion said. "He didn't only convince me," Shimley told Noble, "he convinced the biggest mob in the United States."

Noble steered the conversation toward Mildred's death, pumping Shimley for information about her killers. Shimley repeatedly denied knowing who had killed her, but dropped hints throughout the meeting that he knew more than he was saying. At one point, this brief exchange took place:

> **NOBLE:** Was it three of them?
> **SHIMLEY:** Oh, yes; three of the bastards altogether.
> So I don't—

---

* An excerpt of the conversation, as it appears in the Kefauver Committee records, is included as Appendix 1. The committee considered the conversation too profane to be entered into the record verbatim, and it has been heavily expurgated.

NOBLE: The hell there was. One of them to drive the car, one of them to shoot, and the other to do the job, I guess. The bastards . . .

SHIMLEY: Every one of them ———— bank burglars, ———— knob-knockers, ————.

NOBLE: Who were they, Shimley? You know them.

SHIMLEY: I really don't know their names. No. And if I knew I'd tell you.

Shimley tried to pacify Noble by telling him that the man who was trying to kill him was his brother-in-law, Delbert Bowers:

SHIMLEY: And I'll tell you, you are going to know the son of a bitch that done it.

NOBLE: All right. Who? You know, now.

SHIMLEY: And the son of a bitch, by God, done it was the man that was trying to get you.

NOBLE: Yeh. Who—who is he?

SHIMLEY: You know who he is as well as I do.

NOBLE: No, I don't. No, I don't.

SHIMLEY: You know that bastard down there that got life in the pen as well as I do.

NOBLE: Who, Delbert [Bowers]?

SHIMLEY: You ain't—

NOBLE: He didn't do it by hisself.

SHIMLEY: Well, he done it with some of his goddamn burglar friends.

Throughout the conversation, Noble's reactions remained non-committal, probably because he was aware of Lieutenant Butler and his tape recorder in an adjoining room, but he couldn't contain himself when Shimley told him that Binion would arrange the killing of the men who murdered Mildred. "Goddamn," Noble said, "now we're talking business."

Possibly the true purpose of Shimley's visit with Noble was

revealed in a single exchange, almost never quoted in excerpts of their conversation:

> **SHIMLEY:** If we can get this straightened out and settle this thing, will you be friends enough with the man [Binion] that we can all make money and open the goddamn town?
> **NOBLE:** Yeah.

Ten days later, Shimley's con, whatever it had been, was over.

Shimley called Noble again, this time with a completely different story. The whole charade ten days earlier, he said, had been a ruse to gain Noble's confidence. In fact, Shimley reported, Noble was entirely correct; it was Benny Binion who was trying to kill him. Shimley said that Binion had offered him twenty-five thousand dollars and a Dallas crap game to kill Noble. Shimley told Noble that he hated Binion but was afraid of him.

None of this, of course, came as a surprise to Noble, who had never bought Shimley's peacemaker act to begin with. There was, however, one thing he wanted from Shimley. He begged Shimley to go back to Las Vegas and kill Benny Binion. Instead, Shimley headed for Tulsa, Oklahoma, never to return either to Dallas or Las Vegas.[*]

ON MARCH 31, 1950, Sheriff Bill Decker received a frantic phone call from Tulsa. The caller, a nearly hysterical woman who refused to give her name, said that a man named Tony Barbario, of Peoria, Illinois, had been murdered on the east side of Dallas. Two men had shot him, she said, on Abrams Road, and he had been buried in a shallow grave not far from the car, which had been burned.

---

[*] Shimley died in a mysterious auto accident in January 1954 near Bartlesville, Oklahoma. George Butler believed the accident had been staged to cover Shimley's murder, but his death is officially recorded as "accidental."

Decker led a group of deputies to the location where the woman said the car would be found. Just as she had said, they found the car, a 1949 Ford sedan, riddled with bullets and partially burned. Decker's men searched for three days, even hiring a private plane to fly over the area, but never found the grave.

The car's license plates traced back to a Dallas resident who said he had recently sold it to a local car dealer. The dealer reported that he had sold the vehicle to "two Italians" who refused to identify themselves, saying they planned to register the car in Chicago.

Decker's check of police sources in Illinois, Kansas City, and St. Louis failed to turn up anyone named Tony Barbario, and no other information about the mysterious bullet-riddled car ever came to light. The crime, if there was a crime, remains unsolved and one of the many mysteries of the Dallas gamblers' war.[*]

---

[*] George Butler speculated several years later that the "two Italians" may have been hired by Herbert Noble to kill Benny Binion and may have been killed by Noble because they double-crossed him. Butler was never able to develop evidence to support his theory.

The Plot to Bomb Las Vegas

April 12, 1950

On an unusually warm day for early April, George Butler drove to the Diamond M Ranch to see Herbert Noble, as he did every few weeks to update him on the investigation of Mildred's murder and to tap into whatever information Noble might have picked up "on the grape," as Butler called the underworld grapevine. He found Noble, stripped to the waist, hard at work beneath the wing of a new airplane, a bright red Staggerwing Beech that Noble had bought a few days earlier. As Butler approached, Noble grabbed his carbine and pointed it at Butler, something he had never done before.

"What the hell are you doing, Herbert?" Butler said. "Put the rifle down."

The lawman and the gambler stared each other down until Noble dropped the carbine and sank to his knees in tears. Binion had killed his wife, he said, and Binion had all the breaks. He had influence, money, and power, Noble sobbed. "I never had a chance," he said. Eventually, Noble calmed down enough to explain his plan. It was simple and direct. He planned to bomb Binion's Las Vegas home.

From friends in Mexico, where he had done considerable business in aircraft salvage,* Noble had acquired two military

---

* Noble's aircraft salvage business has never fully explained his trips to Mexico or his connections in that country, leading to considerable speculation that he was smuggling narcotics on his frequent trips across the border.

surplus bombs, one high explosive and one incendiary. When Butler came upon him, he had been busy attaching bomb racks beneath the Beech's wings. The plane had already been fitted with long-distance fuel tanks and, except for loading the three-foot-long bombs, which lay ready near the plane, his preparations were complete. In his pocket he carried a map pinpointing the location of Binion's home and identifying landmarks that could be spotted from the air. Not only were the highways and other landmarks carefully diagrammed, but also there were notes about Binion's habits—what time he ordinarily came home, and when and where he slept. The map, which Harold Shimley had given him on New Year's Eve, was accurate in every detail.[*]

Butler pointed out that Noble, even with the oversized tanks, could never fly to Las Vegas and back without stopping somewhere for fuel. The return trip might be easy enough, but no airport in the country would allow a light plane to take off carrying two bombs. Noble said he had planned for this contingency as well; he had arranged to land and refuel at a private airstrip in Arizona. Sensing that the story was about to become even more outrageous than it already had been, Butler pressed for more detail.

Noble claimed he had made arrangements to land and refuel on his way west at the Grace Ranch, near Tucson, Arizona. The owner of the Grace Ranch, former Detroit underworld kingpin Pete Licavoli, used the spread as headquarters for a huge national bookmaking and layoff[†] operation. Licavoli also controlled gambling in El Paso, Texas, and Juarez, Mexico, as well as large portions of Arizona and New Mexico. Though Licavoli had owned the property for less than five years, the FBI already recognized

---

[*] This is the same map that had been found in Noble's pocket after the New Year's Eve shooting in Oak Cliff. The map had been photocopied and returned without Noble's knowledge.

[†] A "layoff" is a bet taken from a smaller bookmaker who cannot handle all his action. It is the bookmaking equivalent of wholesaling.

the ranch as a regular meeting place for hoodlums from as far away as Cleveland and Chicago.

Noble explained to Butler that Licavoli and his associates had plotted to take over Dallas gambling since the war, but had been frustrated by Benny Binion and his alliance with local law enforcement, particularly Smoot Schmid and Bill Decker. Licavoli was now willing, Noble said, to help kill Binion and install Noble as the new boss gambler in Dallas. In return, Licavoli wanted 50 percent of the take. In Noble's mind, addled by Mildred's death, the plot must have made sense, but in reality there was no gambling to speak of in Dallas to be taken over. Binion's numbers racket, though still lucrative, would never fully recover from the late-1949 raids and felony indictments. The casino action, with the exception of a few sneak games, had been shut down since the 1946 elections, and Dallas civic leaders would never again sanction illegal gambling.

Butler finally persuaded Noble to give up the idea of bombing Binion's home and hand over the map. In doing so, he probably saved Noble's life. If indeed Noble had intended to land at the Grace Ranch on his way to Las Vegas, he would never have left there alive. With Kefauver's investigation scheduled to begin in less than a month, and the Vegas boys on their best behavior, Licavoli could never have allowed Noble to leave the ranch. A spectacular aerial bombing—and Noble's bombs would have been spectacular—of a Las Vegas casino owner's home, probably killing his wife and five children as well as several neighbors, would have been unthinkable, and Licavoli's role in such an enterprise would surely have cost him his own life. If Licavoli ever had agreed to let Noble use his ranch as a fuel stop on his way to Las Vegas, he did so with the intention of luring Noble to Arizona, where he would have died in a tragic plane crash or simply vanished in the desert.

Where the information came from remains unknown, but within twenty-four hours Benny Binion had the whole story of Noble's plot to bomb his home as well as a photocopy of the map.

Not long after, Binion dispatched two of his bodyguards, Louis "Russian Louie" Strauss and Nathan "Nattie" Blank, to Tulsa, Oklahoma, where Harold Shimley was rumored to be operating a horse race book. A few days later, several shots whizzed past Shimley's head as he walked along a Tulsa street. He was unhurt but immediately became very hard to find.

AFTER HIS FAILED plot to bomb the Binion residence, Herbert Noble's behavior became, if possible, even more erratic. He purchased six tiny Chihuahua dogs and let them run loose in the ranch house all night as sort of mobile burglar alarms. "They're not worth a damn as guard dogs," he told a friend, "but they sure raise hell if they hear anything." Besides his increasingly heavy drinking, his narcotic consumption increased as well. Afraid to sleep during the night, he began to take pills to stay awake so that he could roam the house constantly looking out the windows for intruders. At dawn he took his sleeping pills so that he could manage a few hours' rest. Once silver-haired, muscular, and handsome, Noble had lost more than fifty pounds, and his hair had gone snow-white. At forty, he could have easily passed for sixty.

June 14, 1950

Before first light, Franklin Strong and Leroy Goss slipped quietly into a position near the intersection of the Diamond M Ranch road and the county section line road. There they constructed a makeshift hunting blind. Another West Dallas hoodlum, Fleming Van Derrick, waited in a car secluded behind a stand of trees a half-mile away. Armed with 12-gauge shotguns, Strong and Goss settled in to wait.

On one of Noble's increasingly frequent and unpredictable late-night trips to West Dallas, in the late spring of 1950, he had walked into the Austin Café, a diner, beer joint, and hang-out for police characters. There, he confronted Strong and Goss, both burglars and both associates of the late Lois Green. "Where's the rest of you goddamn thugs?" Noble demanded. Strong said something rude, and Noble slammed him on the side of the head with a half-full beer can. Strong, Goss, and Noble all went for their pistols and only the presence of cooler—and soberer—heads prevented a gunfight on the spot. Now Strong and Goss, with their associate hoodlum, Fleming Van Derrick,* waiting in a car hidden a few hundred yards away, figured it was time to settle the score.

Just after 9:00 a.m., Herbert Noble's black Ford turned from the ranch road onto the section line, headed for Grapevine and Dallas. As Noble drew even with them, Strong and Goss stood up from their hiding place and fired. The first load of buckshot exploded Noble's left front tire, and two more shots ripped into the side of his car as he raced away. Noble, who was apparently becoming accustomed to being shot at, drove at high speed to a neighbor's home a mile down the road, where he calmly called the sheriff and then changed the tire.

Sheriff's deputies searched the area where the shots had been fired, but found nothing of value to the investigation except a single footprint, which they judged to be a size eleven. A neighbor told the deputies that she had heard three shots followed by a car driving away at high speed earlier that morning, but she had not seen the shooters or the driver of the car. No arrests were made.

Noble, trying to salvage some benefit from the latest attempt on his life, put out the word that his bulletproof automobile had saved his life. As evidenced by a number of large holes down its side, Noble's Ford was not bulletproof, but he hoped the story might discourage anyone else from shooting at him.

---

* Strong, Goss, and Van Derrick would be implicated a few months later, along with Jettie Bass, in a series of tie-up robberies in Dallas, Irving, and McKinney, Texas. This particularly vicious crew apparently enjoyed pistol-whipping their victims after tying them up.

THE ATTEMPT ON Noble's life by Franklin Strong and Leroy Goss was probably motivated as much by revenge for Noble's altercation with them in West Dallas a few days earlier as by the price on Noble's head, but they certainly would have accepted the bounty had they been successful. The word on the grape had the price on Noble as high as fifty thousand dollars, and others, even though they held no personal animosity toward Noble, began, as George Butler put it, "to sniff at the proposition." By the early fall of 1950, planning to kill Herbert Noble had practically become a cottage industry in Dallas and Fort Worth.

In late October, Lester Pallette held a quiet conversation in a Fort Worth hotel with A.C. "Buddy" Crawford. Pallette, the owner of several Dallas liquor stores, had grown up with Noble in West Dallas and had been his high school classmate. Crawford was also well acquainted with Noble and had operated a crap game with him at a barn that Crawford owned near the town of Grapevine. "Do you want to make ten thousand dollars?" Pallette asked Crawford. "All you have to do is kill Herbert Noble. You can drive right up to the ranch and do it." Pallete patted his pants pocket. "I've got the money right here," he said. "You can have it right now. All you have to do is kill the man."

Crawford declined the proposition, but later began to suspect that Noble had persuaded Pallette to set a trap in order see whether Crawford would agree to kill him. Crawford, not wanting to be caught in the middle, took the story to Runt Noble. Two weeks later, Herbert asked Crawford if the story about Pallette was true, and Crawford told him that it was. A few days after confirming the story, Noble stopped Pallete on the sidewalk in front of the Royal Grill on Commerce Street. "If you want to kill me, you son of a bitch," the drunken gambler shouted, "why don't you just get a goddamn gun and try to do it?" Pallette claimed the whole thing was a misunderstanding, and Noble stalked away; nothing further ever came of the matter.

At about the same time, another Dallas hoodlum, Raymond "Monk" Pannell, was propositioned to kill Noble. Monk and his brother Leroy were well known to the police as professional criminals, specializing in the theft of large quantities of merchandise from warehouses, boxcars, and trucks. In early 1951, the two brothers would be indicted for the theft of the largest quantity of Aspirin ever stolen. The Pannells were also believed in the underworld to be a part of the Noble faction, lending support to the rumors that Noble used the Diamond M Ranch for storing large quantities of stolen goods.

Monk Pannell mentioned casually to a police informer that he had been offered a lot of money to kill Noble but had refused. When George Butler called Monk down to headquarters for a chat, the burglar confirmed the informer's story, but refused to say who had made the offer. In his report, Butler noted that Pannell lived next door to Johnny Grisaffi, and the two seemed to have become close friends, the obvious implication being that Grisaffi had been behind the proposition.

WHILE NOBLE ALTERNATED on sleepless nights between prowling the ranch house and taking drunken, belligerent trips to Dallas, Benny Binion occupied himself with dodging subpoenas from the Kefauver Committee and attempting to avoid extradition to Texas to answer the pending gambling charges. When the senate committee visited Las Vegas, Binion was nowhere to be found, having chosen that time for a vacation at his Montana ranch. Committee staff members missed him by minutes in Los Angeles, where he had dropped in for a visit with his friend Mickey Cohen. The minute Binion stepped off the train, Cohen's men whispered urgently in his ear and presented him with a ticket back to Las Vegas. He left the station less than an hour before the process servers arrived.

In Nevada, in a furious struggle over Binion's extradition to Texas to answer the charges of operating a policy racket, Binion's attorney, Harry Claiborne, persuaded a Las Vegas judge that Binion could not be a fugitive from justice in Texas because he had not been in Texas when the alleged crime had been committed. Under Nevada law, Claiborne's argument was both persuasive and correct, leading Dallas District Attorney Will Wilson to label Nevada "a haven for gangsters." Still, Wilson remained optimistic. "We'll get him someday," Wilson told the press. And he was right.

19

"There Seems to Be a Killing in the Air"

BY THE EARLY 1950s, enforcement of the gambling laws in Tarrant County and Fort Worth had become a civic joke. When religious leaders, particularly the Reverend Frank Norris, a local Baptist leader, and the Reverend Karl Bracker, an Evangelical pastor, demanded an end to gambling, prostitution, and after-hours liquor sales, the authorities replied that, if any such shenanigans were going on in Tarrant County, they would be quickly brought to an end. The only problem, they said, was that there simply was no such activity going on. Sheriff Sully Montgomery and Police Chief George Hawkins assured citizens' groups that they arrested gamblers whenever they found them. They just didn't find them very often.

Assistant District Attorney Stewart Hellman took a more realistic view of the situation. The *Fort Worth Star-Telegram* quoted Hellman as saying, "Tarrant County has been singularly blessed by being free of violence that has marked gambling activity in Dallas." Although scarcely a ringing denial of widespread gambling in Fort Worth, Hellman's statement was correct. Since the killing of Louis Tindall in 1944, little or no gambling-related violence had occurred in Fort Worth. On the surface, the Tarrant County gambling waters seemed smooth.

But just below the surface long standing feuds divided Fort Worth into two separate gambling camps, and violence threatened to boil up at any time. One group, which is now known to have been the Binion faction, included Fred Browning's Top O' the Hill, Tiffin Hall's numbers operation and crap games at several hotels, George Wilderspin's Eastside Club, and Bert Wakefield's 3939 Club on Jacksboro Highway. In the competing faction, Nelson Harris ran crap games at the 2929 Club (also known as the Westside Recreation Center), the Nighthawk Café, and—with Tincy Eggleston and W.D. Satterwhite—the Skyliner and the Annex Club. Jack Blackman had craps and roulette at the Town House Hotel, and Tom Daly ran the games at the Court Hotel. The Harris-Eggleston faction was later reported to have been financed by Herbert Noble, and this may well have been the case. George Butler was told, however, that Harris's backer was not Herbert Noble but Lewis Noble, a Dallas fence who was not related to Herbert. In any case, the Harris group was not popular with Benny Binion, and even the possibility that Herbert Noble was involved with Harris was enough to set him off.

Jim Clyde Thomas had approached Nelson Harris in mid-1949 with an offer to bring Harris into the Tiffin Hall fold. Harris told Thomas that he had no use for Hall or Benny Binion or any of Binion's friends. He and his partners, Harris said, planned to take over Fort Worth gambling, and they had the money to do it. Later, Hall himself tried to merge the two groups. He first approached Blackman and Eggleston with the idea that they should abandon Harris and throw in with his syndicate. Eggleston and Blackman both declined. Hall next contacted Eggleston alone with a suggestion that they take over the entire Harris and Blackman operation, with Tincy, of course, serving as Hall's second-in-command. Tincy didn't go for this proposition, either.

In the late summer of 1950, Jim Clyde Thomas and Frank Cates visited Eggleston again. This time, the message was less subtle. Tincy could either join up with Hall or take his chances on a substantial reduction in his life expectancy. Tincy told the two gunmen that he appreciated the offer, but he was satisfied with things the way they were. Unlike his hot-headed partner, Nelson Harris, Tincy had enough sense not to make threats about taking over Fort Worth gambling. He just said no and went about his business. Very carefully.

Eggleston's business included a wide-ranging strong-arm and hijacking operation. Tincy, typically with the help of one other man, held up crap games all over Texas and in parts of Louisiana and Oklahoma, bursting through the door, shotgun in hand, and taking all the money, jewelry, and watches they could find. When armed robbery opportunities failed to present themselves, Tincy engaged in his own unique brand of extortion. He knew every serious criminal in the Southwest and would approach someone who had just made a big score and demand a "loan." The unspoken assumption was that Tincy would keep his mouth shut, and the loan would never be repaid.

In the early fall of 1950, Tincy and Nelson Harris robbed the game at George Wilderspin's Eastside Club, escalating the existing tension in Fort Worth even further. A few days later, the two smashed their way into the home of Red Oden and his wife. They taped the Odens to kitchen chairs, roughed them up a bit, and took everything of value they could find. Both of these escapades were ill-conceived. Wilderspin, of course, was closely aligned with the Binion syndicate, and Oden worked for Tiffin Hall and Bob Floyd as a dice dealer at the Commerce Hotel. Word soon spread on the street that Benny Binion had a Fort Worth gambler who had gotten a little too independent "on his list."

BY NOVEMBER, TENSIONS in both Fort Worth and Dallas had risen to the boiling point. In the Dallas County jail, Delbert Bowers, Mildred Noble's brother, who was awaiting trial for burglary, announced to anyone who would listen that he held Herbert Noble responsible for his sister's murder and planned to kill him at the first opportunity. Almost every Dallas outlaw who was not behind bars was in Dallas. Late nights in West Dallas, they converged in droves on the Austin Café and the Singleton Club, each person heavily armed, and some even openly carrying sawed-off shotguns. George Butler noted the rising tensions in a daily report: "There seems to be a killing in the air," he wrote.

BENNY BINION WAS in Dallas as well, although not at the West Dallas dives. He had been spotted several times in downtown Dallas with his bodyguard, Russian Louie Strauss. Binion's old nemesis Will Wilson would leave the district attorney's office on January 1, 1951, and word on the grapevine had it that Binion had already made a deal with the new administration to return to Dallas. Harold Shimley's question to Herbert Noble, about getting along well enough with Binion to open Dallas again, now seemed to have the ring of truth.

ON NOVEMBER 18, 1950, two men visited the Noble ranch under the cover of midnight darkness, looking for Noble. But Noble had taken to spending his nights in several different places, in the hope of avoiding an ambush. They returned the next night and set fire to one of Noble's barns, hoping to draw their quarry into the open. Noble didn't take the bait. He stayed inside the ranch house and waited for the fire department to put out the blaze.

ON NOVEMBER 20, 1950, Tincy Eggleston left downtown just before dark, headed for his home in Burleson, a rural community south of Fort Worth. On a long straight road a few miles north of his home, Tincy noticed a fast-moving car gaining ground rapidly behind him. Soon the car was close enough that Tincy was able to identify its two occupants: Frank Cates and Jim Clyde Thomas. Cates and Thomas swerved into the oncoming lane and drew even with Eggleston. When Thomas, in the passenger seat, produced a shotgun, Tincy slammed on his Oldsmobile's brakes and Cates and Thomas flashed past. With this clever defensive maneuver, Eggleston now became the pursuer. Tincy reached for the pistol he always carried above his sun visor and, driving with one hand, began firing out the window at Cates and Thomas as they disappeared in the distance. He didn't hit either man and apparently missed the car entirely as well.

The next night, several hours after dark, Tincy heard gunfire coming from his front yard. He first started to take his pistol and investigate, but thought better of the idea. The way he figured it, whoever was doing the shooting wanted him outside, preferably in the light of the front porch, where he would make a well-lit target. He put his pistol away and went back to bed.

November 22, 1950

On the day before Thanksgiving, Nelson Harris and his twenty-three-year-old wife, Juanita, left their duplex at 3105 Wingate, on Fort Worth's near south side, to do their Thanksgiving shopping. Juanita, due to deliver their first child in less than two weeks, was unable to do the shopping by herself, and Nelson went along to drive and help with the packages. Seconds after they got in their car, windows cracked in an elementary school eight blocks away, and a housewife hanging out her laundry three miles to the south wondered if it was an earthquake that caused the ground to shake and the air to rumble. On Wingate Street, windows shattered and, in one nearby apartment, an automobile battery crashed through a window, narrowly missing an infant sleeping in his crib.

In an eerie repetition of the scene outside the Noble home in Oak Cliff almost exactly one year before, Harris's car sat smoldering and twisted at the curb, the sheet metal ripped from the chassis and scattered throughout the neighborhood by a nitro gel bomb. Behind the wheel, Nelson Harris's charred and nearly decapitated body had been fused to the seat by the explosion. On the lawn near the car, Juanita Harris, still alive but horribly injured, lay where she had been thrown by the blast. She and her unborn child would die less than an hour later.

As Juanita Harris and her unborn child lay dying, Tincy

Eggleston received two phone calls. The first, from a newspaper reporter, told him that his partner had been killed in an explosion. The second, from an anonymous source, warned Tincy that he would "get the same thing" as Harris. In light of this second call, Eggleston decided it would be prudent to examine his own automobile and, when he did so, found the hood of his Oldsmobile slightly ajar. Peering carefully under the hood, Tincy found a quart jar wrapped in duct tape and wired to the ignition. Three hours later, in an empty field, with Tincy and several sheriff's deputies looking on, a military demolition expert set off an explosion that left a crater big enough to bury Tincy's Oldsmobile.

The police immediately identified a suspect in the Harris murders and the attempted murder of Eggleston. The investigation centered on Jack Nesbit, still under indictment for assault to murder Herbert Noble in the 1949 shootout near Noble's ranch. Known as an expert "nitro man," Nesbit had been seen the afternoon before the bombings on a downtown street in deep conversation with Frank Cates and Jim Clyde Thomas, who had attempted to ambush Eggleston just two days before. The police wanted very much to talk to Nesbit, but he had disappeared, just as he had after the gun battle with Noble.

The grapevine whispered that Nesbit had been kidnapped and killed, probably by Cates and Thomas. When Nesbit finally resurfaced about three weeks later, he explained that he had been afraid of some sort of misguided retaliation by Harris's friends and had decided to hole up in West Texas. He denied any knowledge of the bombings and commented that it was a shame about Mrs. Harris.

While the police searched for Jack Nesbit, another rumor about the bombings circulated. This one held that Eggleston and Harris had fallen out over the division of the profits from a con game they had run, and that Eggleston had planted the bomb in Harris's car and then wired his own car to divert suspicion. Most of the underworld gave little or no credence to this theory. Tincy was not known to use dynamite or bombs of any kind, and the plot didn't seem to fit his style. If Eggleston had wanted to kill Harris, they said, he probably would have called on his friend and running buddy, Cecil Green.

The older brother of Lois Green, Cecil, having paid his debt to North Carolina, had returned to Fort Worth, where he and Tincy based a strong-arm, safe-burglary, and hijacking operation that covered most of Texas and extended into Oklahoma and Louisiana. If Tincy had wanted Nelson Harris dead, most felt he and Cecil would simply have taken him somewhere out of the way and shot him.

After finding a nitroglycerine bomb wired to his car's ignition, Tincy decided that his rural residence offered too little protection. With no close neighbors, and miles of isolated roads nearby, Tincy was a sitting duck for anyone with a little patience. He decided to move, at least temporarily, a little closer to town. One of his gambling partners, Jack Blackman, lived in a large house on Crown Road, northeast of downtown Fort Worth. Located on a cul-de-sac, Blackman's home commanded a clear view of anyone coming or going in the neighborhood. Tincy moved in with Blackman, and the two stocked the premises with enough guns and ammunition to fight a small war. With the yard bathed in floodlight, and dogs patrolling the fences, the two gamblers felt safe enough.

Unfortunately for Blackman and Eggleston, Blackman's house sat directly across the street from the residence of Bob Floyd, one of Tiffin Hall's partners in several downtown crap games. Soon, Floyd's home swarmed with tough characters, including, at least for a time, Benny Binion's Las Vegas bodyguard Russian Louie Strauss.* With Eggleston and Blackman holed up on one side of the street, and Floyd, Russian Louie, and others housed

---

* At the time, Binion was thought to be in Fort Worth a great deal of the time and he, too, may have been staying at Floyd's home. Russian Louie was never far from Binion and, if he was there, Binion was almost certainly nearby.

on the other side, the two armed camps spent most of their time glaring at each other and watching cars come and go.

In an effort to end the standoff, Fort Worth attorney Byron Matthews called Eggleston at least four times, suggesting that Tincy should "take a ride" to Dallas with Frank Cates and see a man who could "get this thing straightened out." Understandably reluctant to "take a ride" with Cates, and fearing that Jim Clyde Thomas might be an unwelcome third party on the trip, Eggleston declined.

THE KILLING OF the occasional gambler, especially one with a sleazy history of drug dealing and pimping, might be no cause for alarm, but the murder of a twenty-three-year-old woman and her unborn child was more than the Fort Worth citizenry would tolerate. The public and the press demanded a solution to the murders and expected immediate progress. A grand jury, already sitting at the time of the Harris explosion, began an investigation, but immediately found itself mired in its attempts to sort out the tangled web of widespread illegal gambling in Fort Worth.

In January 1951, District Judge Dave McGee impaneled a new grand jury, instructing them to thoroughly investigate both Tarrant County gambling and the Harris murders. Almost immediately, Ross Hardin, a local attorney, came forward to reveal that Harris had called him the night before his murder and asked to see him on a "life-or-death" matter. The attorney brought with him some of the gambler's personal papers. Among them were two autographed photos of Sheriff Sully Montgomery, personally dedicated to "my friend, Nelson Harris," and a card identifying Harris as a special sheriff's deputy. Another item, a business card, contained, in Harris's handwriting, the names of several ranking Fort Worth police officers with a notation by each name of a certain amount of money. Another witness, a waitress, testified that she saw Harris regularly talking with those same officers in the nightclub where she worked.

Jay Harris and Austin Harris, Nelson's brothers, both appeared before the grand jury and testified that they had been in hiding since Nelson's murder because their own lives had been threatened. Austin Harris told the grand jury that Nelson complained to him constantly about demands for payoff money and the cost of operating illegally and staying out of jail. Jay Harris presented thirteen ledger books with extensive records of crap games and police payoffs. Besides the ledgers, which caused a furor, Jay Harris had another, even more sensational, bombshell to drop. His brother had been killed, he said, because he refused to join Tiffin Hall's local gambling syndicate. Harris went on to say that Hall worked for "Las Vegas racketeer Benny Binion," and Nelson hated Binion and wanted nothing to do with him. The next day's newspaper headlines announced that Tiffin Hall had been identified before the grand jury as the "kingpin" of Fort Worth gambling.

The grand jury, sensing real progress in its assignment, issued a subpoena for Benny Binion. Through his lawyers, Binion advised the grand jury that he feared for his life if he should return to Texas. There were people in Texas, he said, who had threatened to shoot him on sight.* If the grand jurors cared to come to Las Vegas, however he would be happy to tell them anything they might want to know. Although there may have been some degree of truth in Binion's allegations of threats on his life, the real reason that he refused to return to Texas was the outstanding indictment for felony gambling that had resulted from the 1949 raid on his numbers headquarters. Whatever deal might be in the works for his return to Dallas, the Cowboy could scarcely afford to openly appear in Texas during a grand jury gambling investigation. Benny was not about to leave the friendly environs

---

* Recently, a television documentary on the World Series of Poker, aired on the History Channel, suggested that the Texas Rangers had been ordered to shoot Binion on sight. Although Binion at one time told George Butler that he had been "ribbed" that Butler had been hired to kill him, there is no factual basis to support such a plot by the Texas Rangers.

of Nevada—where he had just pleaded guilty to evading his 1949 income taxes in return for a wrist-slap fine—to face his legal troubles in Texas.

Even without Binion's testimony, the grand jury developed a clear picture of Fort Worth gambling and official payoffs. The Kefauver Committee helped put the final piece of the puzzle in place when its investigators supplied the Tarrant County grand jury with the records of a Chicago gambling equipment manufacturer, complete with invoices for sales and shipments to Fort Worth gamblers.

The grand jury finished its work near the end of March 1951 by handing down sixty true bills (felony indictments) against Fred Browning, Tiffin Hall, George Wilderspin, Frank Cates, and more than two dozen lesser gamblers.[*]

The grand jury failed to return indictments concerning the murders of Nelson and Juanita Harris, and those murders remain unsolved. But the grand jury did succeed in dealing Fort Worth gambling a blow from which it never recovered. Within a year, organized gambling on any appreciable scale in Fort Worth had faded into history.

---

[*] Several months later, all of the felony indictments were reduced to misdemeanors, and all of the defendants pleaded guilty and paid fines of $400 or less. Reportedly, the decision to reduce the charges came after George Wilderspin reminded members of the district attorney's staff that he didn't intend "to go down alone," a clear threat to involve the prosecutor's office in the payoff scheme.

"That's the Stuff That Killed My Wife"

JUST BEFORE NIGHTFALL on January 23, 1951, Herbert Noble spotted Jack Todd's black Oldsmobile on the patch of gravel that served as a parking lot for Sonny's Food Store. The Dallas newspapers generally referred to Todd, a close friend of Lois Green and a pallbearer at Green's funeral, as a "police character" and it was widely assumed by both the police and the underworld that Todd stood as the heir-apparent to leadership of the "Forty Thieves."

Minutes later, Todd emerged from the store, and Noble braced him. "Get in the car, Jack," Noble said. "I want to talk to you." Todd shrugged and climbed into the front seat of Noble's Ford. When Noble started the car, Todd, believing Noble planned to take him somewhere and kill him, jumped out and ran for his own car parked a few yards away. Noble chased him down and again demanded that he get in the car, this time pointing his .30 caliber rifle at Todd's chest. "We can talk right here," Todd said. "Get in the car, Jack, or I'll shoot your damn brains out," Noble replied.

Once he had Todd back in his car, Noble started west on Singleton Boulevard toward Irving and eventually Fort Worth. By this time it was completely dark, and Noble, driving with his lights off and trying to cover Todd with the rifle at the same time, ran off the road and crashed into the bar ditch only two blocks west of Sonny's. Still believing he was about to be murdered, Todd lunged across the front seat and grabbed for the rifle, at the same time trying to get to his own pistol. The two men battled fiercely in the cramped quarters of the front seat of Noble's Ford for several minutes, with one or the other leaning on the horn most of the time. Finally, a passer-by heard the commotion and called the sheriff's office. Two deputies already in the vicinity arrived at the scene almost immediately, and separated and disarmed the two combatants.

Noble had taken the worst of the fight. Todd had managed to sink his teeth in Noble's right ear and had nearly gnawed off the earlobe. Before he could be booked into the jail, Noble made another trip to the familiar confines of the Methodist Hospital emergency room, where fifty-six stitches were required to re-attach his ear.

Repaired and in custody at the sheriff's office, Noble told Bill Decker what the ruckus had been about. Several days earlier, Todd had been arrested while attempting to board a New York-bound airliner with a quart jar of nitroglycerine gel in his overcoat pocket. In his luggage, police found a do-it-yourself safe-blowing kit containing several wire fuses and a number of blasting caps. Todd, of course, was arrested and charged with transporting explosives, and the incident made the front page of the Dallas newspapers.

"That's the same stuff they used to kill my wife," Noble told Decker, "and I wanted to make Jack tell me where he got it." Noble denied any intent to kill Todd, but did admit forcing him into the car at gunpoint.

Todd was sent home with instructions to stay away from Noble. Noble was charged with assault and battery and booked into the county jail, where he proved that he had not entirely lost his sense of humor. When asked if he had any identifying marks or scars, he said, "Yeah, I've got 'em all over me. Do you want to see 'em?"

He made bail within hours and went home.

JACK TODD WAS apparently not persuaded by Noble's assertion that he intended only to question him. With some justification, Todd believed he was being taken for a ride and that his questioning would end with a bullet in his head. Todd immediately hired a bodyguard, although his choice may not have been the best.

As his new bodyguard, Todd hired Herbert James "Slick" Goins, who had been handled by the Dallas police for larceny, disorderly conduct, burglary, armed robbery, probation violation, and desertion from the military. Over the course of his criminal career, Goins had served two terms in the Texas State Penitentiary and one each in the Oklahoma and Louisiana state prisons. By the time Todd hired him, Goins was known as both a dealer and a user of narcotics and was generally considered unreliable. One police officer commented that "Slick would kill a man for money, but no one would ask him to."

Already cadaverous and emaciated at just past the age of thirty, Goins only redeeming quality was his abiding loyalty to Lois Green. Just days after Green's murder, Slick gunned down one Holmes "Powerhouse" Davenport on a West Dallas street when Davenport remarked that Green "deserved what he got." The colorfully named Davenport survived a minor wound and declined to press charges.

LESS THAN TWO weeks after Noble and Todd battled in the parking lot, a bomb exploded outside the front door of Sonny's Food Store. Sonny Lefors was not present at the time, and two men sleeping in the back of the store were terrified but uninjured. The store itself, however, was a shambles. The blast blew down most of the shelves and launched canned goods through the ceiling like mortar shells.

No reasonable explanation was ever found for the blast at Sonny's, but, as always, theories abounded. Some suggested that Noble himself had thrown the bomb or, more likely, hired it thrown. Noble's motive was believed to be the presence of Jack Todd at the store two weeks earlier. According to this theory, Noble perceived any contact by his friends with any member of "the Green Gang" as a betrayal of his friendship, and he assumed the purpose of Todd's visit to Sonny's Food Store to be a plot by Todd and Lefors to put him on the spot.

Others believed that the bomb was intended as a warning to Lefors to stay away from Noble, or possibly as a reminder that Benny Binion had spared his life in Las Vegas a year before.

Yet another plausible explanation is that the bombing had nothing to do with either Binion or Noble. Lefors was described in one police report as "closely associated with the old Lois Green gang as well as the West Dallas group of thugs. He [Lefors] is rated as a good case man,* safe maker,† narcotic source, murderer for hire, fence, etc." In the three months before the explosion at Sonny's, at least two members of the old Green Gang had met violent deaths. In December 1950, James "Blackey" Russell had been found in a South Dallas motel, butchered with a razor and a broken bottle. The leading suspect was Forrest "Pinky" Anderson, another Green Gang member. In January 1951, an unidentified blond man gunned down Isaac "Slim" Tomerlin on his doorstep. Tomerlin's wife, standing a few feet away heard the blond man say, "This is from the man in Wyoming," a cryptic statement that has never been explained. Both Russell and Tomerlin had been members of the Forty Thieves, and the police believed both murders to have been motivated by greed, jealousy, and the power vacuum created by Lois Green's death.

The motive for the bombing at his grocery store may well have lain somewhere in Lefors's activities as a fence, or in the drug trade. But it served to keep the Binion-Noble feud on the front pages, especially in view of the events of the next two months.

ON FEBRUARY 13, 1951, at about 3:00 a.m., a huge explosion destroyed most of the ground floor of Herbert Noble's Dallas Airmen's Club. The bomb, which apparently consisted of a large

---

* A case man is a criminal who scouts likely spots for burglary in return for a share of the haul. He is sometimes an insider or recruits insiders to help with alarms, delivery schedules, etc.

† Safecracker.

quantity of dynamite sticks taped together and thrown through the front door glass, was believed to be identical to the one thrown at Sonny's Food Store a week earlier. Once again, no one was injured in the blast, and the timing suggested that the intent of the bombing was property damage and harassment rather than murder. Still, it went on the books as an attempt to murder Noble, although an amateurish and ineffective one.

No arrests were ever made in either the bombing of the Airmen's Club or Sonny's Food Store, and no suspects were ever identified.

AT ABOUT THE same time as the bomb blast at the Airmen's Club, two freelance gunmen drifted into Dallas from Los Angeles. Anthony Trombino and Anthony Broncato, originally from Kansas City, were so nearly inseparable that they were known in the underworld as "the Two Tonys." Between them, Trombino and Broncato had been arrested forty-six times and convicted seventeen times of crimes ranging from rape to armed robbery. The two were also suspected, but never charged, in several murders. Unaffiliated with any particular mob or family, the Two Tonys were outlaws among outlaws and thought no more of taking down a mob-controlled crap game than a corner liquor store.

In Los Angeles, Mickey Cohen's lawyer, Sam Rummels, had just happened to be shotgunned to death during their visit. The Two Tonys were also considered prime suspects in the earlier shotgun murders of Cohen henchmen Hooky Rothman and Neddie Herbert. Both were killed in the course of failed attempts on Cohen's life.

Broncato and Trombino remained on their best behavior during their short stay in Dallas, but their presence was immediately presumed to be connected with the Binion-Noble feud. George Butler assumed, according to his reports, that the Kansas City hoods had come to Dallas to "sniff at the Noble proposition," and quickly added the Two Tonys to his list of those who had attempted or been recruited to kill Herbert Noble.[*]

In this case, Butler's assumption may well have been incorrect. Butler had apparently forgotten Noble's boast several months earlier about hiring "some Italians" to assassinate Benny Binion. The evidence, although entirely circumstantial, gives rise to the strong possibility that the Two Tonys were the Italians Noble hired. If Trombino and Broncato had come to Dallas to collect the bounty on Noble, they certainly would have made some sort of attempt on his life. He was not well-guarded—he consistently refused to hire a bodyguard—and his frequent late-night trips to Dallas made him an inviting target for anyone with enough nerve to walk up to his car and start shooting. The Two Tonys, being the type of gunmen known in the underworld as "cowboys," would not have hesitated to take advantage of an opportunity to gun Noble down, wherever they might find him. Yet no attempts were made on Noble's life while the Two Tonys were in Dallas.

When Broncato and Trombino left Dallas, they headed directly to Las Vegas, where they promptly hijacked a book-making operation being run out of the Flamingo Hotel and belonging to Hy Goldbaum. The Two Tonys either didn't know or didn't care that Goldbaum operated under the protection of Los Angeles mobster Jack Dragna. On August 6, 1951, in Los Angeles, Jimmy "the Weasel" Fratianno, Dragna's top enforcer, emptied two .45 automatics into the Two Tonys' heads.

Some time later, Noble complained to a friend about the "god-damn Italians" taking his money and not doing anything for it.[†] Whether this was a reference to the Two Tonys is unknown, but the implication that Noble hired *some* Italians to kill Binion is clear.

---

[*] Actually, Butler misidentified one of the Tonys as Tony Randazzo, a ranking Tampa mobster. Randazzo was never known to have been in Dallas.

[†] On learning of Noble's statement sometime later, George Butler wondered in his reports if it might have something to do with the burned car found in East Dallas a year before. Nothing came of the speculation.

HERBERT NOBLE HAD frequently told friends that the only place he truly felt safe was in the air. When he traveled by car, he took roundabout routes to his destination, frequently doubling back to cross his own tracks. He never used the same route twice and never announced his plans in advance. He shunned public places and, on the rare occasions when he went to a restaurant, he refused to be the last to leave, always waiting to go out the door with a crowd. He kept his back to a wall at all times and never stood or sat next to a window.

He told a newspaper reporter that he would never hire a bodyguard because he could never trust one. "I might pay some guy $500," he said, "and then some other bastard pay him $600 to kill me."

On his ranch, Noble abandoned the Jeep he ordinarily used to tend his cattle in favor of a small airplane. He would fly over the ranch once or twice a week and, if he saw that work was necessary, dispatch a ranch hand to do whatever was needed. That was his plan on the early afternoon of March 22, 1951. But the instant he cranked the engine, an explosion left the front of his plane a twisted mass of metal.

Nitroglycerin gel had been wired to the plane's generator, in the same manner as in Mildred Noble's and Nelson Harris's cars. Noble survived this, the eleventh attempt on his life, without a scratch. The aircraft's steel firewall had protected him from the blast and, as a bonus, prevented any serious damage to the plane itself, although the engine was reduced to scrap.

The usual group of lawmen from Denton, Dallas, and Tarrant counties, as well as the Texas Rangers, converged on the ranch to investigate the bombing. Beyond the obvious conclusion that someone had tried to kill Noble, the investigation produced no results. The neighbors were questioned, but no strangers had been seen entering or leaving the ranch.

The newspapers sent photographers to take pictures, and reporters to take the usual statements from the police. Noble repeated his familiar refrain about a man "1,500 miles from here" trying to kill him and, within a few days, the incident was all but forgotten.

A WEEK AFTER the explosion in his airplane, Noble, having replaced the engine and repaired the bomb damage, made another attempt to inspect his ranch by air.

Now the plane refused to start, and Noble began an inspection of the new engine. He found that two of the engine's cylinders had been packed with nitroglycerine gel. Rather than exploding, the nitro had simply caused the engine to seize.

As they had a week before, the police came to investigate and left with nothing more than they already knew. This time, the newspapers didn't bother to send photographers, and Noble didn't take the time to make his usual speech about Benny Binion. Having survived twelve attempts to kill him, the weary retired gambler just went into the ranch house and called a mechanic to come and fix his airplane.

"He'll Have to Kill Me to Stop Me"

IN APRIL 1951, the Texas legislature, following the lead of Estes Kefauver and his committee, and prompted by the Harris murders in Fort Worth, launched its own investigation of gambling in North Texas. George Butler presented much of the same information he had given to the Kefauver Committee to the new legislative body, which came to be known as the "Little Kefauver" committee. The Texas Rangers, who had been ordered months before to put an end to North Texas gambling and had failed to do so, were called on the legislative carpet. And, in a secret late-evening session, Herbert Noble appeared to tell his story.

Noble's testimony consisted mainly of a re-hash of the story he had been telling newspaper reporters, sheriffs, and police officers for years. But this time, in the presumed confidence of the legislative chamber, Noble named the "man 1,500 miles away" who had been trying to have him killed. That was Benny Binion, he said, surprising no one except those who believed he would never speak the name publicly. If Noble believed that his testimony was truly confidential, he was wrong. Within hours, days at most, word spread through the underworld that Noble had gone to Austin and told the committee that Benny Binion was trying to kill him.

On his return from Austin, Noble sat down with a reporter, his friend George Carter, and for the first time told his entire version of the story. He refused to talk about his early life, saying only that he had worked as a truck driver, trying to make an honest living. During the Depression, with a family to feed, he had turned to gambling, becoming a "dice hustler" working small games around the Texas oilfields. He met Benny Binion, he said, in the late 1930s and started hustling in crooked games run by Binion and his associates. When he decided to go out on his own, he began paying a percentage to Binion in return for protection from the local authorities. Noble did not mention his employment as a bodyguard for Sam Murray or his widely supposed telephone call to Binion putting Murray on the spot.

After Murray's death, Noble had agreed to finance Raymond Laudermilk in the policy business in competition with Binion. The result had been Laudermilk's murder and Noble's quick exit from the numbers racket. From that time forward, Binion hated Noble and made every effort to run him out of business, first by raising his demanded percentage of the take and later by trying to have the sheriff close Noble's game entirely. Instead of "bowing down to the man," Noble claimed that he sent word that Binion could "go straight to hell."

Noble infuriated Binion even more by backing Steve Guthrie in his race against the incumbent sheriff, Smoot Schmid, who was widely known as "Binion's man." Binion had first tried to have Noble killed in 1946 and had been trying ever since. Noble hinted to Carter that Binion had made a number of attempts on his life that had never been reported, including at least three attempts to sabotage his airplanes, resulting in crashes in Mexico and South America. "I guess he'll get me one of these days," Noble told Carter, "but I'm not leaving my home. If he ever opens up in Dallas again, I will, too. He'll have to kill me to stop me." Noble concluded by telling Carter that Binion's attempts on his life were motivated not by gambling or money but by pride. "I won't bow down to him, and he hates me because of it," Noble said.

In an article written later, Carter portrayed Noble as a tormented man living in a self-made prison surrounded by reminders of his murdered wife, drinking heavily, and waiting to die.

According to Carter, Noble lived only to see Mildred's killers caught and to "get a front row seat at the electrocution."

SINCE 1947 NOBLE had harbored a deep hatred for Steve Guthrie who, he believed, had "turned him around" after accepting a fifteen-thousand-dollar campaign contribution during the 1946 sheriff's election. Noble believed that his payment to Guthrie's campaign fund had at last guaranteed him "the Fix" in Dallas, allowing him to replace Benny Binion as the city's boss gambler. In Noble's mind, as the Dallas gambling kingpin, he would collect tribute from other gamblers for his political protection, just as Binion had done during Smoot Schmid's tenure in the sheriff's office. Noble may also have expected to play a critical, but carefully concealed, role in the attempted takeover of Dallas gambling by Paul Jones and his Chicago associates.

When none of this came to pass, even though his Dallas Airmen's Club seems to have enjoyed a degree of law enforcement leniency that eluded other gambling houses during Guthrie's term in office, Noble blamed Guthrie for double-crossing him.

Perhaps Noble was drinking more heavily than usual when he decided to avenge Guthrie's real or imagined wrongs. A few days after returning from his Austin legislative appearance, Noble offered Bob Braggins $250 to bomb Guthrie's restaurant on Lover's Lane in North Dallas. Noble told Braggins to throw the bomb in the middle of the night, as he didn't want to hurt anyone, he just wanted to "get Guthrie's attention." Braggins enlisted the aid of J.R. Gilreath and Finley Donica and, in the early hours of May 22, 1951, the three men hurled a bomb consisting of sixty-one small sticks of dynamite taped together at the front door of the restaurant.

Considering the size of the charge, the damage, which was confined to the front entrance, was minimal and, since the establishment was empty at the time, there were no injuries. Noble seemed satisfied with his retaliation, but the incident underscores his sense of frustration and impotence. In the old days, if Guthrie had double-crossed Benny Binion, he might have survived his term as sheriff—it's always risky to kill a law enforcement officer while he is in office—but there would have been hell to pay when his term ended. But by 1951, Herbert Noble had been reduced to settling what, a few years before, would have been a blood feud by resorting to little more than a malicious prank.

EARLY ON THE morning of August 4, 1951, at the Blue Top Tourist Court in East Dallas, a porter named Johnny Walker checked one of the cabins to see if it had been vacated. The 1947 Cadillac that the cabin's three occupants had arrived in on the night before was gone and, if the three had left, Walker wanted to get an early start on his cleaning. When no one answered his knock, Walker let himself in with his passkey.

One of the occupants still remained in the cabin, or at least his body did. Sprawled across the bed, dressed only in undershorts, lay the body of a tall, extremely thin white male, his face covered by two motel pillows. In view of the amount of blood soaking the bed and splattering the walls, Walker decided that he could do nothing to help the man on the bed and, leaving the room untouched, went to call the police.

The police soon identified the bloody victim as Owen Nelson "Slim" Hays, Herbert Noble's one-time pit boss at the Dallas Airmen's Club and sometime bodyguard. Hays had been bashed in the side of the head with a blunt instrument that left splinters in a gaping wound, and finished off with two bullets to the back of his head. The pillows had been used to muffle the shots. Hays's face was battered, and his knuckles were bloody and bruised, indicating a recent fight. In the connecting room, the bed sheets were streaked with blood where the police theorized that the killer had wiped down the murder weapon. The Cadillac that Hays and his two companions had arrived in was gone, as were Hays's pants and wallet.

The clerk who had checked the three into the motel the night before described Hays's companions as a white male about thirty years old, with reddish brown hair and a slight limp, and a woman who was young, blond, and apparently a prostitute.

By the next afternoon, the police had located the woman, a twenty-year-old West Dallas waitress named Betty Jack Stevens,[*] and learned the name of the missing man: minor police character George Dycus. According to the woman, she had accompanied Hays and Dycus to the Blue Top Tourist Courts on the evening of August 3, and the three had checked into two connecting rooms. After a night of drinking, an argument erupted into a fistfight between Dycus and Hays. Dycus struck Hays in the head with a rifle and then, with the woman, fled the motel in Hays's Cadillac. She claimed to know nothing about a shooting.

Any possible motive for the Hays killing, other than a drunken brawl with Dycus, remained unclear. In their first statements to the press, police characterized the murder as a "gangland slaying," and, years later, George Butler implied in an interview that the Hays murder was somehow related to Sonny Lefors's visit to Las Vegas and his conversation there with Benny Binion. Butler, however, was mistaken in his recollection of the timing of Hays's killing, which he placed during the same week in late 1949 that Noble was shot on his front porch in Oak Cliff. Hays's murder actually took place almost two years later.[†]

Hays, who had been sent to the Texas State School for Boys at the age of fifteen for cashing stolen checks, had been engaged in one criminal enterprise or another ever since. The Dallas police believed that he had been one of the two men who blasted Bob Minyard in his driveway in 1946 and considered him to be

---

[*] A few months later, Betty Stevens was found murdered, her head and hands missing, near Yukon, Oklahoma, a farming community west of Oklahoma City. The word RAT had been carved in five-inch letters in her torso. Her head and hands were found a few miles away. Her murder was never solved.

[†] George Butler was convinced that Sonny Lefors had agreed to spy on Noble after being threatened with his life in Las Vegas. Butler conceived of the bombing of Lefors grocery store as a reminder from Binion of their agreement and apparently believed that Lefors had killed Hays on behalf of Binion in retaliation for Hays's participation in the murder of Bob Minyard.

one of the "top henchmen" in Noble's gambling operation. The tall, skinny hoodlum was also believed to be a major figure in drug smuggling from Mexico and one of the main suppliers of marijuana in North Texas. He had been convicted in Oklahoma on a federal drug charge in 1949 and, at the time of his murder, had been only recently released after serving nineteen months in Leavenworth. Hays sidelined as burglar as well and, when he was killed, was wanted in connection with the robbery of a drug store in McKinney, Texas, only two days earlier.

Hays's criminal activities, especially his drug smuggling, provided ample motives for his murder, and no real connection between the Binion-Noble feud and his killing has ever been established.

Just a few days after Hays's murder, George Dycus surrendered to police in Topeka, Kansas, still driving Hays's Cadillac. Dycus took police to a spot where he had hidden a bloody rifle with bits of Hays's hair and flesh still clinging to the butt. He told investigators that he and Hays had fought and he had knocked Hays out with the rifle butt. He denied shooting the unconscious Hays. Dycus was returned to Dallas, where he was charged with murder. A grand jury declined to indict him, and the Hays murder remains unsolved.

AT ABOUT THE time Slim Hays was killed, Benny Binion was grappling with his own problems in Las Vegas. After selling his interest in the Westerner, he had been inactive as a casino owner, and thus unlicensed, when the Nevada legislature passed new requirements for the licensing of casino owners. In the early days of Nevada gambling, the city or county could issue licenses without state oversight, and prior conviction of a felony was not a bar to obtaining a license. The new State Tax Commission, however, imposed a requirement that successful applicants must have no prior felony convictions and could not be engaged in any illegal activity outside Nevada. The legislation grandfathered-in those casino operators who were currently licensed, a provision Benny Binion referred to as the "granddaddy" clause.

Because of his 1931 murder conviction and his continuing gambling activities in Dallas and Fort Worth, the commission denied Binion's application for a gambling license for his soon-to-open Horseshoe Casino. Binion's attorney, Harry Claiborne, argued that the real intent of the legislature was to prevent licensing of those who were engaged outside Nevada in activities that were illegal in Nevada. Since gambling was perfectly legal in Nevada, Binion's Texas gambling should not be the basis for denial of a Nevada license. A Nevada investigator determined that there was "no significant evidence" that Binion was "currently" engaged in gambling outside Nevada.

The 1931 conviction for the murder of Frank Bolding presented a trickier problem. Although Binion frequently claimed to have been pardoned for the Bolding murder, there is no official record of such a pardon. The sentence had been suspended, but the conviction was very much a part of his record. When Binion appeared before the commission for the required pre-licensing interview, the Bolding murder naturally came up. "That wasn't nothin'," Binion said in response to the commissioners' questions. "That was just a nigger I caught stealin' whiskey." Apparently this answer satisfied the commission, and the inquiry was dropped. Binion eventually received his gambling license.

On a second front, Binion and his lawyers engaged in a furious battle to prevent the Internal Revenue Service from prosecuting his remaining income tax evasion charges in Texas. Binion had already pleaded guilty in Nevada to charges arising from his failure to pay taxes for 1949 and had received a fine of twenty thousand dollars, a sum that scarcely dented the Binion bankroll. However, the IRS had tax charges pending for three more years and wanted those charges tried in Texas, where Binion's influence had weakened considerably since his move to Nevada. From a legal point of view, both sides appeared to be equally armed. The IRS contended Binion should be tried in

Texas, because that's where all of the unreported income had been earned and that's where all of the financial records and witnesses were located; Binion's lawyers contended that Binion had been a resident of Nevada during those tax years and should not be required to leave his home state to answer a federal charge. Of course, Binion's principal reason for wanting to be tried in Nevada, in addition to his considerable political clout there, was the outstanding felony gambling indictment in Texas. Nevada had already declined to extradite him for trial on that charge, buying Claiborne's argument that Binion could not be a fugitive from justice when he hadn't been in Texas when the alleged crime had been committed and hardly could have fled Texas to avoid prosecution.

This battle would rage on for the next two years.

The Cat's Last Life

August 7, 1951

Dallas and Fort Worth suffered under a crushing heat wave. For
more than a week, temperatures had reached 105° or more, and
the ground was dusty and dry. The skies were cloudless, bleached
white by the midday sun.

At about eleven thirty on that Tuesday morning, concealed
in the scrub oak trees on a small rise about sixty yards east of
Herbert Noble's mailbox, two men sat next to a barbed wire
fence. One of them held a strand of insulated electrical wire
which ran through the grass and weeds to the negative post of
a Delco automobile battery hidden in the brush about twenty
feet from the mailbox. Another wire ran from the positive post
of the battery to a point near the front of the mailbox and then
disappeared underground. That wire was attached to a small
bundle of blasting caps nestled in a box buried a few inches under
the road. The box contained a dozen jars of nitroglycerine gel
and several sticks of dynamite. A hundred yards to the north, a
third man sat behind the wheel of a blue Chevrolet pickup truck,
protected from view by a heavy stand of trees.

The mailbox stood at the top of the "T" formed by the intersection of the two county roads that passed through the Diamond
M Ranch. From their position near the top of the little hill, the
two men commanded a clear view of traffic approaching the
mailbox from any direction. Just an hour earlier, Ralph Millican,
the rural mail carrier, had passed the mailbox on his rounds but

had nothing to deliver. He later remembered seeing the blue Chevrolet pickup parked in the trees north of Noble's mailbox, but thought nothing of it at the time.

At about eleven thirty-five, a cloud of dust announced the approach of an automobile from the direction of Noble's ranch. The two men on the hill watched closely as the car, a black 1950 Ford sedan, stopped at the mailbox. When they were sure the man reaching for his mail was Herbert Noble, one of the men touched the ground wire to the barbed wire fence.

AT ABOUT 1:15 P.M. in Denton, twenty-five miles north of Noble's ranch, County Sheriff W.O. Hodges had just returned from lunch when his telephone rang. Hodges, who had been virtually blinded by a shotgun blast in 1949, investigated crimes in his jurisdiction by interviewing witnesses, talking on the telephone, and taking verbal reports from his deputies. He took all of his notes mentally and, some said, never forgot anything he was told. This call was one he would definitely never forget. Gordon Cunningham, who owned the ranch adjoining Noble's Diamond M, had gone to his mailbox at about one o'clock and had driven up on the scene of what appeared to be a major explosion. He had driven to the nearest telephone to alert the sheriff. Hodges called the Texas Rangers before setting out with one of his deputies for the Noble ranch.

Hodges, Texas Ranger Lewis Rigler, and Ranger Captain Bob Crowder all arrived at the scene of the explosion within the hour. They found a bomb crater four feet deep and five feet across in the road where Noble's mailbox had stood. The twisted chassis of Noble's Ford rested upside down next to the crater. The hood had been blown forty yards to the east. The mailbox itself had come to rest seventy-five feet away.

Pieces of Herbert Noble's body were scattered over an area roughly twenty yards in diameter. Ernest Hilliard, a Denton County commissioner who helped gather the remains, described the gruesome task for news reporters. Only Noble's head, shoulders, and arms were intact, he said. The remainder of his body had been blown to shreds. One of his lower legs had been found in the middle of the road about halfway between the bomb crater and the hill where the killers had waited.

Inside the wreckage, police found about $550 in cash, part of a deck of playing cards, and the barrel of the .30 caliber carbine that Noble always carried. A photograph of the scene, splashed on front pages all over the country, depicted the bomb crater and the demolished car. In the foreground, two playing cards were clearly visible: the ace of diamonds and a joker.

UNDER THE DIRECTION of the Texas Rangers, investigators scrambled throughout southern Denton County, searching for witnesses. Shannon Francis, a summer worker at a neighboring ranch, said he heard the explosion at about 11:45 a.m. and, minutes later, saw two or three men in a blue Chevrolet pickup racing north toward Lewisville. Other witnesses in the area confirmed that they had heard the explosion at about 11:40 or 11:45 a.m. The man closest to the scene, Noble's ranch hand, Lawrence Biggerstaff, had been plowing with a tractor, and the engine noise had muffled the explosion. It was only after the police arrived that Biggerstaff went to see what the commotion was about and learned that his boss was dead.

The Delco battery had survived the explosion intact, and Ranger Lewis Rigler and Denton County Deputy E.D. Davis followed the ground wire to the scrub oak stand where the killers had hidden, hoping to find footprints, cigarette butts, or other clues to their identities. Davis found footprints indicating that at least two men had hidden near the fence, but none of the prints were deep enough for plaster impressions. About one hundred yards to the north, the pickup's hiding place revealed nothing but crumpled weeds and a few broken branches. By the end of the afternoon, it had become clear that the only hard evidence in the Noble murder would be a few strands of electrical wire, a battery, and a blue Chevrolet pickup.

BEFORE EITHER THE sheriff or the Texas Rangers reached the scene of Noble's murder, three men sat down to lunch at a diner in Lewisville, about five miles east of the Noble ranch. The three men, all dressed like farmers, arrived at the Eubanks Café at about noon and all were remembered as being hot, sweaty, and dirty, as if they had been working outside. One was wearing a straw farmer's hat. They were driving a blue Chevrolet pickup.

WHEN WORD OF Noble's death reached reporters, they hustled to call Benny Binion in Las Vegas for a reaction to the story. The *Dallas Morning News* reached Binion at the Last Frontier. He listened calmly to the news of Noble's death* and said, "Well, I don't care one way or the other. I just don't give a damn. But I didn't have a thing to do with it. That's the graveyard truth."

A story in a Houston paper that reported Binion said he was "glad" to hear that Noble was dead drew a vigorous denial from Binion, who repeated, "I just don't have no feeling about it one way or another."

HERBERT NOBLE'S GRISLY death returned Dallas gambling and murder to the national headlines. *Time, Life,* and *Newsweek* magazines sent reporters to Dallas and, during the week of August 20, featured elaborately illustrated stories about the life and death of Herbert "the Cat" Noble. *Life* ran a pictorial history describing each known attempt on Herbert's life. *Time* found an informant identified only as a "convict just released from prison." This convict was quoted as telling "a Dallas cop" that "a certain party was offering $50,000 for Noble. They say this man will buy you a new suit of clothes, give you some running money, a gun—or dynamite, if you want it—and pay you off when you do the job."

Even with all the national attention, clues to the identity of

---

* He had already heard of Noble's death from friends in Dallas. One person present when Binion first heard that Noble had been killed said Binion's face turned ashen, and he said only, "Well, I'll be damned."

Noble's killers were scarce. The battery was not informative. It was new and was the type used in Cadillacs with air conditioning and power-operated windows, but it could be bought in auto parts stores anywhere in the country. The electrical wire offered more promise; it was less common, and there were far fewer dealers to check. A canvass of electrical supply shops in Dallas and Fort Worth began immediately. Besides the blue pickup, the police had nothing else to go on. This murder would be solved on the streets, if it would be solved at all. Rumors would be run to ground. Informants would be squeezed for every drop of information, no matter how seemingly insignificant. Telephone records would be checked. Eventually, lie detectors and sodium pentothal would come into play.

The two men assigned this duty were Dallas detective George Butler and Texas Ranger Lewis Rigler.

GEORGE BUTLER GREW up hoping to become a doctor. He enrolled at Texas A&M University as a pre-med student, but after two years he dropped out, as he put it, "because of marriage and the Depression." Butler tried several jobs, but didn't find one to his liking until in 1936 he joined the Dallas Police Department.

As a patrolman, he worked the streets during the hectic days of the Centennial Celebration when crime, especially "the friendly vices," was everywhere and, for the most part, the police looked the other way. Coming up through the ranks, he learned the secrets of the Dallas streets and alleys, from the high-rolling downtown gamblers to the dingy world of the South Dallas pimps and whores. Though it was outside his jurisdiction, Butler also made it his business to know the comings and goings of West Dallas safecrackers, thieves, and burglars.

Gifted with an eye for the smallest detail and a nearly photographic memory, Butler learned to determine the hangouts and associations of Dallas police characters by watching for their cars as he cruised the city streets. He learned the habits and eccentricities of the local underworld. At any given time, he knew who was broke and who was flashing a roll. He developed a network of informants, not exactly "snitches" in the classic sense of the word, but underground characters that could be trusted to provide accurate information as long as the questions didn't concern their own activities or those of their friends. Butler called these sources his "grapevine" and often referred in his reports to information he found "on the grape." He had a knack for finding out which hoodlum might be mad at another, and he always seemed to know who might be ready "to do a little talking."

A thorough report writer, Butler carefully documented his activities, and his reports are well-organized and remarkably detailed. Butler's language, of course, flavored by the time and his upbringing as a young, white Texas male, was hardly politically correct by later standards. He frequently referred to blacks as "niggers" and "coloreds," and he evidenced a certain disdain for Italians, whom he described as "wops" and "dagos." He described criminals of any age in his reports as "punks" and "boys."

Known to the Dallas underworld as "Hard Fist," Butler had earned a reputation as a tough street cop by the time he became a lieutenant in the detective division. He had also come to be known as something of a maverick in the divisive politics of Dallas law enforcement. During the war years, Benny Binion controlled a large faction of judges, politicians, and policemen. District Attorney Dean Gauldin, Sheriff Smoot Schmid, Under Sheriff Bill Decker, and dozens of police officers as well as most of the local judiciary were widely believed to be in Binion's pocket. George Butler was not a member of this group, but he recognized full well that his continued career on the Dallas police force depended on his ability to look the other way as gamblers and prostitutes plied their trades openly in his city.

It was probably Butler's refusal to join the Binion faction that led Paul Roland Jones to contact him as a go-between for a meeting with newly elected Sheriff Steve Guthrie during the Chicago mob's abortive attempt to take control of Dallas gambling.* During those meetings—which resulted in the conviction of Jones and several others for attempted bribery—both Butler and Guthrie described Bill Decker as Binion's "bagman," and both suggested that, until the 1946 elections, Binion had been in absolute control in Dallas. His work in the Jones investigation made it clear that Butler would not be part of a new axis of Dallas gamblers and politicians.†

It was his undercover work in this investigation that also led to the high profile assignment that established Butler as an expert in organized crime on the national level. In 1950, Butler was detailed to work as an investigator for the Kefauver Committee, and during this assignment he developed a near-encyclopedic knowledge of the American underworld. His work with Kefauver helped expose the Dallas-New Orleans narcotics connection, as well as the workings of the Chicago syndicate in the Dallas juke box and slot machine rackets.

When Herbert Noble died in front of his mailbox, Butler was immediately assigned to work as liaison between the Dallas police and other law enforcement agencies, particularly the Texas Rangers, in the murder investigation.

THE TEXAS RANGERS assigned responsibility for the Noble investigation to Lewis Rigler. As a member of Ranger Company B with responsibility for North Texas, Rigler was stationed in

---

* It was probably Herbert Noble who suggested Butler as a contact. Noble was widely believed to have offered the Chicago mob a large piece of the Dallas gambling action in return for helping him take over from Binion. Noble operated on the theory that any enemy of Benny Binion was a friend of his and, thus, correctly or not, considered Butler a friend and an ally. Noble supported Steve Guthrie for the same reason and apparently expected that he—Noble—would become the boss gambler in Dallas and would control Guthrie and Butler just as Binion had controlled Gauldin and Schmid.

† Several years later, Jones, from his cell in Leavenworth Penitentiary, would threaten to kill Butler for double-crossing him. Several inmates reported that Jones had tried to hire them to kill Butler, but nothing ever came of the threats.

Gainesville, near the Oklahoma border, and Denton County fell within his jurisdiction.

Rigler grew up on a meager Texas farm in the depths of the Depression and watched his father work himself to death farming for shares. He loved animals and wanted to become a veterinarian. After high school, Rigler joined the Civilian Conservation Corps and later enlisted in the Army. After his discharge, he tried selling appliances and soon learned that was not his calling. In 1939 he enrolled at Texas A&M to study veterinary medicine. With a wife and child to support, Rigler, like Butler several years earlier, found the obligations of a family impossible for a full-time student and dropped out.

After working for two years as a driver's license examiner for the Texas Department of Public Safety, Rigler signed on as a state trooper. In 1947 he became a Texas Ranger and was assigned to his post in Gainesville, where he served his entire career.

These two men would spend more than a year of their lives trying to find out who killed Herbert Noble. They would interview hundreds of witnesses and write scores of reports. At one point in the investigation, Butler would write a summary in which he identified forty-two men and one woman who, at one time or another, had tried to kill Noble or hire someone to kill him. At the time of Noble's murder, thirteen of the forty-two were in jail, and six were dead. Eventually, they made a reasonably good circumstantial case for a conspiracy involving five men: Jim Clyde Thomas, Finley Donica, J.R. Gilreath, Bob Braggins, and Sonny Lefors.

In the end, they would learn once again that knowing and proving are two different things.

23

Whodunit?

August 22, 1951

At about noon, Jim Clyde Thomas and a local resident named Hubert Deere stood talking near a mailbox on the main street of Durant, a small town located in the part of southeast Oklahoma known as "Little Dixie."

Hubert Deere had been involved in criminal schemes with Thomas and others for years. The two had stolen cattle, passed counterfeit money, operated gambling games in North Texas and southern Oklahoma, hijacked crap games, and committed at least two strong-arm robberies. In a more legitimate enterprise, Deere and Thomas had been partners with Deere's brother-in-law, George Sanders, in a tourist court in Snyder, Texas,* and another near Odessa. Both tourist courts were fronts, of course, for gambling and prostitution, but they did rent rooms to tourists on occasion.

Thomas had left Fort Worth that morning after telling a friend that he intended to find Hubert Deere "and beat the hell out of him." According to Deere, Thomas accosted him in downtown Durant, near the mailbox, and accused him of failing to return a drill that he had borrowed. During their argument, Thomas also accused Deere of cheating him on a deal to buy a truck. Finally, Thomas told Deere he was coming to get his drill in two

---

* This is the tourist court where Jack Nesbit hid out after he and Thomas attempted to shoot Noble on September 8, 1949.

hours and Deere had better have it ready. Thomas punctuated the conversation by backhanding Deere across the mouth.

Deere left and walked to his home, a shotgun house located about two blocks from downtown. Thomas, still enraged, followed him a few minutes later. Thomas barged into the living room, Deere said, and threatened him again. Deere ran to the bedroom and grabbed a .12-gauge shotgun from behind the door. He walked to within two feet of Thomas and unloaded both barrels. The first load of buckshot struck Thomas squarely in the stomach. The second ripped into his groin and hip as he apparently tried to push the barrel away. The notorious Fort Worth killer died seconds after he hit the floor.

Leaving the shotgun smoking in his living room, Deere walked the two blocks to the sheriff's office (the sheriff was a distant relative) and surrendered.

NEITHER RIGLER NOR Butler had ever been entirely convinced that Thomas had not been involved in the Noble murder, and the news of his death revived their suspicions. Butler suspected that Thomas had been the point man for Benny Binion on the Noble murder plot since Lois Green's death and knew that he had been personally involved in at least one attempt on Noble and probably several others.* Butler figured that Thomas's killing, coming as it did just two weeks later, had to be somehow connected to the Noble murder. If he could find the connection, he could find what he really wanted—the link to Benny Binion.

On the day after Thomas was killed, George Butler went to Fort Worth to question Sam Kimmel, a local jeweler and suspected fence who maintained close contact with both the police and the underworld. Kimmel confirmed what Butler had known for months: Jim Clyde Thomas was as close to Benny Binion as the bark on a tree. Not only had Thomas worked in George

---

* Thomas had made another attempt to ambush Noble that Butler had not yet become aware of. Noble never reported it and may not have known about it.

Wilderspin's Binion-financed gambling operation, Binion had also put up the money for Jim Clyde's gambling enterprises at Snyder and at the Rambling Rose, a nightclub and gambling hall in Odessa.

Later that day, Butler dropped in on Fort Worth Chief of Police Cato Hightower. Several days before, Hightower had mentioned to Ranger Captain Bob Crowder that Jim Thomas had received a Fort Worth traffic ticket while driving a pickup truck, and Butler wanted the details. The officer who had issued the ticket confirmed that he had given Thomas a ticket for driving with a broken taillight. The truck had been a blue Chevrolet with license plates that traced to a Studebaker pickup registered in the Rio Grande valley, hundreds of miles from Fort Worth.

Butler and Rigler decided they needed a closer look at Thomas's alibi.

JIM THOMAS HAD told the police that he and his young wife, Mary, had been on a brief vacation at the Traveler's Courts in Odessa, Texas. They had checked in on August 6, the day before the Noble murder, and had stayed until August 8.

From the desk clerk, Butler and Rigler learned that Thomas had checked in on August 6 and made a show of paying for the room with a hundred-dollar bill. At about ten that morning, Thomas had visited his partner, George Sanders, and the two had talked for about forty-five minutes. At the time, Thomas was driving his new Cadillac. Sanders told the officers that he owned a blue Chevrolet pickup and that Thomas had used it on various occasions. He did not remember loaning it to Thomas on August 6 or 7.

No one else could remember seeing Jim Clyde until sometime after nine o'clock on the night of August 7, approximately nine hours after the explosion that killed Noble.

Jim and Mary Thomas went to dinner that night at the Rambling Rose, located just across the parking lot from the Traveler's Courts. After dinner, Thomas made a scene, refusing to pay his bill. He owned the damn place, he said, and he didn't have to pay for anything. Butler and Rigler decided that this ruckus, which was completely unlike the ordinarily soft-spoken Thomas, had been a ruse intended to help establish his alibi. When the two checked out of the Traveler's Courts on August 8, Thomas again made a show of paying for the room with a hundred-dollar bill.

On the day of Noble's murder, Mary Thomas, alone and driving Jim's Cadillac, had visited her friends Charlie and Joyce Reddens in Odessa. She told the Reddens that Jim had gone to Snyder, Texas, on business and would return that afternoon. He was driving, she said, a pickup truck. Later that night, after the incident at the Rambling Rose, Jim and Mary dropped by the Reddens' home again. This time they were driving Jim's Cadillac.

The two women employed as housekeepers at the Traveler's Courts told Rigler and Butler that they had not seen Thomas anywhere on the premises between August 6 and August 8. Neither one could remember seeing men's clothing or shaving gear in the Thomas's cabin. One of the maids, Mary Jane Snead, reported that Mary Thomas had turned her away when she tried to clean the cabin on the morning of August 7, opening the door no more than a few inches.[*] Wherever Thomas may have been on August 7, Rigler and Butler were certain that he was not at the Traveler's Courts.

During their visit to Midland and Odessa, Butler and Rigler also learned from several sources that Jim Clyde Thomas had visited Las Vegas less than three months before the Noble murder. Several of their sources reported that Thomas had said either that he had gone to Las Vegas to see Benny Binion or that he had happened to see Binion while in Las Vegas. Several months

---

[*] Mrs. Snead was certain that this incident occurred on August 7, a Tuesday, because the other housekeeper was off on Tuesdays, and she was working alone that day.

later, Binion would deny ever seeing or talking with Thomas in Las Vegas.

On October 11, George Butler talked with Foy Crowell, a member of the old Lois Green gang and a previously reliable informant, who told Butler that Jim Clyde Thomas had "pulled the trigger" on Herbert Noble with the help of a local Dallas "character." Crowell refused to name this character from Dallas, but he commented several times during the conversation that Finley Donica was "a very dangerous man."

ON THE DAY after Noble's murder, the Dallas police, following an anonymous telephone tip, arrested Finley Donica. The burly, prematurely graying ex-convict had been known to associate with Noble and, according to the anonymous caller, owned a blue pickup like the one seen at the Noble ranch just after the explosion.

Donica told the police that he had been working on a house in South Dallas at the time Noble was killed (he was a carpenter by trade) and had gone to pick up a load of lumber at about noon that day. Except that he owned a blue Chevrolet pickup, the police had no evidence implicating Donica, and he was released.

Three days later, Lewis Rigler interviewed Donica's wife, Bonnie. She told him that Finley, his brother Robert, and "a boy named Junior" had been working on a new house, but that they worked early in the morning and late in the afternoon, so as to avoid the heat of the day. She thought Finley had gone to the lumberyard to buy lumber at around eleven o'clock on the morning Noble was killed. Her version of the day's events differed in significant detail from the story Donica had told after his arrest. Rigler moved Donica toward the top of his list of suspects.

On August 13, Rigler and Butler went to a ranch about five miles west of Lewisville that was owned by a Mr. and Mrs. J.R. Edmonson. Mrs. Edmondson reported seeing a blue Chevrolet pickup near the Noble ranch on at least two occasions. She described the driver as large and dark and wearing a straw hat "like a farmer wears." She had last noticed the pickup on August 3 or 4, just three days before Noble's murder.

Butler never interviewed a witness without his ever-present deck of mug shots (he often carried more than 250 photos) and he asked Mrs. Edmondson to look through the photos. She picked out two photos, both of Finley Donica. Her husband also identified one of Donica's mug shots as the man he had seen in the blue pickup. Both said they had never seen Donica other than in the blue pickup and that they had never seen him or the truck when they visited the Noble ranch.

On August 24, George Butler got another tip from an informer. It would be a good idea, the informer said, to talk to the folks at the Eubanks Café in Lewisville.

Butler interviewed the café's owners, a Mr. and Mrs. Eubanks, and one of their waitresses, a woman named Jimmie. All three told Butler the story about the three men who had come in for lunch, hot and dirty and wearing farmers' clothes, about noon on the day Herbert Noble had been murdered. All three knew one of the men on sight: Finley Donica. There was no question about this identification. Bonnie Donica had worked there as a waitress, and her husband had been in the café many times.

None of the three witnesses could be sure about the two men with Donica that day. They identified pictures of J.R. Gilreath and Bob Braggins as having been in the café with Donica at other times, but they could not be sure that they were there on August 7. All three remembered hearing about Noble's death on the radio and were absolutely certain that the three men had been in the café that day.

Less than a week later, Bonnie Donica's ex-husband, a man named Leon Kitchens, contacted Ranger headquarters with information about events leading up to the Noble bombing. Kitchens's son, Kenneth, had been visiting his mother at Finley Donica's home on the weekend before Noble's murder. The boy later told his father that he had seen a jar containing several sticks of dynamite under a cabinet in Donica's kitchen. Butler gave Kitchens the pictures of a number of suspects, asking him to show them to his son, and arranged to talk with him again the next day.

The following day, Kitchens showed Butler the photos that his son had identified as being the men who were in his mother's house with Finley Donica. He had picked out Braggins and Gilreath. Butler asked and received permission to question the boy directly.

Kenneth Kitchens had more than dynamite to talk about. On the night he saw the dynamite, the boy said, Donica, Gilreath, and Braggins had gone to a room in the back of the house and locked the door. A few minutes later, a loud bang, "like a giant firecracker," issued from the back room. The three ran from the room laughing, and Kenneth Kitchens heard one of them say, "The cat's in the bag, now." Butler took this to be a clear reference to Herbert "the Cat" Noble. That night, after dark, the three men left and did not return until well after midnight. According to the boy, this took place on the Sunday before Noble's murder on the following Tuesday. The significance of the timing would not become apparent for several months.

Rigler and Butler remained puzzled about the blue pickup that Donica drove and that they believed had been used in the Noble bombing. No such truck was registered to Donica. Months after the bombing, they discovered that Donica had purchased the truck from an ex-convict known as Earl Stewart[*] just a few days before the bombing, but had not registered it. Donica told Stewart that he intended to re-sell the truck and he could get more money for it if it appeared to be a "one owner." Months later Donica still owned the truck and had still never bothered to register it.

Even though the circumstantial evidence continued to mount, the Denton County District Attorney wanted more before charging Donica with the murder of Herbert Noble. Rigler and Butler

---

[*] Stewart's true name was James Earl Wiggington,

continued to work their sources for any scrap of information that would connect Donica directly to the crime. In late 1951, they came close. One of Butler's informants told the detective that Finley Donica had told him that he was paid ten thousand dollars for killing Herbert Noble. The informant, however, stated flatly that he was afraid of Donica and would never testify against him. He would not even allow Butler to use his name in his reports for fear that Donica might somehow learn that he had talked. Butler and Rigler knew they had one of their men, if only they could prove it.

In early 1952, another witness came to light, with still more circumstantial evidence to offer. A minor police character named Henry Grady Walker told two Texas Highway Patrol officers that he had information about the Noble murder. In an interview arranged by the two patrolmen, Walker told Butler and Rigler that he had been at a local auto racing hangout* on South Ewing Street about two weeks before Noble's murder and had heard Finley Donica talking to another man about blowing up Herbert Noble with a land mine.

The man Donica was talking to was J.R. Gilreath.

---

* This was identified as Ben Musick's garage at 1536 South Ewing. One of five racing Musick brothers, Ben had been involved in several altercations with the law, usually involving stolen whiskey, and had at one time raced all over the Midwest and Southwest under the alias "Wild Bill Morris." Musick's garage served as a kind of unofficial headquarters for Dallas racers after WWII and until the late 1950s.

Knowing and Proving—
Two Different Things

JAMES NATHAN GILREATH,* like most other active Dallas criminals, had been questioned briefly in the days following Herbert
Noble's murder, but he had produced a reasonably good alibi and
had been released. Gilreath claimed that, early on the morning of
the Noble killing, he had gone to Ben Musick's garage where he
had spoken to Bob Braggins. He left Musick's at mid-morning
heading for Houston, where he planned to commit a burglary.

A Houston constable had sent word to Gilreath that "a nigger
loan shark" kept a large amount of cash in a safe in his home.
For a cut of the cash, the constable would see to it that no one
interfered while Gilreath cleaned out the safe. Gilreath planned
to "make" the safe on the very night that Noble was bombed.
Gilreath said he had stopped for lunch and had then gone on
to Houston, where he first learned of the bombing in the late
afternoon edition of the Houston newspaper.

By the time Gilreath found the loan shark's house, fate had
intervened. The man had suffered a fatal heart attack, and the
house was crawling with friends and neighbors as well as an
ambulance crew and a few policemen. Deciding this was no time
to make a safe, Gilreath drove back to Dallas.

---

* This is the same man Noble had hired several years before to kill Lois Green.
  Gilreath also participated with Finley Donica and Bob Braggins in the bombing of Steve Guthrie's restaurant.

GEORGE BUTLER PLACED great stock in the criminals' propensity to spend money as soon as they got their hands on it, especially on cars, and after the Noble murder he paid close attention to which of the likely suspects purchased new cars. Almost as soon as Noble had been laid to rest, Gilreath had bought a new Oldsmobile, making the down payment with a handful of hundred-dollar bills. Naturally, Butler wondered where Gilreath got the money for a new car. After talking to Kenneth Kitchens about the dynamite under Finley Donica's sink, Butler was sure that he knew the answer.

In early 1952, the Texas Rangers snared Gilreath in a trap they had spent more than a year setting. In what became known as the "Beaumont Roundup," Rangers arrested more than a dozen safe burglars and cleared more than three hundred Texas burglaries. The operation, based on inside information from one of the safe burglars,* was based in Beaumont, where the Rangers had located a sympathetic judge and sheriff, and bail for anyone arrested in the roundup was set much higher than any of the burglars could raise on short notice. While the suspects were in custody in Beaumont, the Rangers made a deal: if the suspects confessed to every Texas burglary they had committed—all of the details, including accomplices—they would be allowed to plead guilty in every county where they were charged, and all of their sentences would run concurrently. Thus, whatever the longest sentence might be, the time in prison would cover every crime they confessed. There was one catch. If they were caught lying, or concealing a Texas burglary or robbery, the deal was off.

The amount of talking done by the suspects during February and March was monumental. Texas Rangers were assigned to drive the confessed burglars from county to county, allowing them to plead guilty and be sentenced. Lewis Rigler called this "the East Texas merry-go-round."

---

* The name of the informer was never officially revealed, but George Butler's personal papers contain a note strongly suggesting that the informer was Neal Aeby, a Dallas burglar and sometime drug dealer.

It is not surprising, since the burglars on the merry-go-round included Sonny Lefors, Bob Braggins, and Finley Donica, as well as Gilreath, that some of the talking was about Herbert Noble. A flood of new information reached Rigler and Butler by the first of April.

One of the burglary suspects caught up in the roundup was a bootlegger, safecracker, and con man who has been identified only as "Red." * As it happened, Red was the man J.R. Gilreath was to meet in Houston on the day Herbert Noble was killed. Except that, as Red told the story to Lewis Rigler, he and Gilreath were to meet in Houston on the night *before* the Noble murder. Gilreath finally arrived just at dark on August 7, the day of the Noble bombing.†

When Gilreath and Red finally met at the Famous Chicken Café on Houston's notorious Telephone Road, Gilreath said he had been delayed by transmission trouble. According to Red, Gilreath made an effort to make sure that he was noticed.

Late the next day, Gilreath became "very uneasy" when he read that Finley Donica had been arrested. He told Red that he needed to go back to Dallas right away, but he "didn't want to."

As Gilreath and Red drove back to Dallas, Gilreath insisted that they stop several times for beer—unusual, because Gilreath seldom drank. On one of their stops, Gilreath told Red that the bomb at Noble's mailbox had been set two or three days before the murder. This bit of information confirmed the story, which young Kenneth Kitchens had recounted several months before, about Donica, Gilreath, and Braggins going out after dark on the Sunday before the Noble blast and not returning until very late that night.

On another of their stops, Gilreath, who was by now feeling

---

* In contemporaneous reports, this man is identified only as "an informer." Years later, in his book *In the Line of Duty*, Lewis Rigler identified him as "Red." This may have been Red Holt, an associate of both Gilreath and Sonny Lefors.

† Always a stickler for detail, Rigler determined from the U.S Weather Bureau that sunset on August 7, 1951, took place at 7:21 p.m.

his beer, told Red that "Noble's leg flew through the air like a football and, if he wanted to, he could have ran out and caught it." This gruesome piece of information had not been publicly reported, but was corroborated exactly by those who viewed the grim aftermath of the explosion.

Back in Dallas, Gilreath told another of Butler's informants, also never identified, how to set up a car bomb using dynamite and nitroglycerin gel. He described detonating the device with blasting caps connected to an automobile battery, exactly the method that triggered the Noble bomb.

Gilreath had another telling conversation with a Dallas thief who had been given a lie detector test during the Beaumont Roundup. During his polygraph exam, this man had admitted seeing a large amount of explosives at Donica's home the weekend before the Noble murder. Gilreath told him that he had better learn to keep his mouth shut or "one of those damn transmissions would fly up and hit him in the face." The man he threatened was Bob Braggins.

ROBERT EDWARD BRAGGINS liked to hang around tough guys like Donica and Gilreath, probably because it made him feel tough, which he wasn't. The gangly ex-convict had been fairly active in the burglary trade, especially in Mississippi, where he frequently worked as a team with a Dallas thief named Charlie Archer. When he wasn't burglarizing small businesses, he spent most of his time reading detective magazines, or hanging out in West Dallas running errands for Sonny Lefors and talking too much.

A few days after the Noble bombing, Braggins asked for a meeting with Butler. Braggins told Butler that he, Donica, and Gilreath had all given contradictory statements to the police "because they had not had a chance to get their heads together." Braggins went on to say that, shortly before noon on the day of the Noble murder, he and Gilreath had met at Musick's Garage and that Gilreath was on his way to Houston. He also mentioned in passing that Gilreath had been to the cabins at the Noble ranch, a fact Gilreath had repeatedly denied. Braggins asked Butler to keep him informed of developments, so that he might know "what to be on the lookout for." This was the first of several times that Braggins would offer to "assist" in the Noble investigation.

Butler concluded his report of the meeting with this statement: "It was obvious that Braggin [*sic*] had been sent by someone else to gain my confidence."

During his time on the East Texas merry-go-round—he, too, had been nabbed in the Beaumont Roundup—Braggins had voluntarily submitted to both a lie detector test and a sodium pentothal examination. The scores on his polygraph examination were considered completely unreliable, with strong responses to insignificant questions and little or no response to known lies. The examiner concluded that Braggins was drunk, sick, or taking narcotics at the time of the exam.

The sodium pentothal interrogation was little better. Braggins denied having anything to do with Noble's murder, describing himself as Noble's best friend. He claimed that Noble owed him money when he died. Braggins did admit stealing a Jeep with Finley Donica and taking it to Noble at his ranch. He also admitted stealing a key to a school across the street from Lois Green's home and that he was supposed to give the key to Gilreath. He claimed he threw the key away.

Braggins's biggest problem was that he couldn't keep his alibis straight. After telling police he had been at Musick's Garage at the time of the killing, he later claimed that he had actually been at Sonny Lefors's grocery store at the time. Braggins did not know, or had forgotten, that Herbert Noble's brother Gilbert *was* at Sonny's Food Store at the exact moment of the explosion and had told Butler that Braggins had not been there at all that day.

Butler and Rigler could not imagine that Braggins, even as dim-witted as he was, would manufacture an alibi unless he expected it to check out, at least superficially. He obviously thought that Sonny Lefors would lie for him about his presence at Sonny's Food Store around noon on August 7. Could Lefors, they wondered, have been involved in the Noble murder?

CHARLES MELTON LEFORS JR., better known as Sonny, had been a West Dallas crime fixture since his late teens. His grocery store on Singleton Boulevard served as a hangout for burglars, thieves, and petty criminals. Sonny himself was known to the police as a safe burglar and fence.

In one of his reports, Butler summarized Lefors' career this way:

> This man has been involved in all types of crime since he was a boy. He was closely associated with the old Lois Green gang as well as the West Dallas group of thugs. He is rated as a good case man, safe maker, narcotic source, murderer for hire, fence, etc.
>
> At the present time, LaFors [sic] is closely associated with Eddie Smith, Howard K. Tacker, J. B. [sic] Gilreath, Finley Donica, Earl Stewart, Charles Archer, Red Holt, Robert Braggins

George Butler also had him pegged as one of the two shooters who riddled Bob Minyard in his driveway on January 14, 1946. Word on the street also had it that Lefors had been directly involved in the Lois Green murder on Christmas Eve 1949, either as the driver of Herbert Noble's getaway car or as the gunman.*

Lefors had been friendly with Noble for years, and the two had frequently flown in one of Noble's airplanes to Mexico, where Lefors fenced stolen jewelry. After Noble's death, a search of the

---

* It was rumored that Noble himself had shot Green and had an accomplice waiting in a nearby car. If this version of events is correct, Bob Braggins may have been the driver, which would explain why Noble gave Braggins five thousand dollars a few days later.

buildings at the Diamond M Ranch uncovered a large amount of steel stolen in the robbery of the Pioneer Steel Company—a robbery in which Sonny Lefors was the leading suspect.

Shortly after Noble's murder, Lefors left Dallas after telling several friends that he was worried about the "heat" from the bombing. He would never say what, exactly, he was afraid of. Some thought he was afraid of Noble's enemies; others thought he feared Noble's friends.

Butler remembered Lefors's trip to Las Vegas a few days after Lois Green's murder, when Benny Binion and three of his bodyguards had held Lefors at gunpoint and later released him. Could Lefors have been involved in some way in the Noble bombing as repayment for his life? Had the bomb at Sonny's Food Store a few months earlier been a reminder of his obligation to Binion? Butler believed the answers to both questions were to be found in the words of Benny Binion himself.

Butler and Ranger Captain R.A. Crowder had gone to Las Vegas on November 12, 1951, to interview Binion.[*] During their interview, Binion had commented that there were a lot of grateful people in Dallas that would have "sat Herbert Noble down" on a spot should he, Binion, have wanted Noble killed. Butler took this as a reference to Sonny Lefors.

Butler also knew that, for the last months of his life, Noble slept at the houses of various friends, never staying in the same place for more than a day or two. Lefors had followed Noble to the ranch on August 6 and would have been the only person who knew that Noble would be there on the morning of August 7. Butler took this as proof that it was Lefors who arranged to have Donica, Gilreath, and Braggins waiting near Noble's mailbox on that particular morning. Just a few weeks after Noble was killed, Lefors had commenced a large-scale expansion of his grocery market. Where Lefors got the money for the project remained a mystery.

---

[*] Crowder's report of that interview is contained, in part, in Appendix 2.

Rigler and Butler eventually found an informant who told them that he saw J.R. Gilreath and Finley Donica running out of Sonny's Food Store carrying a paper bag and laughing just a few days after the Noble murder.

The last straw, at least in Butler's mind, came when Lefors changed lawyers. For some time, Lefors had been dodging trial on several charges of auto theft. His attorney had been charging him several hundred dollars a month just to keep the cases from going to trial. Suddenly, in the wake of the Noble bombing, Sonny had a new lawyer—none other than Maury Hughes, the man who for years had specialized in keeping Benny Binion and his friends out of jail.

STRANGELY ENOUGH, the Beaumont Roundup served to hinder rather than help the Noble investigation. Most of Butler's sources were either implicated in the roundup or had gone to ground outside the state. The information grapevine dried up, and gradually the investigation came to a halt. No one was ever charged, much less prosecuted, for Herbert Noble's murder. The case remains open.

Many years later, Lewis Rigler said that George Butler always "had a kind of a chip on his shoulder" about the Noble case. A retired Dallas detective who had been sort of a Butler protégé put it even more succinctly: "George never could get anyone to prosecute those guys in the Noble case. The district attorney always said he didn't have enough evidence. It just pissed him off."

25

No One Left to Kill

I N 1953, AS the Noble murder investigation settled into the "open-unsolved" file, Henry Wade* finally made good on his 1946 campaign promise to put Benny Binion in the penitentiary. After three years of legal maneuvering—and with substantial assistance from the Internal Revenue Service, the Department of Justice, and the United States Attorney General—Binion's indictments for income tax evasion from 1945 through 1948 were moved from Nevada to Texas for trial. With Binion in Texas, Wade could have him arrested and held for trial on the outstanding 1949 felony gambling indictment.

On June 8, 1953, Binion returned to Texas, where he was arraigned in San Antonio and formally charged with four counts of income tax evasion. He posted a fifteen-thousand-dollar bond and immediately returned to Nevada.

Finally, with no hope for a minimal fine on the tax evasion charges, and facing the prospect of doing hard time in the Texas prison system, Binion made a deal. He agreed to plead guilty to four counts of income tax evasion, each carrying a four-year sentence in a federal penitentiary, and one count of felony gambling, carrying a four-year sentence in Texas. As a part of the agreement, all five sentences would run concurrently, and the time would be served in federal custody. As Benny put it,

---

* Henry Wade went on to a long and distinguished career as the district attorney in Dallas. He prosecuted Jack Ruby for the murder of Lee Harvey Oswald and gained perhaps his greatest fame as the defendant in *Roe v. Wade*, the landmark U.S. Supreme Court abortion decision.

he agreed to "take a flat four years." Henry Wade put it differ-
ently. If Binion was paroled from federal custody, Wade said,
he would spend the rest of his four-year sentence in the Texas
prison system. On September 15, 1953, the Cowboy entered his
plea of guilty in San Antonio.

On December 6, as a part of his plea bargain, Benny paid his
back taxes. Including penalties and interest, he owed the government $516,541. Five days later, he sold his 97.5 percent interest
in Binion's Horseshoe to New Orleans gambler Joe Brown for
$858,000. The remaining 2.5 percent belonged to Binion's old
friend, the eccentric Robert F. "Doby Doc" Caudill. On his last
day at the Horseshoe, Benny cautioned Doby Doc "not to steal
any more than you have been."

After a three-year legal battle that, according to Benny, cost
him $30 million, Binion was sentenced on December 16, 1953,
to four terms of four years each in the federal penitentiary. In
January 1954, Binion reported to custody at Leavenworth Federal
Penitentiary.

BY THE TIME Benny Binion walked out of Leavenworth, on
October 18, 1957, the Dallas he remembered no longer existed.
During his time in prison, the city had reinvented itself as a
center of commerce, insurance, and business. Cotton and oil had
faded from the limelight; money had replaced them as the city's
most important cash crop. The city fathers, many of whom had
decreed in 1936 that Dallas should "run wide open," studiously
ignored the city's wild and woolly history. By 1957, many of their
names could be found on newly built freeways, parks, and public
buildings. High rollers still wore Stetson hats, alligator boots,
and thousand-dollar custom suits, but they did their gambling
on the stock exchange or the commodities market instead of the
downtown hotel crap games.

The hotel casinos had been gone for ten years. The numbers
racket, Binion's beloved policy business, had fallen into the
hands of others while Binion and Harry Urban wrestled with

their income tax problems. Most of the top gamblers had left town or retired. Ivy Miller bought a ranch and settled in to wait for diabetes to kill him.* Lewis McWillie and R. D. Matthews went to Cuba, where they worked in the swanky Havana nightclubs. Others went to Las Vegas and Reno, where they worked as dealers and pit bosses.

After years of inaction, Big D even annexed its bastard stepchild, West Dallas, providing water and sewage service as well as police and fire protection to that community for the first time in its forlorn history.

In only six more years, the entire history of Dallas, and much of what would come later, would merge in a single instant, signaled by a gunshot in Dealey Plaza.

AT THE WEST end of the Dallas-Fort Worth Turnpike, the Wild West died harder. The 1951 gambling indictments had broken the back of Fort Worth gambling, and most of Fort Worth's gamblers had pulled up stakes. Some, like many of their Dallas counterparts, left town for Las Vegas or Reno, where they could ply their trade legally. Others simply retired to legitimate businesses. Tiffin Hall faded from the underworld scene, contenting himself with operating his chain of Mexican restaurants until his death from natural causes in 1974. George Wilderspin sold his Fort Worth interests and returned to cattle ranching. It was, he said, "the only thing I ever did that made any money."

The Top O' the Hill, Fort Worth's most elegant gambling joint, closed its doors in 1954. The building became first a country club and then a Baptist seminary. The cut-and-shoot joints on the Jacksboro Highway continued to do a booming business in beer and country music through the 1950s, but the after-hours gambling clubs had seen their day.

Even so, with Binion in prison, Herbert Noble and Nelson Harris dead, and Hall and Wilderspin out of the business, a few

---

*   Ivy Miller died on June 3, 1966, at the age of seventy-four.

of Fort Worth's lesser gamblers engaged in a vicious fight over the remains.

Edell Evans, a three-hundred-pound pimp and would-be gambler, tried running crap games out of his home. In February 1955, a Dallas insurance man named Rogers told the police he had been cheated and assaulted at one of these private games. Evans admitted the gambling and eventually admitted the crap game was rigged. Evans had swindled several Oklahoma and Texas high rollers at his friendly home games, and the admission that the games were crooked did not sit well. On the evening of April 5, Evans told his wife that he was going to "meet Cecil" at the Pandora Club on Jacksboro Highway. He never came home. Six months later, Tincy Eggleston's girlfriend told the police where Tincy and Cecil Green had buried Evans's body. It was found exactly where she said it was.

Less than a month after Edell Evans disappeared, Green and Eggleston were ambushed outside the By-Way Drive-In on Jacksboro Highway. The two were caught in a cross fire by two gunmen as they sat talking in Cecil's car. Green was hit by seven rifle bullets and died the next day. When he was shot, he was wearing the same watch his younger brother Lois had worn when he was ambushed on Christmas Eve 1949.

Somehow, Tincy escaped the ambush with no more than a few scratches.* His luck didn't last. A little more than three months later, on August 27, 1955, Tincy's 1952 Oldsmobile was found dripping blood in the parking lot of a supermarket near the Fort Worth stockyards. The police decided that Tincy's habit of demanding "loans" he never intended to pay back had finally caught up with him, and one or more of his victims had decided to eliminate the irritation. A week later, working from an anonymous tip, officers recovered what was left of Tincy from the bottom of a well in rural Tarrant County, not far from

---

* Some less-than-charitable observers suggested that, when the gunfire broke out, Tincy grabbed his friend and used him as a shield. Tincy, of course, denied that any such thing had happened.

the spot where they would eventually find the grave of Edell Evans.

No one was ever charged with the murders of Cecil Green or Tincy Eggleston, but the Fort Worth police were certain that one of the killers had been the notorious hired gun Gene Paul Norris. The other gunman, they were relatively sure, was Norris's partner Bill "Wimpy" Humphrey.

Frank Cates, one of the old-time Fort Worth underworld characters and a partner of the late Jim Clyde Thomas, launched his own attempt to take control of all of the Jacksboro Highway gambling. Other gamblers on the Highway apparently objected, one in particular being Howard "Junior" Dodd, who had set up a casino operation in the back of a Jacksboro Highway joint. Cates ran his own gambling operations out of a tiny rented house in Sansom Park, just off the Jacksboro Highway. One afternoon in the late summer of 1956, Cates answered the telephone, and the house blew up.

Cates survived, largely because the floor he had been standing on when the bomb went off had been reinforced to support a safe, but he was badly injured by flying glass and wood splinters. His treatment at the hospital required four pints of blood, and his recovery would take more than a month.

At the scene of the explosion, the police found an electrical wire running about 250 feet from Cates's house to the parking lot of a nearby diner. The ends of the wire were crimped as if they had been attached to an automobile battery. The operator of the diner told police that two men had been sitting in his parking lot in a blue Buick for several hours. About every half-hour, one of the men would leave the car and make a call from a nearby phone booth. They drove away just after the explosion.

Cates went looking for Junior Dodd as soon as he was able, only to find that Dodd had left town leaving no forwarding address. Cates went back to business as usual, but his luck ran out on October 8, 1956. Cates left home that evening telling his wife he needed to meet a man and would be gone only a few minutes. He didn't come back.

Cates's body was found, still behind the wheel of his car, less than a mile from the well where Tincy Eggleston's body had been deposited. Most of Cates's head had been blown off by two .12-gauge shotgun blasts. The police chalked this one up to Gene Paul Norris as well.

In a fitting end to the violence, on May 22, 1957, Jack Nesbit was shot and killed by his girlfriend, Lois Stripling. The two had quarreled, and Lois had threatened to leave him. If she did, Nesbit said, he would "throw some dynamite" on her mother's front porch. She fired the fatal shot with a pistol that Nesbit had given her. Jack Nesbit, the only person ever indicted in an attempt to murder Herbert Noble, would never go to trial.

EPILOGUE

EVEN THOUGH, after 1953, he never held a gambling license, Benny Binion remained a Las Vegas icon, a living symbol of the town's shady past. Young Vegas entrepreneurs like Steve Wynn came to him for advice. The University of Nevada Las Vegas studied his marketing techniques in its School of Casino Management. With his son Jack, he imported the fledgling World Series of Poker from Reno and turned it into the major gambling event in Nevada.

In typical Benny Binion style, he became enraged when the National Finals Rodeo in Oklahoma City wouldn't let him display his ten-thousand-dollar custom-built, authentic Western stage coach, because it advertised a gambling casino. It took Benny several years of hard work, but in 1985, the premier rodeo in the world was moved to Las Vegas, where it has remained since. The Horseshoe Club's stage coach is prominently displayed each year.

As his age advanced, Benny spent less and less time at the Horseshoe Club, or in Las Vegas for that matter. He spent his summers at his Montana ranch, in the cool air of the country called "the Big Open," where he sold wild horses to rodeo stock contractors.

He enjoyed talking about the old days and even consented to a lengthy recorded interview with the University of Nevada Oral History Program. Naturally, the subject of Herbert Noble eventually came up. As always, Benny denied any involvement with Noble's murder, but he couldn't resist a hint. The twinkle in his eye must have been blinding when he said:

> Well, you know them things. There's a little stuff in
> *The Green Felt Jungle* that they got from records. And

there's a damn lot that ain't, you know. Anywhere there's smoke, is a little bit of fire. I've done nothin' to *no*body that I didn't think it was goin' to do me some bodily harm. There's no way in the world I'd harm anybody for any amount of money. But if anybody goes to talkin' about doin' me bodily harm, or my family bodily harm, I'm very capable, thank God, for really takin' care of 'em in a *most* artistic way.

In March 1989, Benny sat for a lengthy interview with a reporter for the *Houston Chronicle*. Benny summed up his Dallas days in a nutshell: "Used to really live dangerous in them days. And I *was* dangerous. I wouldn't do to be screwed around with. I used to get a kick out of it.

But I don't do that no more."

Benny Binion died in Las Vegas on Christmas Day 1989.

APPENDIX 1

*Expurgated Excerpts of Conversations Recorded on
March 10, 1950, by Dallas Police Department*

SHIMLEY: I've been all over the country. Every ——— place out there, just like I told you. Now, I've made up with some people out there that own the big Flamingo hotel—this eastern outfit that owns that joint. Your name and his name [Binion] is the talk of the ——— country. The man swears by the all God, and hopes that his five kids will all die, if he knows one ——— thing about the whole proposition from start to finish. Now, I'm just going to tell you what the ——— facts are. They know where that Bowers bought the ——— dynamite. They know the whole ——— thing, and the ——— himself claims he spent $10,000 on the investigation, and has it ironclad, and he hasn't had a thing, and swears and hopes his children will die if he's ever had one thing ever done to you in any way, shape, or form.

NOBLE: Now, I—

SHIMLEY: I don't know, you understand, I'm merely telling you what I know and what I've been told.

NOBLE: Well, now—

SHIMLEY: So now Dave Berman tells me—

NOBLE: Who? Who?

SHIMLEY: Dave Berman. Owns the Flamingo hotel. You understand?

NOBLE: I—I know him. I—

SHIMLEY: Now, Dave Berman—said to me—

NOBLE: Just take it slow, now.

SHIMLEY: He says, "Shimley," he says, "do you know this fellow in Texas?" I says, "I've known the man twenty years."

NOBLE: That's right.

SHIMLEY: I says I don't know a ——— bad thing about him. I says that I don't know what in hell this thing is all about, Dave. He says, "We don't believe out here this man is our friend. The man's got the sheriff, the police, the judges—he's got everything in the state—through that outfit that owns everything there." And I says, "Well, I want to tell you something, Dave. I don't know what the proposition is about." He says, "We've got people investigating it now, finding out through our sources of investigation, and—"

NOBLE: Who's he talking about?

SHIMLEY: Talking about you.

NOBLE: Yeh.

SHIMLEY: And he says, "Well, why in the hell don't you get together and straighten this thing up?" And I said, "How in hell can I straighten it up?" "Do you know anybody that's connected with it?" And I said, "Yeh, I know a Jew boy down there that's his friend, that I've known for fifteen years, too." He says, "What's his name?" And I told him ——— who his name was ——— Phillip Stein. Well, he knows about [indistinct] and Jerry and them in the oil business, because he's got some oil leases with old Max Cohn, and things in Oklahoma. So he knows all about you, you understand. Now, how he knows about Phillips, I don't know. So I tell him, so he says, "Well, why in the hell don't you straighten this thing up and get to the bottom of it?" He says, "——— it, and get that ——— all stopped and kill those three ——— down there in Texas." Not talking about you, talking about some other people, understand, connected with this Bowers, now I'm telling you.

NOBLE: Who? Who are they? Tell me.

SHIMLEY: I don't know who they are.

NOBLE: Oh, you do know.

SHIMLEY: No, I don't. I don't know who they are, but I will know who they are, and I think he [Stein] can help me to find out.

STEIN: I don't want to be in on that.

NOBLE: No, no. He's—

SHIMLEY: And the name—

NOBLE: No. Well, now, here—

SHIMLEY: Here, let me show you something.

NOBLE: O.K.

SHIMLEY: Now, here's what this man says—now after Dave gets him, and I talked to him. I said, "Yeh."

NOBLE: What man? Who—who?

SHIMLEY: Dave Berman is the man that brought me in to Benny. Don't you understand? 'Cause I done talked to him. He offered—

NOBLE: But Dave's a big man out there.

SHIMLEY: He's a big man out there. He owns the Flamingo hotel.

NOBLE: I've known him through some friends of mine.

SHIMLEY: Now, now—on top of this, when we get to talking about it, he sits down at the table, me, him, and Dave, and two other people. He says, "I hope my five children will die this minute"—and holds his hand up like this—"if I know one thing on earth about it."

NOBLE: Who—who said that?

SHIMLEY: Oh, Benny [Binion] said that, himself. "Now," he said, "I'm going to get to the bottom of it—this whole ——— thing, and I've got people working on it now." Now, when I left there, I told him that I was coming to see Phillip, not you. Understand what I mean? So that was my mission here, was to try to get you two to talk together over the telephone—and let me and Phillip go out there and Phillip straighten the whole ——— thing out. And he's got to get in the middle of it, because he's your friend, and he can't do any more, and I don't do it by myself.

STEIN: No, Herbert.

NOBLE: No, thank you. Well, even—even after that, the ——— town is in such a mess, how in the hell you going to—

SHIMLEY: Well, you and him know how to straighten it out.

NOBLE: I don't know—

SHIMLEY: Well, by God, he said you could. I'm telling you what the man said. Would you talk to the man over the phone?

NOBLE: Yes.

SHIMLEY: All right.

NOBLE: Yeh, get him on the ——— phone right now. I'll talk to him.

SHIMLEY: I'm going to tell you something. I done stuck my neck clear up to here. You understand.

NOBLE: Yeh.

SHIMLEY: Give me long distance, please. Yes, I want 3669W, Las Vegas, Nev. Nevada, that's right. [Indistinct whispering.]

SHIMLEY: Now, listen, Phillip, you are the only man that can help me with this proposition.

NOBLE: Now, if you ever—tell what name I'm using—

SHIMLEY: Say, listen, don't you worry about me ——— man. Are you afraid of me, Herbert?

NOBLE: No, I'm not. If I was, I wouldn't even be talking to you.

SHIMLEY: Listen, let me tell you something. You know what I've done. Now, I'm just telling you, I don't give a ———. I've spent $6,500 on this.

NOBLE: ——— I still—if—unless he can do something with somebody here—how in the hell—but even at that, I don't see how—

SHIMLEY: By gosh, he can stop it.

NOBLE: That man out yonder?

SHIMLEY: You ain't kiddin'. He'll stop it, or we'll kill all three of them—one or the other. And you won't have to have nothing to do with it, either. You know that man—I mean loves them kids just like you do your daughter.

NOBLE: That's right, that's right.

SHIMLEY: He [Binion] stood like this, Phillip, and he says, "I hope God will kill all five of them, now, if I know one thing about it, at all." He didn't only convince me, he convinced the biggest mob in the United States. If he wanted to get something done, he wouldn't have nobody do it like that. I'll tell you that.

NOBLE: I know he and Mickey [Cohen] are just like that.

SHIMLEY: One of the biggest outfits in the United States.

NOBLE: That's right, that's right. O.K. I know he—he's got a connection that won't quit. Hell, now, I'm not calling him.

SHIMLEY: I'm calling him.

NOBLE: You're calling him.

SHIMLEY: You're ———— right.

NOBLE: Hell, say, I get—

SHIMLEY: Hello, Mrs. Binion? Is Mr. Binion there? This is Shimley—hello, this is Harold Shimley, Harold Shimley. Yes, I'd like to talk to him, please, if you can get him on the phone. Hello, Benny, this is Shimley. Well, I'm in Dallas and I have done what I told you I thought I could do. And I think this whole thing can be straightened out 100 percent. And, of course, I know what I've been told, and you know the whole score from start to finish. I know you wouldn't have spent $10,000 if you hadn't have known. I don't get that from you. I get it from the other people. And this is my friend, just like you are. Now wait a minute. I want you to talk to somebody a minute.

NOBLE: Ask him what he wants to tell me.

SHIMLEY: Well, come on and talk to him. ———— it. Man's 1,500 miles away. Just talk to the ————.

NOBLE: Hello, Benny, this is Herbert. All right, how are you? Oh, I've got a little cold. Yeh, yeh. We are way out in the country, partly, anyway. We are out in the country, partly, anyway. Oh, I'm all right, perfect. Yeh. Well, what about Shimley here? Yeh, yeh. Well, I just wondered—I just wondered—I didn't know what—what the score was. Yeh, wait a minute, then I'll let you talk to him. Yeh, yeh. No, never heard of him. Oh, yeh, I know the son of a ———— hey, I know him. I—I—He gave me some pretty bad write-ups. Yeh—well, I don't know but they—they done something to my wife here in the paper. I didn't like a damn bit. Yeh. Wait just a minute, then, and I'll let you talk to Shimley.

SHIMLEY: Listen, Mr. Binion, I'm here with the only man that—that we can get this whole thing straightened out with—and that's Phillip Stein. Understand? I want you to talk with him a minute. Come here, Phillip.

STEIN: Hello—hello, Benny. O.K. Yeh, well, that's him. I got—I wasn't supposed even to be here, but I am. I—I didn't want to get involved in all of this stuff. Well, I know, but—I mean I'm getting caught in something when I'm an innocent party. Yeh. Well, they just wanted me to talk with you.

SHIMLEY: Let me talk to him.

STEIN: Yeh, I know it. Wait a minute, Shimley wants to talk to you.

SHIMLEY: Now, do I have, just as you said when I left there, the power to go ahead and try to straighten the whole thing out? Well, do you know me now? Well, did you recognize the other two men? Yeh. Well, now listen—now, uh—this thing has gone far enough, just as Dave and everybody out there says, and let—let's straighten the whole thing out. Yeh. Well, then, me and Phillip might come out there to see you. Well, and in the meantime—uh—do you think that fat man—does he know anything about the thing at all? He doesn't—he doesn't? Oh, he don't even know them. Uh-huh, yeh. Well. I'll tell you what I'll do. I don't know just how soon I'll see you, or when I'll call you, but I'll get in touch with you just as soon as possible. And everything will be careful here until we can straighten the whole thing out. Well, every precaution will be taken. Well, no, you won't be responsible, but still, them other people—we've got to take care of that. So then, I'll get right on it and me and Phillip will probably see you within the next two or three days anyhow, maybe tomorrow. All right then, you be good, and we'll see you soon. All right.

That ——— I'm telling you, boy, there ain't no ——— about
it, that Benny is on the square about this thing. And it's the
talk of the ——— country, it's the talk of the ——— country, and there ain't no ——— about it. I mean the talk of the
country.

NOBLE: You know—

SHIMLEY: He said right there over the phone—he said, he said,
"Now, be careful until we can get things taken care of." You
understand?

NOBLE: What did he mean by that?

SHIMLEY: Well, I guess he means that he don't want nobody to
get out in the open, you understand what I mean, and put
yourself in a spot, or something else. Just like you remember,
when I left the house, now you remember this. I'm not bawl-
ing you out or nothing, but you told me you would not go out
that door at night, didn't you?

NOBLE: Yeh.

SHIMLEY: Then you turned right around and did it.

NOBLE: Well, ——— it. Hell. I—I—let's don't go back now.

SHIMLEY: Now, wait—

NOBLE: No; don't go back now—I am going to tell you that's — on
you. When I lost my wife—[Crossed voices.]

SHIMLEY: I know that—I know that.

NOBLE: And ——— it, I'll tell you one ——— thing ———

SHIMLEY: And I'll tell you, you are going to know the ——— that
done it.

NOBLE: All right. Who? You know, now.

SHIMLEY: And the ———, by God, done it was the man that
was trying to get you.

NOBLE: Yeh. Who—who is he?

SHIMLEY: You know who he is as well as I do.

NOBLE: No, I don't. No, I don't.

SHIMLEY: You know that ——— down there that got life in the
pen as well as I do.

NOBLE: Who, Delbert [Bowers]?

SHIMLEY: You ain't—

NOBLE: He didn't do it by hisself.

SHIMLEY: Well, he done it with some of his ——— burglar friends.

NOBLE: I don't doubt your word. Don't doubt your word a bit, but still—

SHIMLEY: I'm telling you, and you're—you are going to find it out for your own satisfaction.

NOBLE: O.K. That's what I want to do, but I don't want to make no ——— mistakes. But—uh—well, here's the thing about it—

SHIMLEY: I know, but I'm telling you, understand? The man thinks that you think it's him. The man is as crazy as any betsy bug you've ever seen, and I saw tears rolling down the man's eyes, about your wife.

NOBLE: Well, ——— it [Indistinct stuttering.] I'm the one. I ain't got my right mind half of the time.

SHIMLEY: Well, I'm willing to try to handle it any way you think. I've told you the truth.

NOBLE: O.K. Well, what's the deal?

SHIMLEY: I say that I think that the two of you ought to get together and go ahead and get straightened, and let these other ——— be taken care of. Understand what I mean?

NOBLE: Yeh.

SHIMLEY: And they will be taken care of from the other end, not from this end. Understand what I am talking about?

NOBLE: Yeh.

SHIMLEY: 'Course, you ain't going to take care of that one [Bowers, in prison] unless you take care of him down there in that joint. [Indistinct.] But he tells me that the ——— can be taken care of down there.

NOBLE: Probably can, if you have the right kind of connections.

SHIMLEY: Well, I don't know about that business, you understand. All I know is what he says. He could get him killed in there if he wanted to.

NOBLE: ———, now we are talking business.

SHIMLEY: And when I'm telling you this, I'm not lying to you. The man sat there and there was five people at the table, and tears rolled down the man's cheeks when he talked about your wife, and talked about the way this thing happened. And when they found out, they know exactly where the ——— even bought the ——— dynamite, and everything, in Fort Worth. And I'll find it out for you and tell you.

NOBLE: That's what I want to know.

SHIMLEY: 'Course, they are never to know that it came from me, understand what I mean?

NOBLE: Hell, there ain't nobody ever know it, Shimley.

SHIMLEY: But I don't want to know it, because here's the thing about it—I don't want to put anybody in the electric chair. I'd rather see a ——— get murdered. I'd rather get killed myself than put a ——— in the electric chair.

NOBLE: No need to talk like that. Let's don't talk about it.

SHIMLEY: Well, here's the thing about it. I'm to straighten the thing out between you and this other man, and I know me and Phillip can get the job done.

NOBLE: I'd rather that you'd just deal around Phillip now, because ——— it ———.

STEIN: Don't pull me in. I don't really want it. You all are pulling me in something that I don't even want, and I told you I wasn't even—didn't want to come in here, and you wanted me to.

NOBLE: Well, well, now, how about this?

SHIMLEY: Well, all right, now look here, ———, you're a friend of mine, and you are his friend, so what the hell?

NOBLE: Well, how about this? . . .

NOBLE: Was it three of them?

SHIMLEY: Oh, yes; three of the ——— altogether. So I don't—

NOBLE: The hell there was. One of them to drive the car, one of them to shoot, and the other to do the job, I guess. The—

SHIMLEY: Every one of them ——— bank burglars, ——— knob-knockers, ———.

NOBLE: Who were they, Shimley? You know them.

SHIMLEY: I really don't know their names. No. And if I knew I'd tell you.

NOBLE: All right.

SHIMLEY: I don't know, I done told you.

NOBLE: I'd expect you to.

SHIMLEY: I don't know, I don't know, you understand. I told you the truth about it, and I wouldn't lie to you, understand, and I'll guarantee that if I can't help you I won't do you any harm. I told you that all the time, from start to finish, and I honestly believe this ——— is telling the truth. I am convinced of it, by God, because he wouldn't lie to them ——— people. They would kill him just like they would me, if they caught the ——— in a lie and a double-crossing ———.

END OF RECORD

APPENDIX 2

*Excerpt of report of Interview of Benny Binion by
Lieutenant George Butler and Captain R.A. Crowder
November 29, 1951*

DURING THE ENTIRE interview Binion's demeanor was cool and collected. He seemed to be sure of himself, looked his questioner straight in the eye, and did not hedge or hesitate in his answers. He was told that many times, that Noble had stated he, Binion, was the man behind the attempts on his life. Binion swears that he had nothing to do with killing Noble and if he had wanted him killed he wouldn't have had it done that way. Binion claimed that he could get professional killers to have shot him for $2500 or $5,000.

Benny Binion stated that while he was in Dallas, prior to leaving in early 1946, had an interest in numerous downtown gambling joints, as well as the policy business. At that time he was connected with Herbert Noble during Noble's operation of the Rose Hotel, the Majestic Hotel, and, for a while, the Campbell Hotel. That he, Binion, had bankrolled those games and Noble had given him a percentage of the profits. During that period he had talked to [Noble] about three or four times personally and a few times over the phone. Binion wanted to know what Noble blamed the trouble on, that existed between them. He was given the same answer that Noble had given out to the papers. Binion denied raising the percentage of take from Noble or doing anything to the man, that would have caused him to react like he did.

In running down a list of suspects, it was explained to Binion that we were going to ask him about some people we knew had made attempts on Noble's life, some people we suspected of attempts, and others that had been reported to us as having been propositioned by him (Binion) to kill Noble. We started off from the first attempt. Binion was told that Bob Minyard, Lois Green, and Johnny Grisaffi were in the car that Noble was shot from. That we had reliable Information to the effect that Green and Grisaffi had been offered some money, as well as an Interest in a large downtown game, if they would get rid of Noble for Binion. That a short time after this incident Green was jumped by Butler one night and Green jumped out of his car with a pistol. That when Green saw who had jumped him he threw the gun down. While Green was still scared he admitted to Butler that he was hot over the Noble shooting, that he expected to be killed, that Binion was not upset over his failure and was going to give him, Green, all the time he needed to kill Noble.

Binion seemed to be surprised over this statement and asked "did that S. B. really say that?" He admitted knowing Green well, but denied ever asking Green to kill Noble. He also stated that he had never known Green to visit in Las Vegas since he had been out there.

Concerning the murder of Bob Minyard, Binion stated that he had never found out who was responsible for Minyard's murder. That be was sure that Buddy Malone was not involved. (Buddy Malone was seen by Dallas detectives Blackie Delk and Baldwin after Malone had wrecked his car near the scene of the murder). Binion said that he, himself, bad been picked up the night Minyard was killed and he went right by the scene of the accident but saw nothing. Binion said he was picked up by a high ranking law enforcement officer at the side entrance to the Southland Hotel that night (of the Minyard shooting) and they had gone to the scene together.

Binion did admit that after Minyard was shot that be had brought Green, Thomas, Cascio, Bass, Grisaffi, and some others to the Southland Hotel to be on the safe side. This was one of the few times he let his guard down and would indicate that he felt, at that time, some uneasiness about the Noble faction possibly killing him. Later, Binion stated that he did not know Bass.

BINION WAS TOLD about the second attempt on Noble and we again pointed out that he, Binion, was the reported ramrod behind that attempt. It concerned the time Jack Darby pulled a gun on Noble at Arthur Thomas' joint, shot into the floor, and tried to make Noble draw his pistol. Buddy Malone had just returned from a trip to Binion's ranch in Montana and was reported to us, as bringing back orders from Binion to have Noble killed right away. Binion denied ever talking to Darby about the trouble with Noble, stating that Darby was just a sucker for dice, that every time Darby came to Las Vegas to play they would break him. He said that Derby had been out there for a short visit recently and had lost $2,800.00.

MANY OF THE suspects we asked Binion about, he claimed not to know, and it is entirely possible that he did not know some of them. When Binion was asked about his reported propositioning of Chinky Rothman, Binion again denied knowing anything about it. He did not know where Rothman was at this time. He also denied having discussed or talked over any such deals with Cliff Helms, Russian Louie Strauss, or Nathan Blank in Las Vegas.

He admitted that when Charley Lefors went to Las Vegas that Cliff wanted to kill him. Both were sure that Charley Lefors had been sent to Vegas to kill Binion, but Bennie (sic) stated that he did not want to kill anyone unless he was sure of what be was doing, and he gave Lefors the benefit of the doubt. Lefors was armed at that time with a .38 super automatic. Binion pointed out that this incident should indicate to us that he was not kill crazy. He also, later on, in the conversation, stated that there were a lot of grateful people in Dallas that would have "sat Herbert Noble down" on a spot should he, Binion, have wanted Noble killed.

WE ASKED BINION if he had ever propositioned, or had been propositioned by Charley Archer, to kill Noble. He denied this and indicated be had no love or confidence in Archer. Noble had

told Butler that Charley Archer bad come to him with the story
that Binion had asked him to kill Noble but he wanted no part
of It, however, if Noble wanted Archer to kill Binion he would
be willing to do it because he hated Binion. Archer was recently
badly beaten in a brawl in EL Paso, Texas.

When asked about his connections with Mickey Cohen,
Binion denied having ever seen or talked with him. Later he was
asked if Cohen had tried to sell him the bullet-proof Cadillac and
he said that it was true. He caught himself right away and stated
that the offer was made through a third party. It will be noted
that there were numerous toll calls made from Cohen's phone in
Los Angeles to Binion's phone in Las Vegas. Also, that Mickey
Cohen was a guest of Paul Harvey, Binion's partner at Odessa,
Texas. There has been no verification of any connection between
these two, Cohen and Binion, except as stated above. Binion
denied any dealings with Jack Dragna, stating that Dragna was
an old man that sometimes hung around Las Vegas.

In regard to Jim Thomas having made a visit to Las Vegas,
Binion stated that as far as he knew Jim had never been there, if
he had, he had never been around Binion's place. He did say that
he knew Jim Thomas back in Dallas some years ago, that Jim was
hanging around the Blue Bonnet Hotel crap game, and when
Binion found out who he was, he told Thomas to leave, that he
was too hot, and that Jim left without any comment or trouble.

Binion commented on his dealings with Paul Harvey. He
stated that Paul Harvey said some things from the stand before
the Texas Crime Committee that he shouldn't have said, and
some of the things Paul said were not true. He did admit that he
had a third interest in the place, at that time. He told about meeting Harvey in Denver and giving Harvey the money to operate
on. Binion stated that Harvey wouldn't hurt a fly but past records
indicate that Harvey has more nerve than a Government mule.
Binion denied having any interest in Harvey's place at this time.
It is reported that Harvey has put his show place up for sale.

When asked about "Big Boy" Burton, Binion declared that

he did not know Burton was Jim Thomas' father-in-law, until be learned of Jim's death. He stated that Burton was not too happy about his daughter marrying Jim Thomas, but was afraid of Thomas personally. Burton worked at the "Rail Road Pass" game near Boulder City, Nev. He also worked for George Wilderspin in Ft. Worth. Binion described Burton as an old man, sick and broke. (Burton took a handful of hundred dollar bills to Durant with him to pay for Jim Thomas' funeral).

We asked Binion about his connection with Ralph Campbell. He stated that he did not know the man but had heard about him. (Campbell was one of the men called by Jim Thomas from Ft. Worth, Texas to Tucson, Arizona). Binion admitted that he knew Pete Licavoli at Tucson but stated that he bad never visited with him.

Binion claimed that he did not know Louie LeForce that if LeForce was in Las Vegas or had been there, he did not know it. He denied knowing any of the West Dallas punks that we have known to discuss Noble's murder for money. He said that if Lois Green had propositioned any one to kill Noble it was not at his instruction. He denied knowing anything about Pete Norris' brother. Gene Paul Norris. He admitted knowing Bud Mace, Tincy Eggleston, and other Ft. Worth characters but denied knowing Jack Nesbitt.

We asked Binion if he had ever heard of any reason that Jack Nesbitt or Jim Thomas would want to kill Noble except for money. He said that he had never heard anyone say anything about any other reason, but again, denied hiring these thugs to kill Noble. He was asked if he had ever heard anything about Noble being involved in the dope business, but he said "not that he ever knew of."

Again, he denied knowing Tony Trombine, Tony Randazzo, or Bob Pinkerman from Kansas City, nor had he ever known anyone to proposition any one of them to kill Noble for him.

In answer to the question about Russian Louie Strauss and Nattie Blank going to Tulsa with the intention to kill Hal Shimley, Binion stated that as far as he knew, neither of them had ever gone out of the State of Nevada since last year. Information had been received from a reliable source that Shimley had been shot at in Tulsa and the two punks bad attempted to kidnap Shimley off the Tulsa streets in broad daylight.

He denied knowing Donica, Gilreath, or Braggin. He saw in the paper where Donica had been arrested. He stated that he did not know Hubert Deere and had never heard of him until Jim Thomas was killed.

WE QUESTIONED BINION about Hal Shimley. He stated that Shimley was an opportunist, that he was playing both ends against the middle. He, Binion, admitted that he had been taken in by Shimley and had paid for Shimley's doctor and hospital bills when the man was in Las Vegas, sick. That Shimley told him he could get the matter between Binion and Noble straightened out. He denied making Shimley any proposition to kill Noble, nor promising Hal anything for his work. He did say he gave Shimley some money. He was asked about the map found on Noble one time when he was shot. Binion stated that he had been sent a photostat copy of the map, which covered the area around his home. He did not admit that be knew who bad made the map but indicated that it could have been Shimley. One of the Las Vegas Deputy Sheriffs close to Binion had already told us about Shimley drawing the map and giving it to Noble.

Binion was asked if he had ever heard of anyone being propositioned to have him, Binion, killed for Noble. He stated that he had not.

When asked if he was attempting to return or wanted to return to Texas, Binion stated that he would like to raise his children in Texas, but the State was too hot against him now for him to return. He was asked if he had ever been approached by any of the so-called syndicate mob to return with him to Texas when he decided to come back. Binion said that none of them had ever talked to him about it. He denied any such conversation with Dave Berman as related by Hal Shimley to Herbert Noble.

Binion did say that Dallas was a great town and the reason it was so good was because he or any other man could borrow all the money they needed from the banks. He said that they would shake you down for a brokerage commission extra, in addition to the usual interest. That the banker would send you upstairs to see some friend of his but he managed to always get his loan through. He also stated, strictly off the record, that, since he had been to Las Vegas ha bad been instrumental in obtaining loans amounting to about $4,000,000.00 for local Vegas people from Dallas, Texas banks. For this favor, he, Binion, had been given a 5% brokerage fee.

Bennie (*sic*) denied any gambling interests in Dallas at this time. He did not deny having money Invested in Ft. Worth during the time George Wilderspin was running the Eastside Club. He stated that he never knew George Wilderspin to have anything to do with Jim Thomas or Jack Nesbitt. (Hubert Deere, the man who killed Thomas, told us that both Nesbitt and Thomas had gone to Wilderspin's home when he was along with him. He was in the cattle business with Wilderspin.)

Binion stated that Ivy Miller had recently visited him at Las Vegas, that the old man was sick and had bought a ranch and was about ready to retire.

In regard to the reported shooting incident in Las Vegas recently, Binion said that it was true, that he was shot at. However, be bad a tendency to shrug it off by giving us the following story.

A square-John friend of his offered to take him home one night, the night of the shooting. The friend's car was parked some distance from the Horseshoe Club, in a dark spot. They got in the car and started home. Some car drove up behind them at a high rate of speed. When the other car approached within 100 yards some one began shooting in their direction, and kept shooting until it passed. This car was described as an old model Chevrolet, about a '39. It Is Binion's opinion that the car either contained some drunk soldiers going back to the Army base or some half drunk cowboys In town for a spree. After this description by Binion, we were inclined to agree with him. Be did not give us the friend's name nor did we ask him for it.

This incident occurred a very short time before some action was due on his application by the State Tax Commission for a new gambling license. Other people in Las Vegas were inclined to think the shooting was an effort by a competitor of Binion's to embarrass him and have his application turned down.

We asked Binion if it were true that his boy, Nathan Blank, had left him after the shooting took place. He said that Blank was still with him. We did not see Blank during our visit. Blank has many times been mentioned as Binion's bodyguard.

Binion admitted that he was taking care of himself and had some people around him that could take care of almost any situation. In addition to his regular bodyguards, Binion now has two ex-officers hanging around him. Both are well known for their nerve. One is reported to be a former Officer (whom we did not see), and the other a former Border Patrolman named Agee. Binion said that Agee could knock the eyes of a gnat out with his pistols. He did not discuss his other protectors but did seem curious that we knew something about them.

Cole Agee was formerly a peace officer in Texas and New Mexico. He was recently working in Roswell and killed a man there. Details of that Incident are not known at this time. Agee is not only an expert shot but an expert craftsman with engraving tools. He makes good money engraving and decorating pistols. He is described as about 45 years old, 5' 10", 175 pounds, graying brown hair medium dark complexion, wears western style clothes, very likeable.

Binion did not discuss any Dallas officers in any manner that would indicate corruption on their part. He did say that be had many friends among the officers and didn't have to buy them. (He was not pressed as to who sent him the map found on Noble's body at the time Noble was shot off his front porch on Conrad Street.)

BINION TALKED MORE freely than we expected him to do. He was straight-forward with us and did not hesitate in his answers,

We told Binion that Noble came to town (Dallas and Ft.

Worth) on occasions and got drunk. He would have accidents, drive into a telephone pole, ditch, or parked car. It would have been easy for some killer to follow him around and shoot him after he left a beer joint. The word had got around that Noble could not be killed in Tarrant or Dallas Counties. Binion was asked, Doesn't the fact that Noble was killed like he was, and in Denton County, indicate to you that it was a contract killing? Binion admitted that it looked that way.

BINION SAID THAT most of his play at the club came from people In Texas, Oklahoma, and Louisiana. That Ray Ryan had come to his club recently and lost some money. (The story going around Las Vegas was that Ray Ryan went into Binion's joint and put up $40,000.00 on the table. Then asked Binion if it would be alright to shoot it. Ryan shot and won, then shot the $80,000 and lost. Informant, who worked at the Golden Nugget, a competitor of Binion's, stated that this large stake gambling was the source of a lot of jealousy and envy by the other clubs because the big players were going to Binion and a lot of smaller players were going there to see the big stake gamblers.) Binion verified reports that Bondy Hall had recently been there and had won $96,000.00.

BINION STATED THAT Senator Kefauver was considered quite a guy in Las Vegas, that Kefauver was not a blue nose (or words to that effect). The people there admired the man, but Binion stated that they considered Kefauver's timing as wrong, politically, because if he had waited until this year to make his bid he may have obtained the nomination for the Presidency. Binion said that he thought Kefauver would make a good one.

When asked about the big mob being in Texas or coming into Texas, or Dallas, Binion stated that they were already there but did not elaborate. (We think he would help us along these lines if talked to more). The only other comment he made about them, was to the effect that they had been in Texas since 1946 and had not been run out yet.

APPENDIX 3

Progress report—Herbert Noble Murder

Dear Sir:

The *first attempt* on Noble's life occurred on January 15, 1946. Noble was followed from his club at 1710 ½ Live Oak, trailed by a car out the Grapevine Highway, and after a long running chase, during which he was shot at many times, wrecked his car, crawled under a house, and escaped with a bullet in his back. Reported to have been in the car (owned by George "Jr." Thomas), were Lois Green, Johnny Grissaffi, and Bob Minyard. No prosecution was requested and no arrests were made in this case. Bob Minyard was killed two days later.

The *second attempt* was made at about 3:00 A.M. on August 19, 1946, at Arthur Thomas' gambling joint located at Travis and Knox, Dallas. Jack Darby was a partner of Noble's at the time and had gone to Thomas' club to collect $12,000.00 owed to them by Eddie Gilliland, which they had won in a crap game. Darby, was drunk. When Noble entered the place, Darby met him at the downstairs door, pulled a snub-nosed pistol on him, cursed him, fired several shots into the floor at Noble's feet, and threatened to kill him. Apparently, Darby "chilled" and he was disarmed. Gilliland was later killed. Reliable information received to the effect that Darby had been promised, by Binion, a large roll of money and a big percentage in the downtown crap game "if he would get rid of Noble". Buddy Malone was reported to be the go between in this attempt as Binion was in Jordan Montana. No prosecution was requested in this case and no arrest was made.

The *third attempt* occurred on the night of May 20, 1948 when Noble was shot as he drove across the cattle guard at the entrance to his ranch at Grapevine. His right arm was riddled with buckshot and the end of his nose was powder burned. Lois Green was considered the prime suspect in this attempt. No arrests were made.

The *fourth attempt* took place on Feb. 14, 1949. A friend of Noble's happened to see a man under Herbert's car, ran upstairs to the Airman's Club, 1710 ½ Live Oak, and told Noble about the incident. Two Vice Squad officers examined the car and found a quantity of dynamite wired under Noble's car. Many pictures were shown to the witness but no identification was made. No arrests after this incident.

The *fifth attempt* was made on the night of September 7, 1949 near Noble's Grapevine Ranch. This attempt was made by Jack Nesbitt and Jim Thomas, and Noble was shot in the left leg. Nesbitt was arrested but was not indicted by the Tarrant County Grand Jury. Information received to the effect that Thomas and Nesbitt had been hired by Binion with George Wilderspin acting as go between.

The *sixth attempt* happened on November 29, 1949 in front of Noble's home on Conrad Street in Dallas. Mrs. Noble was killed by accident when her husband used her car and she stepped into his Mercury. Information received to the effect that Lois Green, R. F. Matthews, and Jettie Bass were the men who set this bomb. Matthews was arrested but there was very little evidence and no case was filed.

The *seventh attempt* on Noble occurred when he was shot as he stepped out on his front porch at his Conrad Street home on the night of December 31, 1949. This attempt was reported to be another attempt by Jim Thomas and Jack Nesbitt. No arrests made in this incident.

The *eighth attempt* was made while Noble was in the Methodist Hospital on February 6, 1950, recovering from his serious wound received on December 31, 1949. This attempt failed when he was shot at through the Hospital window, and the gunman missed. No arrests in this incident.

The *ninth try* happened on June 13, 1950 as Noble was driving toward Dallas near his ranch. His car was riddled but he was not hit. This attempt was made by Leroy Goss, Van Derrick, and Franklin Strong. Noble, while drunk a few nights previously, had stopped and cursed those punks in west Dallas.

The *tenth attempt* took place about January 10, 1951, when Noble pulled a motor out of one of his planes because it would not start. Later examination showed the cylinders to contain two large chunks of Nitro "jelly".

The *eleventh try* occurred when Noble tried to start his plane on March 22, 1951. The motor blew up but failed to kill Noble. In addition to the above mentioned attempts, Noble had several forced landings in his planes. Examination showed that it had been tampered with. The tampering had apparently been done by someone not familiar with airplanes.

Information was received two years ago to the effect that Lois Green and some of his gang had carried a case of 100% dynamite up to the Noble ranch and hidden it there with the intention of blowing Noble up as he drove over his cattle guards. Green has been flown over the Noble ranch by Roy Goss on several occasions in order to get a better idea of the area.

Noble was killed on August 7, 1951, by a land mine near his mail box at his ranch.

In addition to the above mentioned attempts there were numerous times when Noble spotted cars in the vicinity of his ranch driven by suspicious people. When Noble tried to check more closely, the cars would drive off at a high rate of speed and leave him. One night a sheriff from an outlying county was visiting a girl in the neighborhood of Noble's ranch and was shot at by mistake.

Since 1945 information has been received by this investigator that the following listed characters had been propositioned to kill or, had attempted to kill, Noble: Bob Minyard (dead), Lois Green (dead), Jack Todd, Jarrell "Fuzz" Carter, B.J. Few, Gladys Harvey, Jettie Bass, Sam Landrip, George Thomas, Johnny Grissaffi, Franklin Strong, Leroy Goss, Norman Eugene Wright, Finley Donica, J.R. Gilreath, Bob Braggin, Tommy Pate, Nick

Cascio, Jimmy Montgomery, Duane Smith, Jack Darby, Foy
Crowell, Louis La Force, Van Derrick, Charlie Archer, Tex
White, Albert Dupree (dead), Herbie Farris. Fort Worth connections report that Tincy Eggleston, Bud Mace, Jim Thomas,
and Jack Nesbitt had all been contacted for this job. In Las Vegas,
sources stated that Cliff Helms, Chinkey Bierman, Bothman,
and Hal Shimley were just a few of the characters propositioned
by Binion to kill Noble. It is understood that from Kansas City,
Robert Pinkerman, Tony Randasso, and Tony Trombine, were
all called to Dallas to look over the Noble proposition. A brother
of Pete Norris, now living in Oklahoma, was also called here by
Green to look over the deal.

In checking through the above list of former suspects the
following are known to be dead: Bob Minyard, Chinkey Rothman, Albert Dupree, Tony Trombine (Killed in Los Angeles
the night before Noble was killed). Jim Thomas was killed two
weeks after the Noble murder.

In further eliminating the suspects it is known that the fol-
lowing were in jail or the Pen at the time of the killing: Jack
Todd, Jarrell Fuzz Carter, George "Jr." Thomas, Franklin Strong,
Leroy Goss, "Monk" Norman Eugene Wright, Tommy Pate,
Nick Cascio, Duane Smith, Van Derrick, Cliff Helms, Robert
Pinkerman, Herbie Farris.

Characters also considered as suspects although not listed
above are Slick Goins, Richard Blankenship, Francis Jessie
Parvin, Victor Estill. A rundown of suspicious actions by those
people will be noted later..

Considered among prime suspects from the first were Bob
Braggin, Finley Donica, and J. R. Gilreath. Investigation showed
that Donica and Braggin had been to the Noble ranch on several
occasion. They stated that the purpose of their trip was to help
Noble destroy sections of a Jeep he had stolen. Braggin took
Donica up to burn the frame and body of the jeep with a torch.
Very little of their alibi held water. Friends of Noble told of see-
ing them at the ranch. A woman near Lewisville saw Donica a

few days before the killing riding, bareheaded, in his blue pickup truck along the road near her place. She remembered him distinctly because she had met Donica at Noble's ranch. On the day of the murder, Donica stopped, with two other men, at a café near the Circle, just about noon. He seemed hot and thirsty. Donica's wife formerly worked at this café and he was well known to the personal. They picked out pictures of Gilreath and Braggin as being the men with Donica, stating that they were almost sure about it, but they were sure that they had been in the place with Donica previously.

Gilreath had told us that he was enroute to Houston and had stopped at Fairfield for dinner about noon. That the first he knew about the killing was when he arrived at Houston about 2:00pm and read the Extra newspapers there.

Braggin stated that he had called Gilreath at his home and he made arrangements to meet him at Musik's Garage on South Eving, that both of them were there at that time. He changed his story laters. Donica's alibi was also vague.

In addition to the above-mentioned facts we found a witness that was at the Donica home a few days before and after the murder took place. This witness stated that he saw a large jar, described as a 2-gallon pickle jar, full of dynamite sticks with colored wires sticking out of it. That Bob and Donica set off something that sounded like a firecracker or gun in one of the rooms where the witness was not allowed to enter. This was the same day the murder took place.

All three of these suspects have taken a lie detector test. Donica was the first. He showed definite reactions when questioned about setting the trap, furnishing the explosives, running the wires etc. However, there was no indication that he apparently talked to Donica and were prepared to some extent for some of the questions. It was obvious that they were trying to "beat" the machine. In Braggins case, he was either sick or drunk the night before the test and did not react to normal questions, as he should. See Dee Wheelers report on these subjects. Highway patrolmen in the grapevine area talked to one of their informer who stated to them that he was present at Musik's garage when he heard Gilreath and Braggin talking about killing Noble. Later, when asked personally by Captain Crowder, the informer changed his story. He is very muchly afraid of Gilreath killing him. In all instances where we questioned witnesses regarding these suspects there was a decided fear to face the suspects personally, nor did the witnesses want the suspects to know what had been told or who had told it.

It may be significant that Braggin has made a determined and more or less constant effort to convince Robert Noble, brother of Herbert, that he, Braggin, was at Sonny Lefors grocery store at the time Noble was killed. Herbert's other brother, Gilbert, was at the store at the time, talking to "Sonny" Charles Lefors and is sure that Braggin was not there.

It also may be significant that Braggin told Robert Noble that "he had told Herbert many times how to kill old Binion". When asked by Robert how he instructed Noble to get the job done, Braggin said "just steal a car—pack it full of 100% dynamite)—park it alongside Binion's car—and when Binion got into his car just blow the Hell out of it"—"of course," he added, "you would have to kill a couple of his old body guards at the same time".

On the way back from Austin, after taking the polygraph test, Braggin denied to Ranger Rigler and Butler as having had any proposition or conversation with Noble to kill anyone. He did say that Noble had propositioned him to put Jack Todd on the spot where he could pick him up and talk to him. All three of these suspects have bought new cars since the murder. However, there is little doubt that they have been very active in the safe burglary racket, which may account for some of their money. These three suspects have been placed at the scene of the murder a few days before it happened—in the vicinity a short time after it happened—were on the other side of the fence from Noble—and are considered plenty capable of murder. Gilreath admitted he knew all about land mine deals from his army experience. A close watch and check is constantly being made of these people. They are unpopular in the local underworld and we may get a break.

In regard to Jim Thomas and Jack Nesbitt: Nesbitt has been cleared by Captain Crowder. Jim Thomas went to Odessa, Texas, on August 5th, and registered into one of the finest operated Tourist Camps in the nation, he signed in and pulled a $100.00 bill to pay for his cabin. He checked out on August 8th, 1951 and again pulled a $100.00 to pay for his cabin. He had supper on the night Noble was killed at the Rambling Rose and made some kind of scene at the place over paying for his check. We accounted for most of his time in Odessa except from about noon on Monday, August 6th until about sundown August 7th. A check of phone calls made from Jim Thomas' residence in Ft. Worth showed that, on August 6th, Mr. Thomas had called Mrs. Thomas, in Odessa, Texas. We checked the number called by Jim and found it to be a friend of both Mr. and Mrs. Thomas. When we contacted these people we were told that on August 7th, the following incident took place:

Mrs. Joyce Reddens, wife of Charles Reddens, an employee of Paul Harvey received a phone call after lunch from Mary Thomas who asked if she could come over to see Mrs. Reddens. Joyce Reddens stated that she did not want Mrs. Thomas in her home and told Mary that her husband, Charlie, had the car and she wouldn't be able to come over to get her. Mary replied that Jim went to Snyder in the Pickup and that she had the Cadillac—so if it was alright she would be over. Mary later called the Tourist Court several times from Mrs. Reddens house but Jim had not arrived. Mary left late in the afternoon, driving Jim's Cadillac, and they both, Jim and Mary, returned to the Redden's home about 10:00 P.M., that same night for a short visit. It is the opinion of both Mr. and Mrs. Reddens that Jim Thomas killed Noble and was going to use them for an alibi. Is there any point in these people lying about what had happened?

Also to be considered in this phase of the investigation were a check of phone calls made from Jim Thomas' home: Several calls were made to Tucson, Arizona, to a Ralph Camel or Campbell. Two calls were made to Jack Darby's phone in Dallas. One of the calls made to Darby was made on the day Jim Thomas was killed and almost immediately after the Thomas family in Ft. Worth was notified about the murder. A check of phone calls from Jack Darby's phone showed that he had been called by a Mr. Burton, Tucson, Arizona on July 30th, a week before Noble was killed. A check on the Tucson phone line has been requested, about 6 or 7 weeks ago, from the FBI, but as yet no reply has been received. A request was also made to the P.O. Department, Inspector George Gray, but as yet no response has been received. It is known that Binion had a strong contact in Tucson and has been known to spend a lot of time there.

When interviewed, Mary Thomas denied that Jim had been away from her at night, nor had he gone anywhere in the pickup truck. She had the advantage at that time, of talking to George Sanders, Jim's partners in the Tourist camp deal at Sprayberry, and knew what Geo. had told us. When interviewed, Jack Darby did not deny the story about his threat of Noble in 1946 but passed it off as a joke. *However*, he did deny seeing, or talking to either Jim Thomas or "Big Boy" Burton, Thomas's father-in-law. Both phone checks from Darby's and Thomas' phone showed that he did talk to Burton. Darby's denial of the conversation and his dealing with Burton is very suspicious. It is entirely possible that these men acted as a go between in the killing. Both formerly worked for Binion at the Eastside Club in Fort Worth, and have been known to have contacted Binion before and since the killing. The significance of the call immediately after Hubert Deere killed Thomas stands out like a light, the call being made from the Thomas home to Jack Darby. When asked to take a lie detector test. Darby became alarmed and turned white. He stated that he would not sign anything nor would he take any kind of lie test.

In regard to the Pickup possibly used by Thomas when, as his wife told Mrs. Redden, Jim went to Snyder: Jim Thomas was arrested in a dark Chevrolet pickup truck in Ft. Worth, Texas, several months ago for not having a tail light. The pickup belonged to George Sanders, Jim's partner at Sprayberry. George Sanders stated that, as far as he knew, Jim had not used his pickup truck during the August visit. Senders is a hard looking character, himself, and is now bootlegging whiskey at Sprayberry.

We interviewed a gravel hauler working on the Grapevine Dam Grapevine, Texas. This man had also done some hauling for Herbert Noble. Noble asked him to keep a lookout along the roads and if he saw anything that looked suspicious to let him know. It was due to this request, said the gravel hauler, that he was probably more observant than he would have ordinarily been. He saw two men in a car stopped at the bridge across Denton Creek, near the Noble Ranch. They had the turtle back open and the hood of the car raised. When they saw him watching, they closed both the hood and turtle back, jumped into the car, and took off. He looked through a large group of pictures and picked out Jack Darby's picture. He stated that the other man looked like "the fellow that was killed the other day in Oklahoma" (Jim Thomas)—that he had seen Thomas's picture in the paper and thought how much he looked like the man he saw on the bridge.

Darby has been broke until very recently when he showed up with a new 1951 Cadillac sedan and moved into a nice apartment. He formerly worked for Binion and did not deny making a three week visit to Las Vegas recently, right after Noble was killed. However, he did deny talking to Binion. Darby's activities, phone calls, contacts, and general denial of known facts seem to indicate that he has guilty knowledge of this murder. Jim Thomas and Jack Nesbitt were definitely tied in with the previous attempts. Thomas told Hubert Deere about making an airplane trip out to see Binion a short time ago.

There has been a lot of loose talk that Thomas would not work with anyone on a job. This is well disproved by Thomas' participation in the Rosebud Bank job, where he killed Lon Holley and his other partner when he found out that they were going to stool on him. He has also been known to work with Hubert Deare, Jack Nesbitt, and others.

Further checking is being made of the above-mentioned characters who may be involved in this deal.

An average of about four interviews a day has been made during this investigation, so far. Arrangements have been made, with informers, to cover some of the suspects mentioned. Every effort is being made to eliminate suspects.

> Respectfully submitted,
> George Butler, Lieutenant
> Dallas Police Department
> Dallas, Texas.
> GB: mep

cc: Colonel Homer Garrison, Jr., Director
     Texas Department of Public Safety
     Austin, Texas.

     Carl f. Hansson, Chief
     Dallas Police Department
     Dallas, Texas.

SELECTED BIBLIOGRAPHY

BOOKS

Alvarez, A. *The Biggest Game in Town*. San Francisco: Chronicle Books, 1983.

Arnold, Ann. *Gamblers and Gangsters*. Austin, TX: Eakin Press,1998.

Demaris, Ovid. *The Last Mafioso*. New York: Times Books, 1981.

Fitzgerald, Ken. *Dallas, Then and Now*. San Diego, CA: Thunder Bay Press, 2001.

Gatewood, Jim. *Decker*. Garland, TX: Mullaney Corporation, 1999.

Govenar, Alan B. & Jay F. Brakefield. *Deep Ellum and Central Track: Where the Black and White Worlds of Dallas Converged*. Denton, TX: University of North Texas Press, 1998.

Greene, A.C. *Dallas, USA*. Austin, TX: Texas Monthly Press, 1984.

Kefauver, Estes. *Crime in America*. New York: Doubleday & Company, 1951.

Leslie, Warren. *Dallas Public and Private*. New York: Grossman Publishers, 1964.

Malsch, Brownson. *Lone Wolf Gonzaullas, Texas Ranger*. Norman, OK: University of Oklahoma Press, 1980.

McDonald, William L. *Dallas Rediscovered*. Dallas, TX: Dallas Historical Society, 1978.

McLeRoy, Sherrie S. *Black Land, Red River*. Virginia Beach, VA: The Donning Company, 1993.

McManus, James. *Positively Fifth Street*. New York: Farrar, Straus, Giroux, 2003.

Meed,Douglas V. *Texas Ranger: Johnny Klevenhagen*. Plano, TX: Republic of Texas Press, 2000.

Payne, Darwin. *Dynamic Dallas, An Illustrated History*. Carlsbad, CA: Heritage Media, 2002.

———. *Big D*. Dallas, TX: Three Forks Press, 2000.

Preston, Amarillo Slim. *Amarillo Slim in a World of Fat People*. New York: Harper Collins, 2003.

Reid, Ed and Ovid Demaris. *Green Felt Jungle*. New York: Trident Press, 1963.

Rigler, Lewis C. and Judyth W. *In the Line of Duty*. Denton, TX: University of North Texas Press, 1984.

Rumbley, Rose-Marie. *The Unauthorized History of Dallas*. Austin, TX: Eakin Press, 1991.

Russo, Gus. *The Outfit*. New York: Bloomsbury, 2001.

Scheim , David E. *Contract on America*. New York: Sapolsky Books, 1988.

WPA Writers' Program. *The WPA Dallas Guide and History*. Dallas, TX: Dallas Public Library and University of North Texas, 1992.

MAGAZINES

Life

Look

Newsweek

Texas Monthly

Time

Western Horseman

NEWSPAPERS

Daily Oklahoman

Dallas Dispatch

Dallas Morning News

Dallas Times Herald

Fort Worth Star Telegram

Houston Chronicle

Las Vegas Review Journal

Las Vegas Sun

Tulsa Tribune

COLLECTIONS

Butler, George. Papers. Dallas Police Department Museum. Dallas, Texas.

Dallas and Texas History Collection. Dallas Public Library.

Genealogy Collections. Dallas Public Library.

Smoot Schmid Collection. Dallas Public Library.

Special Collections. University of Texas, Arlington.

Texas Rangers Museum and Research Center, Waco, Texas.

INDEX

ACKNOWLEDGMENTS

I **WOULD LIKE TO** thank the staffs of the Dallas Public Library, Texas/Dallas History and Archives Division; the Texas Rangers Hall of Fame and Museum; and the University of Texas Arlington Special Collections Division. Without the assistance, advice, and expertise of these three fine organizations, this book would not have been possible.